21 Days to Unlimited Power with People

James K. Van Fleet

PRENTICE HALL
Englewood Cliffs, New Jersey 07632

Prentice-Hall International, Inc., *London*
Prentice-Hall of Australia, Pty. Ltd., *Sydney*
Prentice-Hall of Canada, Inc., *Toronto*
Prentice-Hall of India Private Ltd., *New Dehli*
Prentice-Hall of Japan, Inc. *Tokyo*
Prentice-Hall of Southeast Asia Pte., Ltd., *Singapore*
Whitehall Books, Ltd., Wellington, *New Zealand*
Editora Prentice-Hall do Brasil Ltda., *Rio de Janeiro*
Prentice-Hall Hispanoamericana, S.A., *Mexico*

© 1992 by

PRENTICE-HALL, INC.

Englewood Cliffs, NJ

10   9   8   7   6   5   4   3   2   1

Library of Congress Cataloging-in-Publication Data

Van Fleet, James K.
   21 days to unlimited power with people / by James K. Van Fleet.
     p.   cm.
   Includes index.
   ISBN 0-13-948365-9
     1. Success—Psychological aspects. 2. Interpersonal relations. 3. Control
(Psychological) 4. Leadership. I. Title. II. Title: Twenty-one days
to unlimited power with people.
BF637.S8V275   1992
158'.2—dc20   91-45550
                                                   CIP

0-13-948365-9

0-13-927724-2   (PBK)

 PRENTICE HALL
Professional Publishing
Englewood Cliffs, NJ 07632
Simon & Schuster. A Paramount Communications Company

PRINTED IN THE UNITED STATES OF AMERICA

What This Book Will Do For You

This book will enable you to turn your life around completely. You'll develop the ability to gain remarkable and spectacular achievements instead of accepting average, even mediocre, results.

Instead of taking orders and doing whatever you're told to do, you'll be able to take over the leadership role yourself and be in complete charge. You *can* gain unlimited power, influence, and control over people if you read and put into practice the principles and techniques presented in this book.

By reading just one chapter a day, in only twenty-one days—less than a month—you will learn how to control the key individuals in your life and achieve success.

Here are some of the marvelous benefits that will be yours when you gain this unlimited power with people:

1. You'll become a leader of people—not just a clever manipulator, but a true leader. People will want to do virtually anything you ask them to do.

2. You'll attain a degree of personal power greater than anything you've ever experienced before. Prestige, respect, and influence will become yours. Even formerly unfriendly people will be willing to do what you ask of them.

3. You'll be able to master even the toughest of bosses, obstinate customers and clients, stubborn authorities—anyone who has been holding you back from the success that is rightfully yours.

4. You can be the leader in all the social, business, political, and neighborhood activities in which you participate. You can easily be elected to the presidency and chairmanship of clubs and groups as a result of your unlimited power, influence, and control over others. Wherever you go, you will be hailed and recognized as a leader of people.

5. Your unlimited power with people will open the door to an amazing development: the emergence of a brand-new you. Your true individuality (probably suppressed for many years) will begin to surface. This new you will be different in manner, speech, poise, confidence, bearing, and most important of all, *power*.

6. Your new personality will begin to pay off for you immediately. For instance, you'll see how you'll be able to speak your mind in a way that everyone always wants to, but nobody has the courage to. Perhaps there are many things you've been wanting to speak up about, but you've been hesitant to do so in the past. Now you'll have what it takes to stand up before any group and put them entirely under your complete control.

7. Your power at this point will become self-generating. It will start multiplying of its own accord. You'll find that your great new personality will act like a magnet drawing people to you. Your personal magnetism and charisma will grow and grow beyond belief.

8. If you will look in the mirror you will see a completely new person, one with new talents, power, and influence who commands respect wherever he or she goes—a person who now gets everything he or she wants. That person is *you*, and you can now enjoy to the fullest your whole new station in life. I know this sounds like a miracle, but it can all be true.

Let me explain that I often use the pronouns *he, his, himself* not only for the sake of convenience, but also, to prevent any awkward and clumsy wording. However, please understand that everything I'm talking about applies equally to both men and women.

Now, without any delay, let's get right into Twenty-one Days to Unlimited Power with People.

James K. Van Fleet

Contents

v

Chapter 2 ✳ *The Second Day*

HOW TO SET THE PERSONAL EXAMPLE FOR OTHERS TO FOLLOW, 17

Chapter 3 ✳ *The Third Day*

SUCCESSFUL TECHNIQUES FOR ACHIEVING SELF-IMPROVEMENT, 31

Chapter 7 ✳ *The Seventh Day*

HOW TO FIND THE SECRET MOTIVATORS FOR PREDICTING AND CONTROLLING PEOPLE'S BEHAVIOR, 78

Chapter 8 ✳ *The Eighth Day*

THE POWER PLAY THAT NEVER FAILS TO GET RESULTS, 91

Chapter 13   ✳   *The Thirteenth Day*
HOW TO CORRECT A PERSON'S MISTAKES WITHOUT CRITICIZING,   157

Chapter 14   ✳   *The Fourteenth Day*
HOW TO BUILD AN ARMY OF LOYAL FOLLOWERS,   169

Chapter 15   ✳   *The Fifteenth Day*
HOW TO GET OTHERS TO GIVE THEIR ALL FOR YOU,   181

Chapter 16 ✳ *The Sixteenth Day*

HOW TO PERSUADE PEOPLE TO YOUR WAY OF THINKING AS IF BY MAGIC, 193

Chapter 17 ✳ *The Seventeenth Day*

THE MASTER FORMULA FOR POWERFUL WRITING AND SPEAKING, 206

Chapter 18 ✳ *The Eighteenth Day*

HOW TO CONTROL A PERSON'S EMOTIONS AND TURN OFF HIS ANGER IMMEDIATELY,   220

Chapter 19 ✳ *The Nineteenth Day*
HOW TO GAIN COMPLETE CONTROL OVER PROBLEM PERSONS, 231

Chapter 20 ✳ *The Twentieth Day*
HOW TO BUILD UP YOUR DEFENSES AND KEEP PEOPLE FROM OVERPOWERING YOU, 246

How to Develop Your Personal Powers

Almost everyone wants to control others and achieve power with people without first gaining power and control over themselves. But it doesn't work that way. To control others, you must first learn how to control yourself. This requires self-discipline and a complete understanding of your own motivations.

Part I, therefore, discusses the points that are most important in developing your personal powers. For example, in Chapter 1, which constitutes the first day of the program, you will learn the *Eleven Personal Qualities That Will Make You a Powerful Leader of Others*. Be assured of this: If you want to gain power with people, you must first become their leader.

On the second day of the program, you will learn why it is so important for you to set the personal example for others to follow. Everyone tends to do as his superior does, not as his superior tells him to do. Only by setting the example to be followed can the image of the leader be created.

On the third day of this program, you will find that you must never be satisfied with the status quo. To develop your personal powers so you will be able to control and manage others, you should always seek self-improvement. This does not mean that you should be dissatisfied with your performance, but that you should always want to do better.

On the fourth day of the program, you will be shown how to project the power of your personality so you can gain power with others through the use of body language. You will learn why nonverbal language is so important to understand. You will also be shown how to look the part of a commanding and powerful personality. You'll learn how to develop confidence in yourself and how to radiate that self-confidence to others. You will also learn how to build up your self-esteem.

On the fifth day of the program, you will learn the guidelines that will help you develop your leadership qualities to control and influence the actions of others. I learned these techniques many years ago from a man whom I deeply admired and respected. Over the years, the guidelines have never lost their importance to me. I have done my best to follow them at all times.

Although Part I—How to Develop Your Personal Powers—is much shorter than Part II—How to Develop Unlimited Power with People—its brevity is not to be construed as an indication of a lack of importance. It is just that in dealing with others, there is a greater variety of methods and techniques that can be used.

So now, let us get right on into Chapter 1, the first day, so you can learn the eleven personal qualities that will make you a powerful leader of others.

Chapter 1 ✳ *The First Day*

ELEVEN PERSONAL QUALITIES THAT WILL MAKE YOU A POWERFUL LEADER OF OTHERS

You cannot be a leader unless you have some followers to lead. As Mark Twain said, "You should be thankful for the indolent, for without them, you could not get ahead."

To get ahead and gain power with people, you must first be a leader. There are eleven personal qualities you must have and develop to be able to lead and control others:

1. Character
2. The power of decision
3. The wisdom to plan and order
4. The courage to act
5. The capacity to manage
6. Integrity
7. A sense of responsibility
8. Reliability
9. Loyalty (to both superiors and subordinates)

10. Enthusiasm

11. Initiative

Although leaders are not born, but made, these eleven qualities of leadership must be pronounced and positive characteristics in a person if he or she is to lead others.

If even one of these qualities is noticeably lacking, that person will have extreme difficulty in succeeding as a leader. If all eleven are present and prominent, that person can develop into an outstanding and powerful leader of people.

The Benefits You Will Gain

1. You will be well qualified for leadership positions and promotion, for these eleven personal qualities are the specific characteristics that are looked for when people are being selected for leadership positions or for promotion to a job with more and higher responsibilities.

2. When you develop these eleven personal qualities of leadership, your people will respect you, trust you, and have full confidence in you.

3. They will give you their willing obedience, their loyal cooperation, and wholehearted support.

4. You'll have people who will stick by you when the going gets rough.

5. Your people will work just as hard as you do to get the job done.

Let's look more closely at how the eleven personal qualities can help you to lead others.

1. Strength of Character: Your First Essential Trait   Character applies to the moral qualities that determine the way a person thinks, feels, and acts in the important matters of life, especially in relation to the basic principles of right and wrong.

If you have character, you will instinctively know the difference between right and wrong. Not only will you know the right thing to do, but you will also have the moral courage to do it. You will be a person of honor. You are to be trusted. Your word will be your bond. You will not lie, cheat, or steal, no matter what advantage you would gain by doing so.

As you can see from this, character is the derivative of personal decision. It is the jewel within the reach of every person who has the moral will to attain it. Every individual is the architect of his or her own character.

And so, in a sense, every nation is the architect of its own character. As Eddie Rickenbacker, an American war hero, once said, "The four cornerstones of character on which the structure of this nation was built are *initiative, imagination, individuality*, and *independence*."

2. The Power of Making Sound and Timely Decisions   Elbert Hubbard, author of many fine works, including the timeless and inspirational essay, "A Message to Garcia," once said, "It does not take much strength to do things, but it requires great strength to decide what to do."

You must be able to make a sound and timely decision if you want to become a powerful leader of people. When you can make sound and timely decisions, people will trust you and have confidence in you. They will be motivated to do their best for you.

It is not enough that you use logic and reasoning in making an estimate of the situation. Many people can do that. But only a rare few have the strength of character it takes to make that decision at the right time and then announce it without hesitation. Today's problems will never be solved with tomorrow's solutions.

Remember that you cannot pass the buck to someone else if you make the wrong decision. As President Truman always used to say when he was in the White House, "The buck stops here!" You might as well accept that fact right now that making sound and timely decisions means that you'll have to stick your neck out once in a while. But you will never learn to make your own decisions if you constantly turn to someone else for answers. Sooner or later you'll have to fly on your own.

3. The Wisdom to Plan and Order   Once you have made your decision, you must develop a workable plan to carry it out. Definite and specific tasks must be given to your people. Your plan must answer certain questions: What is to be done? Who will do it? Where will it be done, when, and how? The wisdom to plan and order is one of the essential characteristics you will need if you are to lead, control, manage, and gain unlimited power with people.

When it's time to issue your order, make sure that it is easy to understand. Your choice of an oral or a written order will depend upon what's to be done and how complex the job is. If a lot of people are doing the work and there are a lot of deadlines to be met, then at least you'll need a notebook to keep track of who's doing what and when they're doing it.

To issue clear, concise, and positive orders that are easy to understand, follow these simple guidelines:

1. Fit your order to the job to be done.
2. Use simple words and simple terms.
3. Concentrate on a single point.
4. If it's a written order,
    a. Use your own language.
    b. Develop your own style
    c. Don't worry too much about grammar.
5. If it's an oral order, *always* have it repeated to you.

4. The Courage to Act   Even though you have the power of making sound and timely decisions, of making excellent plans to accomplish your mission, and formulating the necessary orders to get the job done, you will still be far from gaining your goals unless you have the courage to act.

The brilliant thinker with the faint heart invites only disaster through his inaction or his hesitancy to move. You must have the courage to do what has to be done, despite the costs, the hardships, the hazards, and the sacrifices.

As one of my superiors once told me, "Do something, even if it's wrong; don't just stand there. If you don't do anything, nothing will ever get done. But if you do something, even if it's wrong, you have the opportunity to correct your mistake so it will come out right in the end."

Although you might have the vision to see what needs to be done and the wisdom of Solomon to help you in making your decisions, you will never influence the result of the action unless you have the courage to act when that action is required.

5. The Capacity to Manage   To be a strong and powerful leader of others, you must develop the capacity to manage. The capacity to manage is the systematic approach to the attainment of specific goals. It requires administrative skills and know-how. Management is a tool of good leadership and a key to power with people.

It is quite easy to take the perfect combination of abundant and well-trained people, all the desired supplies and equipment, unlimited funds, and indefinite time to complete a project. That's no challenge at all; anyone can do that. The real challenge to your management ability comes when you have to make the best use of whatever you have on hand to get the results that you want. You will be measured more by what you actually get done under such circumstances than by what you can do under ideal conditions. Let me give you an example now of how many executives select their top management people.

"Technical knowledge and know-how are, of course, musts when a person is being considered for selection or promotion to a key management position," says Jane A. Andrews, an executive vice president with a large U.S. corporation. "I expect a manager to know his job. So do his subordinates. If he does not know his business, he invites only ridicule and contempt from those who work with and for him.

"But technical knowledge is not the total answer. It alone will not earn a person the job. The individual I select must have much more than that to offer. For instance, I would expect this person to have an aptitude for long-range planning. He must be inventive and creative and able to bring new ideas to the company.

"A manager in a key position in our company should also have certain desirable character traits. Above all, he must possess integrity. He should have a personality that inspires confidence and respect. And he must be people oriented. By that I mean he should have a natural leadership ability and a talent for judging people and placing his subordinates in positions that will maximize their strengths.

"I also look for intelligence, an open mind, the flexibility to learn from experience, the self-confidence to take calculated business risks, the ability to handle stress, the courage to make difficult decisions and to carry them out."

6. Integrity: A Must for Leading Others   In the example I just gave you, Ms. Andrews mentioned several desirable character traits she felt that key managers should possess. One of these was integrity. In fact, she said that above all else, the person must possess integrity.

I, too, personally consider integrity to be one of the most important qualities you need to develop to become a powerful leader of people. It is also one of the most important character traits you should look for when you are hiring someone for a management position or when you are considering an individual for promotion. Henry Peterson, a top-level company executive, feels the same way and here's what he has to say:

"Integrity is one of the first qualities I look for when I am hiring a person for a top management position," Mr. Peterson says. "It is one of the most important character traits an individual can possess. It is absolutely essential if a person is ever to supervise and control people and rise to the top levels of management.

"A person with integrity is always able to determine right from wrong, and he will have the moral courage to do what is right. He or she will be a person of honor, one who can be trusted, a person of his word. That individual will not lie, cheat, steal, or chisel. Integrity is an absolute must for the person who wants to succeed as a manager or an executive."

Other top executives whom I've talked with confirm Mr. Peterson's statements. They, too, feel that integrity is one of the most important character traits to look for when selecting a person for a key management position.

I'll have even more to say about integrity in the next chapter, How to Set the Personal Example for Others to Follow, when I give you five guidelines to help you develop high standards of personal integrity. But for now, let's move on to why a sense of responsibility is also required of you.

7. How to Seek and Take Responsibility for Your Actions   If you want to become a leader and gain unlimited power with people, you must learn to seek responsibility and to take responsibility for your actions. You should actively seek every bit of responsibility that you can possibly handle. Accept and welcome that responsibility gladly. You will never go up the executive ladder by avoiding the tough assignments.

When you do look for added responsibility, you will raise your confidence in yourself and in your own abilities to do the job. Your superiors will also have increased confidence in you, and so will those who work for you.

People always respect a boss who has the courage to take a few chances, make a sound and timely decision, and accept responsibility for that decision. Those who are not willing to take chances and stick their necks out once in a while will never gain unlimited power with people or become leaders of others. People have no use for a superior who always tries to pass the buck and avoid responsibility for his or her actions. Even if you are wrong, even when you make a mistake, your subordinates will still respect you and have confidence in you simply because you had the courage to try.

Now here's a big benefit you'll gain when you take responsibility for your actions: When your people know you are not trying to evade your responsibility, when they know you are willing to take full responsibility for your decisions and your actions, you will gain their willing obedience, their loyal cooperation, and their full support. You'll be able to motivate them to do exactly what you want them to do, and that, my friend, is unlimited power with people.

"One of the best signs that you're developing maturity is when you are willing to accept responsibility for your own mistakes," Dr. Wayne Morrison, a professor of psychology at a Midwestern university, once told me. "It takes both courage and wisdom to admit your errors, especially when they are very stupid and foolish.

"I make mistakes every day and I suppose that I will keep on doing so the rest of my life. However, I try not to make the same one twice in the same day, but even that's too hard for me most of the time.

"But I console myself every time I see a pencil. I figure that when people stop making mistakes, they'll stop making pencils with erasers."

Here are twelve guidelines you can use to learn how to accept responsibility:

1. Learn your profession thoroughly while you are developing your capacity for accepting responsibility.

2. Learn the duties of your superior and be prepared to accept his or her responsibilities on a moment's notice.

3. Prepare yourself physically, mentally, and psychologically to shoulder heavy responsibilities.

4. Always seek diversified management assignments so you can gain and develop a broad experience in the acceptance of varied responsibilities.

5. Take full advantage of every opportunity that offers you an increased responsibility.

6. Perform every job assigned to you, large or small, to the best of your ability.

7. Accept just and honest criticism when it is warranted.

8. Stick to what you think is right; have the courage of your convictions.

9. Accept full responsibility for the failures of those who work for you.

10. Assume complete responsibility for your decisions, your actions, and your orders.

11. Remember that it is as important to accept the responsibility for *what you do not do* as well as what you do.

12. In the absence of any orders, seize the initiative and take the action you believe your superior would direct you to take if he or she were present.

8. How to Prove Your Reliability to Others   Reliability is a personal quality you'll have to develop if you want to gain unlimited people power with both your superiors and your subordinates. Reliability means to be trustworthy and dependable. It means that you will always do what is required with only the minimum supervision, if any, from your immediate superior.

Reliability can also be defined as your superior's faith in your present and your future performance of duty based upon the known facts of your performance in the past.

If you want to be thought of as being reliable, your boss must be able to depend upon you to carry out actively, willingly, intelligently, and immediately, his or her orders and directives in all things, both large and small.

Now you'll notice that I used four big words here telling you how to carry out your superior's orders and directives. I meant to use them. These words are *actively, willingly, intelligently*, and *immediately*.

Just keep those four in mind when you are carrying out your orders, especially those you don't quite agree with, and I will guarantee you will always be considered to be reliable in your work. Your boss will always be able to depend on you.

Now to be reliable, to carry out the orders of your superior willingly and voluntarily does not mean that you are supposed to give him blind obedience. You should not be a yes man or woman. Blind obedience from you can easily lead to trouble for him. He should listen to your suggestions and your advice just as you should listen to the ideas and opinions of your subordinates. The best rule to follow when giving advice to your boss is to *tell him what he has to hear, not what he wants to hear.*

But once he has listened to your suggestions and given due consideration to your ideas, you are entitled to nothing more from him. Remember that *command can never be by conference. Only one person can make the final decision.* So when your boss makes that final decision, even though it might be the complete opposite of your recommendations, he is then entitled to your complete, wholehearted, and energetic support. Don't you expect the same thing from your subordinates?

Here are six specific guidelines you can follow to develop the personal quality of reliability:

1. *Never make excuses, never alibi; accept the blame.*

2. *Don't evade responsibility by passing the buck.* Don't try to blame others for your mistakes.

3. *Do every job to the best of your ability.* Strive for excellence no matter what your personal feelings are.

4. *Be exact and meticulous about doing the minute details of your work.* The tiny, monotonous, and tedious things are important to do, or they shouldn't be there in the first place. If they are important, do them, no matter what the size. If they are not important to the satisfactory completion of the task, then get permission to get rid of them.

5. *Be punctual.* Form the habit of always being on time. Being late indicates carelessness and a lack of self-discipline and self-control. You cannot be late and be thought of as being reliable.

6. *Carry out the intent and the spirit as well as the literal meaning of any order.* If you do what you are told to do grudgingly and with resentment, you are going to let yourself down sooner or later. If you feel there is some sort of conflict between the letter and the spirit of the order you've been given, then get a clear ruling on it from your superior. But once you have his or her interpretation, then stop quibbling. Accept that decision with good grace and get on with it.

9. How to Develop Loyalty to Both Superiors and Subordinates
Loyalty is a must if you want to gain unlimited power with people. Unless you keep your people well informed, you are asking for their blind loyalty.

This will not work. Only after you've proved to them that you are dependable, trustworthy, and loyal to them will they give you their loyalty without question. But at first you'll have to earn it.

"I used to think that loyalty was required only by my employees," says Lloyd Stone, a general foreman in an Ohio industrial plant. "I figured they owed me that, but I didn't realize that I had to earn it. I didn't think I owed them anything. But when the chips were down and I needed their loyal support, they wouldn't stick up for me, and I lost my job. I learned about loyalty the hard way.

"Today I know that loyalty is a door that swings both ways. It goes from an employee to the boss and from the boss to the employee. If you want your people to stick up for you and support you when the going gets rough, then you have to protect them and defend them from unwarranted criticism and abuse from above. You have to absorb their blows and protect them. I do that now."

If you want to develop the personal quality of loyalty, then follow these six guidelines:

1. *Always know who your superior is and who his or her superior is.* You are entitled to know who your immediate boss is. You must also know who his or her superior is. By the same token, your people must know that you are their direct superior. Every person must know who his or her immediate superior is. No person can serve two masters and following this guideline will prevent that from happening.

2. *Be quick to defend—and always defend—your subordinates from all mistreatment and abuse from above you.* Always protect your people from criticism and abuse from your superiors. In fact, it is up to you to absorb that criticism and abuse for them.

3. *Never show the slightest hint of disagreement with the orders of your superior in front of your people.* If you feel that you must question your superior's actions and orders, then take the matter up with him or her in private. But never do so in front of your people.

4. *Never criticize your superiors.* Questioning your superior's actions is one thing, but criticism of his or her actions is another. Don't criticize him, even to yourself. If you do, you'll never be able to keep your feelings toward him from coming to the surface and creeping into your work. You can't develop loyalty by criticism.

You must wholeheartedly support your superior's decisions, no matter what your own personal feelings are. Criticizing your boss is just another way of passing the buck upstairs.

5. *Never discuss the personal problems of your people with others.* Never violate the confidences your people have placed in you. Don't gossip or be a rumor monger. It's your job to squelch rumors, not to spread them.

6. *Stand up for your superiors, your subordinates, your associates, and your whole organization when any of them have been unjustly accused.*

10. How to Be More Enthusiastic and Optimistic Enthusiasm implies that you have a cheerful and optimistic attitude. If you are enthusiastic in your work, you will always try to do the best job you can under all conditions, no matter what they might be. Your cheerful enthusiasm can set the example for others to follow.

Enthusiasm and optimism are especially important when you're doing detailed work that tends to become tedious, boring, and monotonous or in any complex and intricate situation that requires you to have a great deal of patience.

Some people have the wrong idea about what enthusiasm actually is. You don't have to go around bubbling all over the place calling everyone *dear, darling,* or *sweetheart* to be enthusiastic.

But a good smile, now, that's different. It can be worth a great deal at times. Doesn't cost you a thing either. It can be that spark of enthusiasm that is needed at the moment to motivate one of your people to do the right thing.

If you want to develop a cheerful and enthusiastic attitude about your work and your company, then follow these seven guidelines:

1. *Know and understand every detail of your work so you can sincerely believe in what you are doing.* Need more be said?

2. *Be optimistic.* Keep a positive mental outlook on your work and life in general. Don't be a pessimist or a chronic complainer about everything. Life is what you yourself make out of it.

3. *Explain to your people why they have to do a certain job.* Tell your people the why and the wherefore of every task you give them to do, especially those that seem dull, uninteresting, and distasteful.

If you will do this, much of the unpleasantness can be taken out of an undesirable piece of work. Just make sure that the person knows *why* the job has to be done. If you can't explain that to him, you'd better check on it yourself. Does it really have to be done? Just how important is that job anyway?

4. *Always be quick to capitalize upon success.* Nothing will build enthusiasm in your people more quickly than success. Always let them know about the successful accomplishments of the organization.

5. *Keep enthusiastic even when things are not going your way.* It's ever so easy to be enthusiastic when you are successful and when everything is going exactly as you've planned it. But it's tough to be enthusiastic when everything is piling up on you and you can't see your way out. That is when you really have to stay right in there and keep at it. Never, never give up.

6. *Don't let yourself become stale.* If you want to keep up your enthusiasm about your job and your work, then never allow yourself to become stale. Set aside a short period each day when you can completely free your mind from all business matters.

Relax completely, even if it is only for a few minutes. But do it. Take off your mental shoes and wiggle your intellectual toes freely for a bit. You'll snap back refreshed.

7. *Whatever you do, do it vigorously, cheerfully, and forcefully.* Many an improper order has been brought to a successful conclusion by enthusiasm. So don't use any half-way measures about anything. If that job is worth doing at all, it's worth doing well, or it shouldn't be done. If it's worth doing, then do it. If it isn't, then don't.

11. How to Improve Your Initiative and Ingenuity Today we have transistors in our radios, our television sets, stereo systems, tape recorders, and CD players to replace the old-fashioned vacuum tube. Why? Because some ingenious person came up with a better idea.

Transistors, solid-state systems, and computers are but a few examples of the tremendous technical progress that's been made simply because someone had a better idea or a better way of doing things. All the good things we enjoy today came into being because of some person's initiative and ingenuity.

Never underestimate the brainpower of your people just because they happen to be your subordinates. Good ideas come from a person with an active imagination, no matter who he is or what he does. Things we take for granted had to first start in someone's mind: simple things like the paper clip, safety pin, zipper, Velcro fastener.

Let me give you now ten guidelines you can use to develop your initiative and ingenuity for yourself:

1. *Stay mentally and physically alert.* You simply cannot grasp the initiative or see what has to be done if you are physically or mentally asleep at the switch or are walking around with your eyes closed. A tired mind and a tired body are not conductive to developing new ideas.

2. *Train yourself to recognize what needs to be done.* Once you see what has to be done, don't hesitate to do it. Don't wait to be told. Never use the excuse that you didn't know what to do because your superior hadn't told you.

3. *Think up new approaches to problems.* Let your imagination soar. Do some brainstorming with others to get some new ideas.

4. *Learn to anticipate by thinking ahead.* Plan ahead for the unexpected. Always think in terms of "what will happen if...". By doing this, you will reduce the risk of being caught off guard to the bare minimum.

5. *Make the most of promising new ideas or plans.* Give each new idea a fair trial before making a final decision about accepting or rejecting it.

6. *Look for and readily accept responsibility.* This forces you to use your abilities to the utmost. Many people try to look the other way when responsibility comes along. Don't be afraid. Look for responsibility and then readily accept it when opportunity comes your way.

7. *Put into operation worthwhile suggestions made by others.* Don't hold up because you didn't think of it first. Just be glad the person who thought of the idea works for you. That way, you can at least get some reflected glory out of it.

8. *Constantly encourage people to try new methods and new ideas.* You can't improve the status quo without trying new procedures.

9. *Use all your available resources* in the most effective and efficient way possible.

10. *Be adaptable.* Always be flexible enough to adjust to new and changing situations. Develop your ingenuity. Don't be afraid to venture into the unknown. Always be ready to take that calculated risk. Look for answers and solutions to problems, no matter what the obstacles might be.

You now know the eleven personal qualities you should develop so you can become a powerful leader of others on your first day to unlimited power with people.

Why don't you place a checkmark under A, B, C, D, or F, whichever you feel indicates your present capability in your leadership ability for each personal quality. Then periodically review your checkmarks so you can change them to reflect your improvement in each quality.

	A	*B*	*C*	*D*	*F*
1. Character					
2. The power of decision					
3. The wisdom to plan and order					
4. Courage to act					
5. Capacity to manage					
6. Responsibility					
7. Integrity					
8. Reliability					
9. Loyalty					
10. Enthusiasm					
11. Initiative					

Chapter 2 ✳ *The Second Day*

HOW TO SET
THE PERSONAL EXAMPLE
FOR OTHERS TO FOLLOW

Being a writer of business management and applied psychology nonfiction books brings me all sorts of unique fringe benefits, benefits I would not otherwise enjoy. For instance, I'm often invited by the chief executive officer, the president, or general manager of some company to come with him or her behind the scenes and see what really goes on in a firm.

I've been fortunate enough to see the internal operations of big department stores, large factories, automobile assembly plants, airports, shipyards, TV and radio stations, newspaper and magazine editorial offices. Such visits are both fascinating and profitable, for they give me a wealth of material to draw from for my writing. Sometimes I can even help them out too.

Several months ago, Jeffrey Barnes, the manager of a huge rubber and tire plant, took me on a tour of his place. He wanted me to see some projects that had been added and to look at some new equipment he'd had installed since my last visit. As we walked through the various departments, I saw several things that Jeff didn't point out to me.

For instance, I saw a foreman jump up on a guardrail and leap over a running conveyor belt despite a big warning sign not to do so. A young chemist—a junior executive with the research and development department—was supervising some experimental work at a rubber mixing mill.

17

He wore no face mask to filter out the powder and carbon black that filled the air, nor did he have on the required plant-approved safety shoes with metal toe caps. He also wore a four-in-hand tie that was strictly forbidden when doing mixing mill work, according to the safety poster on the wall directly over the mill.

I saw an accountant from the controller's department hitching a ride on the front of an electric fork lift by standing on one of the blades. This practice is strictly forbidden in every plant that I've ever been in.

Then I saw a supervisor enter a section of the plant that was undergoing construction. He failed to stop and put on a hard hat, although he passed right by a dozen or so of them on a table that had been put there especially for people entering that dangerous area. I knew he should have worn one, for a sign mounted on an A-frame in front of the table read:

ALL PERSONNEL STOP HERE. PUT ON HARD HAT BEFORE ENTERING CONSTRUCTION AREA.

Back in his office, Jeff said, "Well, what do you think of the operation, Jim?"

"I think you have a high-accident rate," I said.

Jeff frowned and said, "Well, actually we do have, but how do you know that?"

I told him what I had seen, and then, since we've known each other for a long time, I risked our friendship by saying, "And I would bet that your production is off—both in quality and in quantity. You're probably running a high rejection rate in your quality control department, maybe even getting a lot of customer complaints about your products."

"You're absolutely right," Jeff replied. "To tell you the truth, the head office in Atlanta is on my back all the time over it. What do you think I ought to do?"

"Well, this is right off the top of my head, Jeff, and I would much rather have a couple of weeks to go over your whole operation in complete detail before giving you an answer, but from what little I've seen this morning, I would say that your executives and management people are not setting the proper example for your employees to follow."

"Evidently they feel the rules don't apply to them, for I've seen safety rules and regulations violated all over the place this morning. And if your management people are careless about safety, then your employees will be careless, too—not only about safety rules, but also about everything else as well."

"Get your management people to set the personal example for their subordinates to follow, Jeff, and see if things don't improve almost immediately for you."

Last week Jeff called me. "You were right, Jim," he said. "Things are improving all over the plant. Production is up and so is quality. The accident rate is down to almost zero and customer complaints are almost nonexistent.

"And all because I talked to all my management people right after you left and told them what you had said. Maybe you'd better make setting the personal example for others to follow a chapter in your next book, Jim."

And so I did as Jeff recommended. I figured if it helped him that much, then it would help you too.

The Benefits You Will Gain

1. *You'll inspire all your people to achieve that same high state of perfection.* All you need do is to follow the maxim of General Robert E. Lee, the South's great hero of more than a hundred years ago, and you'll never go wrong: "Do your duty in all things. You could not do more. You should not want to do less." Time has not dimmed the wisdom of his remarks. It never will. Follow this principle and you will inspire your people to do the same.

2. *Always set the personal example to be followed, and you'll gain unlimited power with people.* If you will always set the personal example for others to follow, you'll be able to gain the respect, the confidence, the willing obedience, loyal cooperation, and full support of all your people. You'll be able to motivate each one of them to do his or her level best for you. And that is unlimited power with people.

How You Can Make Setting the Personal Example for Others to Follow Work for You

There are eight techniques I'm going to give you in this chapter that you can use to set the example for others to follow. There are others, perhaps, but if you can achieve perfection in these eight, you'll never need worry about not setting the example anymore.

Use these techniques, apply them daily, and you will soon be able to develop these personal qualities to the point that your own subordinates will follow your example. You'll motivate them to do their best for you. You'll be able to get them to do what you want them to do and that's true leadership with the end result of unlimited power with people.

You should always remember that *leaders are examples to be followed, not models to be admired.* Setting the personal example for others to follow is not an easy task. It means that you are going to have to strengthen some of those "old-fashioned" personal qualities you and I used to hear about in Sunday School when we were children.

Setting the example means developing such personal traits as courage, integrity, tact, unselfishness, dependability, and others that I discussed in the previous chapter. Setting the personal example for others to follow also means sticking to what you know to be morally right, even when it would be much easier for you not to do so.

But as Albert Schweitzer, the medical missionary to the country of Gabon in west central Africa and winner of the Nobel Peace Prize, once said, "Example is not the main thing in life; it is the only thing." So set the proper example for your people to follow, and you'll not have to lecture them or preach them a sermon. They'll need only follow in your footsteps to do the right thing.

Your people will always look to you as their leader for the example to be followed. Because of your own superior performance of duty and your exemplary conduct, your subordinates will have respect for you, pride in you, and a strong desire to live up to your high standards.

There are eight techniques you can use to gain the benefits I have mentioned:

1. Set high standards for your people to follow.
2. Set the example by working hard yourself.
3. Be physically fit and mentally alert.
4. Master your emotions completely.
5. Maintain a cheerful and optimistic outlook and attitude.
6. Conduct yourself at all times so your personal habits are not open to censure or criticism.

7. Always use tact and courtesy with everyone.
8. Your word must be your bond.

Now let's discuss these eight techniques.

How to Set High Standards for Your People to Follow

"I must set the standard in everything I do for my people to follow," says George Crawford, manager of one of the biggest retail stores I've ever seen in Orlando, Florida. "And my confidence in the successful completion of a difficult job or the achievement of a specific sales goal is one of the most important ways that I, as the store manager, can set that example for my employees.

"By everything I say and do, I must show my complete confidence in the successful outcome of a tough project. If I show the least bit of doubt, I'll most certainly cause my employees to have doubts and fears of failure too. Success, then, is not likely to follow. So setting a high standard of confidence is an important part of my job as a manager. I'm sure it must be an important part of your job too, no matter what it is."

This same concept applies to many other relationships with your people also. For example, you'll expect them to be courteous, respectful, loyal, and cooperative. So you must set the standard for them to follow by showing them courtesy, respect, loyalty, and by cooperating with them first. You must first lead the way and you can do that by setting the example for them to follow.

If you are irregular in your own work habits, if you are late for appointments, careless about safety rules and regulations, apparently lazy and bored with your work, the people under you will act just as you do.

On the other hand, however, if you are on time coming to work and punctual with your appointments, if you obey the safety rules, if you are enthusiastic about your work, and if you set a high standard by your own exemplary performance of duty, they will be eager and anxious to follow your good example of leadership. You'll gain unlimited power with people by so doing.

Keep in mind that any organization is an accurate mirror of the viewpoints, strengths, confidences, fears, and shortcomings of its leader. It is inescapable that you must set the standard and be the example for them to follow in everything that you say and do. It can be no other way.

How to Set the Example by Working Hard Yourself

"One of the best ways I know of to set the example for others to follow is to work hard yourself," says Dale Foster, the safety director for a Cleveland, Ohio, manufacturing firm. "Few things will attract more attention from your boss than plain old-fashioned work. I'll never forget what the first boss I ever had told me. He said, *'Rule by work...don't work by rules.'*

"So stop thinking about what you can get out of your job and concentrate on what you can put into it for a change. Put out some extra effort. Skip your coffee break or carry it back to your desk and keep right on working. Shorten your lunch hour. Come to work early some of the time. That first boss I had always was the first person in the plant in the morning, usually 20 to 30 minutes ahead of everyone else. Stay until your desk is clear at night.

"Be willing to go beyond the call of duty—to go the extra mile. Try these few things for just one month. Your job efficiency will skyrocket. And let me tell you this, too. Your boss will most definitely take notice of you. The person who works hard—every day of the week and every hour of the day when he's on the job—is still rare enough to stand out in any group."

Mr. Foster gives you a clue about *how to work hard* in that last sentence, and that is to make every minute count while you are on the job. Don't have any lost motion; don't make any false moves. Never read the same piece of paper twice. Avoid telephone traps. Stay away from the crowd at the coffee maker or the water fountain. Don't waste your precious time in idle or malicious gossip.

Be friendly with visitors, of course, but when you are interrupted, get back to work as soon as possible. A business friend of mine has a sign on his desk that says it very succinctly. IF YOU HAVE NOTHING TO DO, PLEASE DON'T DO IT HERE! This really cuts down on any congestion in his office.

Five Guidelines for Developing Your Mental and Physical Endurance

Endurance is a part of being physically fit. You must have the ability to stick to the job that needs to be done, no matter what happens. Endurance is a

part of being both physically fit and mentally alert. It is a personal quali.
you will need to develop to be a leader of others and gain unlimited power
with people.

Actually, endurance is closely tied in with courage. It is that staying
power you need when things are really rough. It's the ability to run the mile
as well as the hundred-yard dash. Endurance can also be thought of as the
physical and mental stamina that's required to withstand the stress of pain,
fatigue, hardship, and even verbal criticism.

Endurance is your ability to perform successfully under extreme
mental and physical stress for long periods of time. It's that extra effort
you'll need for the long haul. It's your second wind. And it's an important
personal quality of leadership you'll need to develop if you want to have
unlimited power with people.

"Endurance and courage are compatible," says Bill Bales, a high
school football coach I know well. "Often a lack of endurance can be
confused with a lack of courage. You need physical stamina as well as
mental stamina to develop the endurance it takes for playing football.
Sometimes, a fellow can be mistakenly taken for a coward and a weakling
because of his poor physical condition and his lack of endurance."

True enough, you may not need endurance in a physical way as
some others do on their job. But whether you do or not, it will still take lots
of adrenalin and blood glucose to stick to a given job and see it through to
a successful conclusion, no matter what obstacles you might encounter.

To develop your mental and physical endurance, follow these five
guidelines:

1. *Don't indulge in activities that tend to lower your physical and
mental efficiency.* Too much smoking will cut your wind, if nothing more.
Scientific studies prove it will do a lot more to you than that.

Too much alcohol will lower your body's physical resistance. It
will decrease your ability to think clearly and to function properly. In the
end, it could result in drastic physical and mental changes, and all for the
worse.

Few, if any, heavy drinkers have ever become successful managers of people or gained unlimited power with them. Most temporarily
successful executives who drink too much have been toppled from their
high positions of authority and responsibility by becoming alcohol de-
pendent.

I'm not beating any drum for total abstinence here. I'm simply stating facts. What you want to do about it is entirely up to you.

But you will never be able to think and function properly when your physical stamina, your health, and well-being are not completely normal, no matter whether it's due to alcohol, cocaine, or some other cause. Try making a sound and timely decision when you're sick or, say, after the fourth or fifth martini.

2. *Develop physical training habits that will strengthen your body.* Aerobic or isometric exercises seem to be the current answer for those of us who are chained to a desk. But no matter what kind of physical exercise you use to keep fit, try to build up your endurance by using the overload principle.

The overload principle is simply the proven scientific fact that muscular development and improvement depend upon the demand you impose on your muscles. *The demand must increase as your ability increases if you expect improvement to continue.*

3. *Learn a sport you can play by yourself and still enjoy it as you grow older.* Baseball, tennis, volleyball—all these are wonderful group sports when you are young enough to take it. Golf, bowling, hunting, and fishing are sports you can enjoy with others as well as by yourself. Personally, I have always liked bowling better than golf. I never have to hunt for my ball; someone always throws it back to me.

One of the best exercises you can do by yourself, especially as you grow older, is walking. Most health authorities recommend a vigorous pace, not a leisurely stroll, of at least 20 minutes no fewer than three times a week. I walk at least 30 minutes, sometimes 40, no fewer than five days a week, to keep in shape.

4. *Test your mental endurance by frequently forcing yourself to do strenuous mental work.* Push yourself to work sometimes when you are deathly tired and your mind is sluggish and worn out. It's the only way you'll ever learn to operate under extreme pressure. This again is using the *overload principle.*

5. *Finish every job you've been given to the best of your physical and mental abilities.* This is usually the best test of your endurance. It's the one that takes courage as well as endurance.

Why You Need to Master Your Emotions Completely

"A person is just as big as the things that make him mad," says Robert Duncan, a retired Midwestern restaurant owner now living in Florida. "And in the restaurant business, a lot of things happen that could really get you down if you'd let them.

"I always tried to keep two things in mind when I was in business and dealing with people to make my living. One was this: *Never let someone else's inferiority overcome your superiority.* The other one was: *When things go wrong or someone makes you real angry, instead of flying off into a great rage, fly off into a great calm.* It's a heck of a lot better for your disposition as well as for your stomach and your heart."

If you can't control your temper, or if you are subject to deep periods of depression, I can say without any hesitation, you'll never be able to control others. In fact, you will never gain the loyalty or respect of those who are under you. They will never know for sure what your reactions are going to be, especially if they bring a difficult problem to you to solve. As their superior, you must be both calm and consistent if you want their trust and respect.

Above all, don't swear or yell at your people. Never let your emotions enter the picture when you are correcting someone. *Always criticize the act, never criticize the person.* The moment you become angry in your attempt to correct someone's actions, the issue becomes cloudy and obscure. The result will be nothing more than a shouting match between two combatants.

"I've learned a few things in my life of working with others, and one thing I have learned is this," Carl Evans, the director of industrial relations for a large Georgia manufacturing firm, told me:

"Never yell at a person unless he's so far away you have to shout to make him hear you. And even then, make sure he understands that's why you're shouting or yelling at him. Shouting or yelling at a person at any other time has no value whatever that I can see. It only creates trouble."

Five Ways to Maintain a Cheerful and Optimistic Outlook

Norman Vincent Peale has spent a lifetime showing people how to be enthusiastic and think positively. His books tell people how to get more out of life by using a positive and enthusiastic approach.

Most successful people believe firmly in the need for enthusiasm. Take Roberta Putnam, vice president in charge of public relations for an Illinois company, for instance. "Enthusiasm often will make the difference between success and failure," Roberta says. "A faulty order carried out enthusiastically with vigor has a much better chance of succeeding than does the best order carried out carelessly without spirit or drive."

Here are just a few of the ways you can be enthusiastic and set the example for others to follow:

1. *Give yourself your own pep talk.* Who motivates the motivator? You do! The motivator of others must be self-motivating. He must inspire himself and be his own self-starter. If you, as a manager, need your boss to come along and give you a pep talk to fill you with fire, enthusiasm, spirit, and drive, then I seriously doubt that you should be a manager. Managers and those who lead others must motivate themselves. So give yourself your own pep talk.

2. *Associate with enthusiastic people.* Mix with those who are excited about their work and interested in the future. Some of their enthusiasm is bound to rub off on you. If you can't do that too well on the job, then do it when you're off duty by associating with enthusiastic and optimistic people.

3. *Read some positive thinking books to fire up your enthusiasm.* It's hard today to think positive thoughts when the newspapers and TV news are filled with reports of war, crime, pollution, and poverty. But you can use part of your free time to read some positive, forward-thinking, self-help books that show you how to improve yourself and get more out of life. If you don't know how or where to start, get a copy of David Dunn's book, *Try Giving Yourself Away,*[1] and try some of his ideas. They helped me; I'm sure they will help you, too.

---

[1] David Dunn, *Try Giving Yourself Away* (Englewood Cliffs, NJ: Prentice Hall, 1970).

4. *Be enthusiastic about your job.* When our new house was being built, my wife and I used to go out every so often to watch its progress. One day I asked one of the bricklayers a question about construction, and he said, "I don't know. Better ask the foreman. I'm only a bricklayer."

"And a masterful one, too," I replied. "I've been watching you work. You make bricklaying an art. You certainly add the touch of the master's hand. I could never begin to do it as well as you do."

He was still beaming and bubbling enthusiastically over his work when I left an hour later.

5. *Think of all the people who depend on your example.* Whenever your enthusiasm lags, remember that you are the motivator; your people are the motivated. You are the leader; they are your followers. Keep that idea in mind and it will perk you up like magic when you realize how much your people need you and depend on you.

How to Conduct Yourself So That Your Personal Habits Are Not Open to Criticism

To set the personal example, to have an excellent bearing so that you will not be open to censure or criticism, you must always be dignified. Many people think that dignity is reserved only for ministers and undertakers. They feel that being dignified means you must have a long, sad face, always wear a black funeral coat and tie, and never get any fun out of life.

Well, between you and me, I don't think that is dignity at all. Some persons might call it solemnity, but it's surely not dignity.

Dignity, first of all, means a state of being worthy and honorable. It means that one possesses complete control over his or her emotions and actions at all times.

For instance, the manager who makes a complete fool of himself through loud and boisterous talk, obscene jokes, and vulgar language, excessive drinking, or the complete loss of emotional control in fits of anger is surely not dignified at all.

Such a person is nothing but a complete fool. He'll sooner or later, and usually sooner, completely lose the respect of his people. He's not meant to be a manager, an executive, or a supervisor, and if he is, he won't be one for long. *Once you've lost the respect of your people, it's almost impossible to regain it.*

Seven Techniques You Can Use to Be More Tactful and Courteous

Tact is your ability to say or do the right thing at the right time without offending anyone. It takes a lot of skill and tact when you're dealing with difficult persons or touchy situations. You must always have a quick and delicate sense of just what is best fitting for the occasion.

To be tactful, you must have a good understanding of human nature and a sympathetic consideration for the feelings of others. Tact will be important to you in all your personal relationships with others.

Courtesy is also a part of tact. You simply cannot afford to be discourteous in your relationships with either your superiors or your subordinates. No, not even with your associates. Who knows, that associate might some day be your boss.

If you demand courtesy from others, but you fail to return that courtesy in full measure, you show only arrogance, a lack of interest in others, as well as no breeding.

Here are seven techniques you can use to develop tact and courtesy:

1. Always be cheerful and optimistic in your manner.
2. Be considerate of others in everything you do.
3. Study the methods of people who are skilled in the art of human relations.
4. Cooperate in spirit as well as in fact.
5. Maintain a tolerant attitude toward others; live and let live.
6. Don't criticize or talk about others.
7. Know when your presence is wanted, both on and off the job.

Why Your Word Must Be Your Bond

If you are going to gain unlimited power with people, you must be as good as your word, and your word must be your bond. To make sure that your word is your bond, keep these three points in mind:

1. Never make a promise you cannot keep.
2. Never make a decision you cannot support.

3. Never issue an order you cannot enforce.

Personal integrity is a must if you are going to make your word your bond. Without integrity, you'll never be able to set the example for anyone to follow. Integrity, which I touched upon in the previous chapter, is that quality or state of being of sound moral principle. Integrity stands for uprightness of character, absolute truthfulness, candid honesty, and deep sincerity. Above all, *you must be honest with yourself.*

Let me give you now five guidelines that will help you develop the highest standards of personal integrity and moral character:

1. Practice absolute honesty and truthfulness in everything you do at all times.

2. Be accurate and correct in everything you say and do.

3. Your signature on any document is your certification as to the honesty and truthfulness of that document, be it your personal check, a letter, a memorandum, or a report.

4. Stand for what you believe to be right. Have the courage of your convictions, regardless of the consequences. Never compromise your standards; don't prostitute your principles. *To thine own self be true.*

5. Duty and honor should always come first. If you are ever tempted to compromise your principles, then you must place your sense of duty and personal honor above all else.

If you can grasp, understand, and practice the ideas of duty and honor, you cannot help but develop personal integrity and your word will be your bond.

Before I close this chapter on setting the personal example for others to follow so you can gain unlimited power with people, I want to list for you again those eight techniques I've given you to use.

To sum up these techniques and this chapter, then

1. Always set high standards for your people to follow.
2. Set the personal example by working hard yourself.
3. Be at all times physically fit and mentally alert.
4. Learn to master your emotions completely.
5. Maintain a cheerful and optimistic outlook and attitude.

6. Conduct yourself at all times so your personal habits will not be subject to censure or criticism.

7. Always use tact and courtesy with everyone.

8. Make sure your word is your bond.

I recommend that you review these eight techniques at the end of the day to see whether or not you have set the personal example to be followed. If you find that you have failed in some particular technique, determine what you did wrong so you can correct it and not make that same mistake the next day.

Now let us move on to Chapter 3, the third day in the program to gain unlimited power with people, where you will learn that to develop your personal power with people, you must always seek self-improvement.

Chapter 3 ✳ *The Third Day*

SUCCESSFUL TECHNIQUES
FOR ACHIEVING
SELF-IMPROVEMENT

It goes without saying: To gain unlimited power with people, you should know more than they do. And to do that, you need to seek constantly to improve yourself, not only in your handling of people, but also in your own chosen field. Never let a day go by without learning something new. If you don't do that, you'll not be just standing still, you'll be going backward because every day you live you forget something you learned previously. Let me give you two specific examples of that:

Allen Norman was a bright industrial engineer who once worked for a large firm in Los Angeles. An MIT graduate, Allen was earmarked for early promotion and advancement. But he left the company in less than five years. Let me tell you what happened to him.

Allen used to spend nearly three hours a day getting from his suburban home to work and back again. As he drove, he listened to the latest musical hits from the top 40 on his tape player.

Allen thought about taking some night courses at UCLA and doing some graduate work, but he never quite got around to it. He also gave some consideration to taking a correspondence course from the university or, at the very least, subscribing to some of the best scientific journals in his field so he could keep up to date. But he seemed to be so tired from work and from driving to and from the office every day that after a couple of drinks and dinner about all he could do was flop down in his favorite easy chair and watch TV for an hour or so.

When the company offered to send him back to college at the firm's expense so he could get his master's degree, he asked them to postpone it for a couple of years as he was "all worn out with going to school and studying," as he told them. And when the company offered a Dale Carnegie course for their junior executives and young management personnel, again all at company expense, he declined because his wife was pregnant and needed him at home every night, or so he said.

He'd often thought about joining the Los Angeles chapter of the Society of Professional Engineers. They met on Friday nights to discuss new developments in the industrial engineering field and to exchange ideas, but after all, that was his poker night with the guys in the neighborhood, and he didn't want to miss that.

And what with Saturday morning on the golf course, doing some odd jobs around the house in the afternoon, driving into the city with Marian to see a movie and have dinner at a good restaurant on Saturday night, and then catching up with his sleep on Sunday, well, somehow Allen never did seem to be able to get around to doing anything at all about learning any more than he'd known the day he got his sheepskin from MIT. So the company let him go. "Not qualified for further advancement or promotion," he was told.

Now Jeri Wallace came to the company at the same time that Allen did. Jeri had not graduated from as prestigious a school as MIT. In fact, she got her engineering degree from a small college in Oregon.

Nor were her scholastic achievements as impressive as Allen's had been. Jeri had a 2.5 average on a four-point scale, but she had paid for 100 percent of her college expenses by working as a cocktail waitress. She had also worked as a bartender, which impressed the senior company recruiter, Howard Richmond, who said, "Shows she has guts to get the job done. And she knows how to talk with people and get along with them, too. Anybody who can listen to a drunk's problems without getting upset has to have a lot of ability to handle people."

Jeri also drove to and from work several hours a day. But she used her driving time to listen to prerecorded tapes (including some of mine[1])

---

[1] "The 22 Biggest Mistakes Managers Make and How to Correct Them," "Power with People," "Hidden Power: How to Unleash the Power of Your Subconscious Mind," and "Managing for Results," for example.

from Success Motivation Institute (SMI), a Waco, Texas, firm, the world's leading producer of personal motivation, supervision, leadership development, executive, and management courses.

Of course, Jeri and her husband, Clark, did set aside some of their leisure time for a round of golf, some tennis, a movie now and then, or some other form of weekend entertainment, but they budgeted their free time carefully for self-improvement.

Jeri continued her education by taking some extension courses from UCLA, and when the company offered to pay for her master's degree, she took advantage of the opportunity. She also subscribed to the Bureau of Business Practice in Waterford, Connecticut, and became a member of two Prentice Hall book clubs in Englewood Cliffs, New Jersey, The Business Leader's Book Club and the Management Books Institute, so she could keep up with the latest ideas and developments in the executive and management field.

All in all, Jeri used every possible method she could think of to keep up with developments, not only in her own specialized engineering field but also in the "people field" as well. Today, just a little less than ten years after joining the company, Jeri is the vice president in charge of research and development. But she hasn't quit. She is still working just as hard as ever to improve herself, both as an industrial engineer and an executive and manager of people.

The Benefits You Will Gain

1. When you seek to improve yourself by keeping abreast of the latest development in your own field, you'll always be ready for promotion at a moment's notice. And you must always train yourself to be capable of taking over the next higher position at any time. If you are not ready, someone else will be!

2. When you are the expert and the authority in your own field, your people will look up to you. They will admire and respect you. They'll turn to you for advice and help. It will be much easier for you to gain the obedience, cooperation, and full support of your subordinates. And your superiors will take notice of you, too, for they'll respect your abilities and have full confidence in you.

3. When you seek self-improvement, your job will be more interesting and worthwhile. And, of course, you'll gain many material benefits when

you keep up with the latest developments in your own field. But perhaps even more important—although I do have a healthy respect for money, too—you will not wither away to stagnate and vegetate as you grow older. You can always keep your work new and exciting, and that in itself makes self-improvement worthwhile.

Now to help you achieve these benefits and to keep you from making the mistake Allen Norman made of failing to keep up with his chosen profession and to seek self-improvement, let me tell you about some of the methods Jeri Wallace and many other successful executives and managers have used to become successful, not only in their chosen professions, but also in gaining unlimited power with people as well.

There are six techniques you can use to achieve these benefits:

1. Analyze yourself objectively and realistically.

2. Prepare yourself for advancement.

3. Ask for the advice and opinions of others who can help you improve.

4. Always accept managerial and executive training when it is offered to you.

5. Develop a deep and genuine interest in people.

6. Actively search for ways to improve yourself.

How to Analyze Yourself Objectively and Realistically

As hard as it might seem to you to do, you must honestly and forthrightly evaluate and inventory yourself so you can recognize and identify your own strengths and weaknesses.

Here, I am referring to the improvement of your technical and professional abilities as well as improving your personal qualities and character traits. Both of these are important if you are going to gain unlimited power with people. However, let me point out that even though you are striving for perfection, never let it lead you to frustration when you miss your mark slightly.

Both areas, your personal leadership qualities and your technical and professional development, must be constantly improved if you want to become completely successful in the art of motivating others to do what you want them to do.

However, you can't set out on a self-improvement program unless you know and fully understand your own capabilities as well as your own limitations. That is the only way you'll ever be able to strengthen your good points and get rid of your weak ones.

You must be self-motivated enough to want to achieve improvement. But you cannot be wishy-washy about improving yourself and getting rid of your weak points. You really have to have courage to do it. You must certainly be the master of yourself before you can ever hope to master others and gain unlimited power with them.

If you really are serious about improving yourself, take a good long objective look at yourself in the mirror. Have plenty of courage when you do. Take a true inventory to find your strong points and to isolate your weak ones. Then make the honest effort to overcome your weak ones. Improve and strengthen those where you are already strong.

Be completely honest with yourself; take a complete and unbiased audit. To lie to yourself at a time like this will accomplish absolutely nothing for you at all.

Then continue to take this personal inventory at definite time intervals, say, weekly or monthly. And keep right on doing so for the rest of your life if you want to keep on improving yourself day by day.

A friend of mine, Carl T., a recovering alcoholic and a member of Alcoholics Anonymous for eleven years now, tells me that A.A. has twelve suggested steps for its members to follow.

"Our tenth step says that we should continue to take a personal inventory, and when we are wrong, we should promptly admit it," Carl says. "The tenth step is the 'here-and-now' one. I can't afford to take a personal inventory on a weekly or monthly basis. I must do it not only daily, but the moment something goes haywire that is my fault. That usually means I must make amends or apologize to someone immediately for what I did. To delay will only make things worse."

After listening to Carl, I, too, have found that it is better for me to practice this idea of a personal inventory almost on a minute-to-minute basis as the situation warrants or as the occasion demands.

If I were to let my mistakes and my resentments pile up for a week, a month, or more, I'm afraid I would never get an honest inventory completed. I would be far too busy taking everyone else's inventory in those long intervals between.

How to Prepare Yourself for Advancement

"If you want to be considered for promotion up the corporate executive ladder, you must take the necessary action to prepare yourself for advancement," Jeri Wallace says. "Without a doubt, the biggest obstacle to success for most people is the improper use of their leisure time. So your first big step is simply to learn how to *budget your time properly.*

"If you work forty hours a week and sleep eight hours a night, you still have seventy-two hours a week left over. True enough, part of that time might still be thought of as work hours, for you'll have to use some of them getting to your job and back home again, but even those driving hours don't have to be wasted.

"You can listen to prerecorded tapes from SMI or Prentice Hall just as I do. Or while you're home, you can record certain data that you want to hear again, perhaps even commit to memory, and play them on your car's tape player while you're driving to work."

Let me mention one set of tapes that could be extremely valuable to you. The Prentice Hall Audio Division has put one of my books, *The 22 Biggest Mistakes Managers Make and How to Correct Them*, into a dynamic four-audio cassette edition that will help you get ahead in the executive and management field. The package is available from Prentice Hall Audio, Business and Professional Publishing Division, Englewood Cliffs, New Jersey 07632.

My own family physician, Dr. Wayne Shelton, tells me that he memorized every muscle in the body while riding a streetcar to Washington University while he was attending medical school in St. Louis, Missouri.

"Didn't have tape recorders in those days," Doc says. "At least not the kind you carry around with you or put in a car. So I would type all the information about muscles on 3 by 5 cards. The name of the muscle would go on one side; its bony attachments, nerve and blood supply, and function would be on the other. I kept shuffling them from my left pocket to my right pocket as I memorized them. Used a lot of valuable time on those old streetcars while I was going to medical school that otherwise would've been wasted looking out the window daydreaming or reading the comic strips and the sports page."

I realize you can't use every spare waking moment for self-improvement, although some people seem to do so. Chet Atkins, for example, one of the finest guitar instrumentalists in the world, often carries his guitar to the dinner table and keeps right on working on a new arrangement for a song even while he's eating.

But you must leave some leisure moments for "fun and games" like golf, bowling, swimming, tennis, handball, or whatever it is that you like to do. And keep some time open for your spouse. Do what he or she wants to do—at least part of the time.

If you're the husband, you should also reserve some time for those inevitable odd jobs around the house, taking out the trash, mowing the lawn, getting the car fixed, going to the grocery store with your wife, and the like.

And perhaps I don't even need to say this, but in view of the current divorce rate of 50 percent, perhaps I should. Save some time for making love with each other. Don't let your marriage fall apart because of an obsession to succeed, no matter what.

If you do budget your time properly, I'm sure you will find that you still have about three hours four or five nights a week that you can use to good advantage instead of watching television. Which leads me to this simple recommendation:

Stay Away from the Boob-tube. Television is a wonderful source of entertainment, but it can also turn you into a living vegetable, or a couch potato, as the saying goes. I usually watch the evening news, although sometimes because of its contents, I wonder why. Once in a while a special catches my eye or an old movie stirs a memory, but normally speaking, I'm settled down in my study with a good book by seven o'clock in the evening, Monday through Friday, five nights a week. I learned to love books as a child when there was no TV to watch and I've never gotten over it. I feel I still have a great deal to learn, and not nearly enough time to do it in.

There's Absolutely No Substitute For Knowledge. Lack of knowledge never has been and never will be an insurmountable obstacle to anyone, no matter how much or how little formal education a person has. Lack of knowledge is usually used more as an excuse than as a valid reason for not doing a job.

You can acquire knowledge about any subject in the world if you have enough interest and desire to do so. You can ask questions, search for facts, pursue new ideas. Your age, your job, your health, even your financial status have no bearing on your ability to learn. If you want to gain specific knowledge and information on any given subject, simply *look for it—find it—learn it.*

You can gain information and facts about anything simply by developing the public library habit. By being selective in your reading, you can become a private student and have the greatest teachers in the world right at your fingertips. Or you can take advantage of your state university's extension courses. Enrollment and study in a correspondence course can make you the master of whatever subject you choose.

Ask for the Advice and Opinions of Others Who Can Help You Improve

Be sure that you listen when the advice you've asked for is given to you. Just remember which one of you is asking for help. Be certain to explore all possibilities to gain information for your continued improvement. A lot of good advice can come up to you from the actual working level, that is, if you are not too high and mighty to listen.

Lee Horne is the vice president of marketing for a large oil company in Tulsa, Oklahoma. Here's what Lee says about how he helps out younger executives in the company when they come to him for advice.

"I have a lot of the junior management people come to me for help and advice," Lee says. "I tell each one that I'd like to think the problem over for a couple of days before I give the person any concrete recommendations.

"During that time, I get out and talk to his own employees about his particular problem, and sure as anything, I always come up with an answer from his own people!

"And I almost always find out something else, too. Nine times out of ten, that same suggestion I got from the employee was also given to the person who came to me for help, but he wouldn't listen. He thought his subordinates couldn't possibly have the answer to such a weighty problem, especially since he couldn't think of a solution.

"When they come back to me and I give them the same advice I got from their own people, they look impressed and they say, 'What a brilliant idea. Now why didn't I think of that?'

"Oh, they'll catch on to me one of these days. And when they do, they'll have learned an extremely valuable lesson about where to get their advice. I had to learn that lesson the hard way, too. Today I know that the person who is actually doing the job always knows more about its problems and how to solve them than anyone else does."

Take Advantage of Managerial and Executive Training Offers

Remember how Jeri Wallace accepted the company's offer to help her get her master's degree and how Allen Norman refused? I at first thought that Allen was the exception to the rule, but after talking to Charlie Johnson, the director of management training for a Paterson, New Jersey, company, I found this was not the case at all.

"Our company really goes all out to help our executives get a college degree," Mr. Johnson says. "For instance, Columbia University has an adult education course called Master's Degree for Executives, although you don't need a bachelor's degree to enroll. However, several years of midlevel or top-level administrative experience are required.

"The sponsoring company must certify that the applicant is headed for higher-level responsibilities. We also have to pay a $7,500 fee for the course. The individual must pass a standard admissions test for graduate study in business.

"The course itself consists of classes one day a week, three full-week sessions each quarter, and fifteen hours of homework every week. The studies last for two years, and upon successful completion of the course a Master's Degree is awarded.

"Now wouldn't you think that people would jump at a chance like that? Well, amazingly, they don't. They give a variety of reasons for not being able to go, but in the final analysis, the most common one of all is the loss of free time because of the fifteen hours of homework every week."

If you want to get ahead, then, take every opportunity that is offered to you for self-improvement. It's one of the surest methods you can use to gain unlimited power with people.

Develop a Deep and Genuine Interest in People and Their Problems

If you want to be successful in motivating people to do their utmost for you, you'll have to develop what is called the *human touch.*

If you're going to be a successful executive—a leader of people, the master motivator—you simply have to know how to stimulate them to do your bidding. And remember that you have to lead people, not push them. Pushing people is like pushing a piece of wet spaghetti. It can't be done. So remember that you have to pull people, not push them.

And if you don't like people, if you cannot develop a deep and sincere interest in them and in their problems, you'll never make a top-notch executive. You'll always be a loner, even when you're in the middle of a big crowd.

Consider the following example of someone who makes this technique work for him. Having a deep and genuine interest in people is the main reason why George Gregory has been so successful in operating his large Chicago department store. When George was a youngster helping wait on customers in his father's small dry goods and notions store, he learned the value of placing the interest of his customers first.

Women especially liked to have George wait on them for he was polite and patient, and he always respected their desires. Not only that, George had a lasting memory for names and faces. Of course, his memory was helped along by a small black book in which he made notes about all his customers, their spouses, their children and their ages and names, their special likes and dislikes. George's sincere interest in people has paid rich dividends for him.

"That's the biggest secret of salesmanship," George says. "If you want to be a supersalesman, *find out what the other person wants and then help him get it.*"

Take a tip from George. That secret also works in gaining unlimited power with people, that is, finding out what the other person wants and then helping him get it. Do that, and you will be successful every time.

Three Ways to Improve Yourself

When you get right down to bare-bone facts, it's up to you not only to keep up with technical development in your own specialized field, but also to teach yourself people management skills so you can gain unlimited power with them. You can be sure of becoming successful with such a two-pronged attack. Here are three techniques you can use for self-improvement.

1. *Reach out for more responsibility.* You really start to grow when your job is just a little too big for you to handle easily without effort. If your present duties are no longer a real challenge to you, then it's time for you to look around, *especially above you*, for new fields of conquest.

For instance, tell your boss you'd be glad to relieve him of some of his routine daily problems so he can have more time for high-level policy decisions. Of course, you'll probably not fool him. He no doubt will be wise enough to know that you are looking for increased responsibility. After all, he came up the same way himself. And you can bet he'll reward you with more work, too, and he'll keep his eye on you to see how you handle it.

2. *Be your own taskmaster.* Management experts learned a long time ago that you cannot train an executive or a manager in the same way you teach a person to be a typist or a file clerk or a secretary. Remember: *Technicians work with things, executives work with people.* Executive development is primarily self-development even though your company might go all out to provide ideal conditions to help you grow in your mastery of people.

This is important for you to remember for many young executives think that managerial skills and know-how can be learned only in a college course or at a management institute.

But what you learn on the job and through well-planned homework becomes even more important because it teaches you self-development through *practical application* of what you've learned in school. We all learn best by doing, whether it's swimming, riding a bicycle, playing a piano, or managing people.

3. *Let yourself grow on the job.* Alice Dennis is an executive vice president for a large Dallas, Texas, corporation. Her job is that of an executive recruiter. She knows her work, enjoys it, and does it well, for of the people she's selected during her years with the company, seventeen of them have risen to the position of vice president. One has become the corporation president and chief executive officer, another, the chairman of the board.

"When a young person starts to work for us as a junior executive, he finds his duties are more administrative than managerial," Alice says. "In other words, he finds he's pushing paper more than he is leading people. But as he goes up through successively higher levels of management, he finds that the nature of his duties undergoes a change.

"He discovers that his position at the top requires him to use leadership and management of people to get the job done. Of course, he is still concerned with market reports, sales charts, and production figures, but he is no longer concerned with actually doing them himself. His job now is much broader than that.

"Much of his work now has to do with the philosophy of management, the leadership of people, and presenting the proper corporate image to the general public."

To sum up this idea in a nutshell remember that *technicians work with things, while executives work with people.* If you are going to be an executive and a leader of people rather than a technician, make that decision early in your career and stick to it. Remember that you cannot be both; you cannot serve two masters.

For example, I have a nephew who was trained to be a tool and die maker. But he learned that this was not his field of expertise for he didn't like to work with things. He went into the life insurance business because he liked working with people and helping them. An excellent decision, for today he is one of the top insurance people in the state of Iowa.

Chapter 4 ✳ *The Fourth Day*

HOW TO PROJECT THE POWER OF YOUR PERSONALITY WITH BODY LANGUAGE

You can project the power of your personality with body language to control people and gain unlimited power with them. Body language is often used to let another person know subtly how you feel about something. It can also be used in the art of persuasion. However, one of its most valuable uses is in projecting the power of your personality.

I'm sure you are already familiar with certain aspects of body language and its uses. For example, you know that a smile projects joy and happiness while a frown can display displeasure, dissatisfaction, or anger.

There are techniques you can use to project the power of your personality to others to influence and control their actions. You will also learn how to detect those unspoken signals when someone else uses them on you, not only in business situations, but also in social conversations as well.

The Benefits You Will Gain

1. You can project the power of your personality to others by your physical appearance, your demeanor, and your bearing. For example, an erect posture with your head up and your chest out shows you have supreme

43

confidence in yourself by your self-assured manner and bearing. As a result, others will have full confidence in you too.

2. The way you look at a person can control a bad situation and get things back under your control quickly without your ever having to say a single word. I'll give you a specific example of how to use the power to control people and their behavior later in this chapter.

3. You can use simple body language to discipline your employees subtly and get them to do a better job for you. Your physical presence alone is enough to stimulate people to get to work. All you need to do is stand with your hands on your hips, your feet slightly apart, and just watch the work that is going on. You need not say a word. To see and be seen is an effective supervisory tool, for it never fails to work.

4. You will gain the reputation of being a "born leader," when you use body language to project the power of your personality. People will automatically turn to you for advice and assistance.

5. When you learn how to read another person's body language, you'll learn his secrets easily. He won't have to tell you what he is thinking; you'll know. This knowledge will give you a powerful advantage over him.

Seven Body Language Signs to Watch For

According to Suzanne Kramer, a clinical psychologist, there are seven body language signs to be aware of.

"*Eyes* give you one of the biggest clues to what's really going on in the person's mind," Suzanne says. "No matter what his mouth says, his eyes will tell you what he's really thinking. If the pupils widen and open up, then he's heard something pleasant. You've made him feel good by what you've just said. If his pupils contract, then just the opposite is true. He's heard something he does not like. If his eyes narrow, you've probably told him something he doesn't believe, so he feels that he has cause not to trust you or what you say.

"*Eyebrows* give you another clue as to what the person is really thinking," Suzanne says. "If he lifts only one eyebrow, you've told him something he either doesn't believe or that he thinks is impossible. Lifting both eyebrows shows surprise.

"*Nose and ears* can also furnish a clue as to what he is thinking. If he rubs his nose or tugs at his ear while saying he understands what you want, it means he's puzzled by what you are saying and probably doesn't know at all what you want him to do.

"*A person's forehead* can also give you a clue as to what he is thinking," Suzanne goes on to say. "If he wrinkles his forehead downward in a frown, it means he's puzzled or he does not like what you've just said. If he wrinkles his forehead upward, it indicates surprise at what he has heard.

"*Shoulders* also furnish a clue about his thoughts," Suzanne says. "When a person shrugs his shoulders, it usually means he is completely indifferent to what you're saying. He just doesn't give a hoot for what you are saying or what you want.

"*Fingers* drumming or tapping on the arm of the chair or the top of a desk indicate either nervousness or impatience.

"*Arms* clasped across the chest usually means he is trying to isolate himself from others or that he is actually afraid of you, at least psychologically if not physically, and he is trying to protect himself from you."

This gives you an idea of what body language is all about and how it can be used, not only to project the power of your personality, but also to know what others are thinking in spite of what they are saying.

Why Nonverbal Language Is Important to Understand

Nonverbal communication has less deceptiveness than does the spoken language. We find it much easier to lie with words than with our bodies. For example, have you ever tried to hold your hands still and keep from biting your lips, chewing your fingernails, or sighing deeply when you were extremely nervous and worried about something? Impossible, wasn't it? One of these mannerisms will no doubt fit you, and no matter what you may have said, your body told others what you were really feeling.

When someone is talking with you, especially about a subject that you're a bit suspicious of, you usually watch the other person's face intently to see if the expression actually matches what is being said. Then you listen to the tone of voice to see if you can find any hidden meaning there. Finally, you actually listen to the person's spoken words. Even if these spoken words are cynical or sarcastic, you will no doubt accept them as a joke if the speaker's face is jovial and happy.

For instance, my children always knew that if I said Robert instead of Bob, Lawrence Lee instead of Larry, or Teresa Lynne instead of Teresa in a louder-than-normal voice, they had done something wrong and a serious conversation was about to take place. You are communicating nonverbally not only when you use gestures, but also when you change the volume or the tone and intensity of your voice.

If you think that nonverbal communication or body language is not important to understand, remember this: Studies indicate that over 90 percent of the meaning of any message is transmitted nonverbally. So it becomes extremely important to you not only to know how to use body language yourself to project the power of your personality, but also to be able to read another person's body signals.

How to Look the Part of a Commanding and Powerful Personality

To have the look of power and command so that people will always give way to you on sight, you need not be 6 feet tall or built like a professional athlete. *The way you carry yourself is the key.* I know a man, less than 5 feet 6 inches tall, who has built a financial empire in computers from scratch. His people respect him and admire him, and I know full well that most of those in his organization are taller than he is.

I myself am only 5 feet 7 inches tall, yet since the age of 23 I have had people under my supervision who were taller and physically stronger than I was. There has never once been the slightest hint of disobedience from any of them. I have always had complete cooperation and full support from all those whom I supervised, commanded, or controlled.

I have also seen tall physically strong men turn and run in battle, while small shorter ones stayed and fought the enemy with courage. Power comes from within and is primarily a matter of mental attitude, not muscular development.

Of course, there are certain physical characteristics you can develop that will help you project the power of your personality: a steady unflinching gaze, a tone of voice that implies total confidence in yourself, an expectation of immediate obedience, and above all, a solid no-nonsense attitude that lets people know you are exactly where you ought to be.

Fred Olson, a business leader in our city who is well respected by all says this: "If you show confidence in yourself and always act as if it were impossible to fail, people will gain strength from your example. Your physical appearance and manner must reflect a confidence sometimes even beyond what you might actually feel. But by controlling your voice and your gestures, you will be able to exert a firm and steadying influence on your colleagues and your associates as well as your subordinates.

"People always have the greatest respect for the leader who remains cool in the midst of trouble," Fred goes on to say. "But they have no use whatever for the one who panics at the first sight of something gone wrong."

You, too, can increase people's confidence in you when you view a tough situation with a calm and cool presence of mind. By assuming such a positive attitude, you appear to take the entire burden on your own shoulders. You give your subordinates the feeling that there is no cause to worry and that the problem, no matter what it is, can be solved.

Your people will then have confidence in your strength, courage, and ability to set things straight. You will be able to project the power of your personality so that they will quickly obey every one of your orders and commands without fail.

How to Use the Steepling Technique to Project Power

Wise people who know how to project the power of their personalities without saying a word often make a steeple with their hands. Watch a group of people during a business conference. As the boss listens to a subordinate's suggestion, he will often steeple. This action shows that he is thinking seriously about what the other person is saying. As his thoughts become deeper and more profound, he may steeple in a higher and higher position with his hands until the steeple nearly hides his face.

"Medical doctors, psychiatrists, and psychologists are all avid steeplers," says Harry Kronman, a professor of psychology. "The impression that they want to leave with people is that they are deep thinkers and extremely intelligent and important people."

If you use the steepling technique yourself, people will draw the same conclusions about you. This technique is a powerful adjunct you can use, not only to project the power of your own personality to gain unlimited power and control with others, but also to turn off another person's play for power.

How to Expand Your Control by Establishing Your Own Turf

In big companies and corporations, the general rule is that the more powerful you become and the more people you supervise or control, the larger the physical area that you can call your own. Low-ranked employees may work together as a group in one large room. Their supervisor might have only a glassed-in cubicle from which he can both see and be seen by his subordinates.

A young executive can be blessed with a private, although small, office. As a member of the power elite, even if you are only a junior one, you will be entitled to that at least.

"Although things have changed a lot in the workplace, you still have to fight for what you get if you're a woman," says Jessica Lawrence, a corporate vice president. "No matter how small your office might be, you can expand your space of power and authority by placing visitors' chairs against the farthest wall as far as possible from your desk. Another person should never be able to *invade* or *encroach* upon your territory by putting his arms on your desk.

"If you do have the authority to pick the furniture for your office, always pick soft easy chairs or a low sofa for your visitors. When you are sitting in the power position behind your desk, and your visitor is slumped down or sprawled out in an easy chair or low sofa, even if he's your boss, he is immediately at a disadvantage. It is much easier for you to retain the upper hand psychologically when your visitor is sitting in a weaker position."

How to Use Relaxation to Your Advantage

You already know how to use the steepling technique to project the power of your personality so you can gain unlimited power with others. Another way you can project the power of your position is to appear completely relaxed and at ease.

For example, in an interview, the power person, that is, the interviewer, is relaxed and at ease in his posture and his manner. He can choose to sit, stand, even stroll around while talking to the other person. If a man, he might even straddle a chair or put his feet up on the desk. If a woman, she can place her hands on her hips and spread her feet slightly to project her power. This position is a strong expression of power, especially for a woman.

But the person being interviewed, man or woman, is powerless to do any of these things. He or she is limited to sitting up straight, usually on the edge of the chair, in a completely motionless position.

You can also project the power of your personality by maintaining a completely neutral facial expression. At a high-level meeting of business executives, the ranking individual or the person in charge rarely smiles, even when greeted cordially by others. Less powerful people will almost always smile—even though nervously—throughout the entire meeting.

The Trick To "Staring Down" Another Person

The powerful person is accustomed to staring down another individual as a way of invading his private territory. Usually, if the boss stares at an employee, the employee will lower his eyes and only glance up now and then to sneak a quick look at his superior.

There's a trick to this technique of staring down another person. *Never, never look directly into the other person's eyes.* You can't win if you do that. Instead, pick a spot in the middle of his forehead just above the level of his eyebrows. Keep your eyes glued to that one spot, and no one will ever be able to stare you down. Eventually, the other person will have no choice but to lower his gaze.

How Body Language Can Reveal Your Innermost Thoughts

A person doesn't have to say a word to let you know what he's thinking or how he feels. His hands, eyes, mouth, and body give away how he really feels inside. Roberta Underwood, a psychologist from Orlando, Florida, has this to say about how a person's body language can reveal a person's inner thoughts and feelings.

"A person's hands can indicate fear and anxiety in a number of ways," says Dr. Underwood. "For example, fingers twitching or drumming the knees or arms of the chair, palms wet and clammy, hands visibly nervous when holding a pencil or cigarette, clenched fists, hands gripping the arms of the chair so firmly the knuckles actually turn white, all these show his anxiety.

"The face can reveal a great deal about the person's thoughts and feelings," Dr. Underwood goes on to say. "Eyes can show fear by shifting anxiously back and forth as if looking for escape, refusing to meet the other person's gaze, or by excessive blinking. The mouth can show fear when a person bites his lip or has a tightly clenched jaw. The body held stiff and rigid indicates a deep-seated anxiety. So does excessive perspiration or constant deep breathing with heavy sighs.

"A man's abdomen is also used in body language. In courtship, a man will tighten his abdominal muscles and pull in his belly to display his masculine strength and virility. When he is downcast and depressed, he will often overrelax those muscles and let his stomach sag visibly downward. The degree of tension of the abdominal muscles will tell a great deal about the emotional and mental state of a man. One way to tell if a person is really listening to you or not is to watch the position of his head while you are speaking to him," Dr. Underwood says. "If he works for you and is really attentive to what you are saying, he will usually tilt his head to one side. Less powerful people will often do this when they are listening to instructions from their superiors.

"The less powerful person, as your employee is, for example, will also mirror exactly the body posture of the more powerful person," Dr. Underwood says in conclusion. "For instance, if you lean forward and cross your arms, he will often do the same. If you cross your legs, so will he. If you look anxious while speaking to him, he will soon show body language signs of anxiety, too."

How You Can Stop Trouble Without Saying a Single Word

Henry Brockman, a high school principal, knows the quickest way to squelch potential or actual trouble in the classroom without ever saying a single word. Here's exactly how he does it:

"Maintaining order and discipline in the classroom is usually the hardest job a teacher has," Mr. Brockman says. "But the instructor can eliminate between 70 and 90 percent of classroom disruption if he will use this system. When the system is used properly, discipline is almost invisible, and that's the best kind. Let me give you a specific example of how you can make it work.

"Let's say a teacher tells her class to begin working on their arithmetic problems. But in a few moments, Johnny decides he'd rather do something else.

"Seeing this, the teacher walks over, leans over Johnny with her hands planted squarely on his desk, looks him straight in the eye, and tells him quietly to get back to work so he can turn his assignment in before he leaves at the end of the period. Johnny suddenly develops a deep interest in arithmetic again.

"Close physical proximity is one of the most important elements in maintaining discipline," Mr. Brockman goes on to say. "So is a quick response to disruption. A lot of teachers think that if you ignore the problem, it will go away. But that is simply not true. Immediate corrective action is necessary to retain control of the class.

"So respond quickly. Then it's mostly how you project the power of your personality through your body language by facing the student directly, having a tone of voice and a facial expression that shows you absolutely mean business. Eyeball-to-eyeball contact is also extremely important. The use of body language also helps the teacher keep his mouth shut. When he doesn't talk, he can't end up with his foot in his mouth or make a fool out of himself in front of the entire class."

If you will note, the close physical proximity Mr. Brockman talks about is an invasion of the student's space. This serves to deflate his ego and makes him more susceptible to direction from the teacher.

How to Project Power over the Phone

Although you cannot use the body language of your hands or eyes over the phone, how you use your voice and choose your words can still vividly project the power of your personality. For example, never refer to yourself by your given name. If you call someone on the phone, don't say, "Hi! This is Joe." Don't even say, "This is Joe Davis." Instead say, "This is Davis."

The use of first names encourages unwanted familiarity in the workplace. In power circles, familiarity is an invasion of privacy and space. It punctures your space bubble. Be courteous and polite, of course, but keep people at arm's length if you want to gain power with them.

When you answer the phone, don't use your title. To do so implies that you cannot get by on your own and that you need a crutch. Don't say, "This is *Mr.* Davis, or *Superintendent* Davis, or *Doctor, Professor, Major,*" or whatever. Just say, "Davis," "Davis here," or "Davis speaking." When introducing yourself to someone, simply say, "I'm Davis," or "My name is Davis." That's enough.

If you are a woman, follow the same procedure. This immediately places you on the same power level as your male associates. Never refer to yourself as Miss, Ms., or Mrs. This invites too many chauvinistic remarks, especially about the title Ms.

Telephone selling, or telemarketing as it is also called, has increased dramatically in recent years, probably because of the increased cost of driving a car. Many companies and corporations today use the phone instead of the traveling salesman to get orders and do business. So do a lot of retail firms.

I usually get from two to four telephone calls a day from local stores or firms wanting to sell me something. Most of those calls come when I'm eating supper, watching the evening news, reading the newspaper, whatever, and I don't want to be disturbed by anyone. It takes a powerful personality with a terrific message on the other end to get my undivided attention. The caller has to offer me a great big benefit of some sort right away to arouse my interest.

Many of the calls I get sound like this: "I'm going to be in your neighborhood tomorrow checking on (water purity, roofing, sidewalks, siding, grass, whatever). Could I drop by and see you so I can show you what I have to offer?"

My answer is usually that I'll not be home. That kind of call offers me no benefit whatever. The only benefit appears to be to the caller. In other words, it will be convenient for him to call on me since he's going to be in my neighborhood anyway—or so he says.

As Elmer Wheeler, one of America's greatest salesmen once said, "Your first ten words are more important than the next ten thousand." His statement is especially applicable to telephone selling.

So if you want to be successful in telemarketing, you must grab the person in the first few seconds by offering him a benefit he can't possibly refuse. There's simply no other way to be sure of getting him interested in your proposal.

Two Words to Eliminate from Your Vocabulary

Whether you realize it or not, certain words and phrases automatically place other people above you when you use them. You can bring yourself up to or above their level immediately by eliminating these words completely from your vocabulary.

I'm referring specifically to the use of the words "Sir" and "Ma'am." Never use these words either alone or in the phrases so often heard: "Yes, Sir," "No, Sir," "Yes, Ma'am," "No, Ma'am."

The use of "Sir" and "Ma'am" immediately places you on a lower level than the other person whether you realize that or not. These two small words imply *submissiveness* rather than courtesy and respect. You can still be courteous and show respect for the other person without being submissive. For example, if your boss asks if you've completed a certain task, don't answer with "Yes, Sir!" Instead, say, "Yes, Mr. Jones, I have."

Don't reply with only "Yes" or "No" when answering a question. It sounds too curt and brief and borders upon being insolent and discourteous. Answer "Yes" or "No" in a short sentence just as I said a moment ago. If the person to whom you are speaking has a title, use that, too, in place of "Sir" or "Ma'am." For instance, you can say, "Yes, Doctor, I have..." or "No, Professor, I have not."

How to Interpret Body Language in Social Activities

Wayne Thompson, a lecturer and an authority on body language and its interpretation, says it is very important for you to be able to interpret body language at social activities, especially in business or at office parties to keep yourself from making the wrong move or stepping on the wrong person's toes.

"For instance, if your boss and some of the other top-level brass have formed a tight circle that excludes everyone else, don't try to invade their area unless you are specifically invited to do so," Dr. Thompson says. "You can easily tell when they don't want others to be included in their conversation if they are sitting on a couch and the two at each end are 'book ended,' that is, turned inward to enclose the person or persons in the center and with their backs to the outside. This serves to lock out intruders, for the implication of this kind of grouping is, 'This is a closed discussion...keep out...you are not invited.'

"If they are standing in a group, elbow to elbow in a 'circle the wagons' posture, it also means they want to be left alone. Sometimes one man will put his foot up on a coffee table to prevent any outside intrusion into the group. Men will also tend to protect a woman by placing her in the middle of their circle or by placing themselves between male visitors and the female.

"If men and women are forced to sit very close together, face to face, and they are not on close terms, they may cross their arms and legs protectively and lean away from each other while talking, almost as if they had bad breath.

"You can learn a great deal about a person simply by watching his body language," Dr. Thompson says in conclusion. "He often gives away his thoughts and feelings without ever saying a single word."

Six Valuable Body Language Signals for Communicating Your Power to Others

When you want to communicate equality with your associates (this is especially important to a woman), you can use these six simple but powerful body language signals. These are also valuable to project the power of your personality to your subordinates, or to your boss as well, or to assert your status as an executive or a manager. Whatever your position is, these six tips will help you to gain unlimited power with people.

1. *Don't smile unless you are genuinely happy.* This does not mean that you have to walk around with a frown on your face as if you were carrying the weight of the whole world on your shoulders. It means exactly what it says. Don't smile unless you are truly happy. A neutral facial expression best conceals your inner thoughts, feelings, and emotions.

2. *Don't allow other people to interrupt you.* If someone does interrupt you, even if he or she is your superior, simply say, "Excuse me, but I wasn't finished yet," and then resume speaking at once where you were cut off.

This is usually enough to stop the other person in his tracks unless he is abnormally obtuse.

3. *Don't restrain your body gestures.* If you need to use your hands or arms to make a point, do so. The only thing to avoid here is pointing your finger at someone as if you were accusing him of some wrong. This turns everyone off.

4. *Look people straight in the eye.* I've already told you that the trick to this is staring at the spot in the middle of the forehead just above the eyebrows. This is one of the most effective techniques you can use to make the other person back off. If he is trying to argue with you, saying nothing but staring at him in this way will cause him to become nervous and flustered. You can make your point without ever having to say a single word.

5. *Use your space bubble effectively.* Many young executives fail to do this and then wonder why their personal private space is always being invaded. The proper placement of office furniture is often the key here.

6. *Be completely relaxed.* I don't mean that you should be sloppy or casual about your dress or careless about your appearance. The key to being relaxed is self-confidence. If you know your job, you don't have to be nervous and filled with tension or apprehension about doing it. You can relax and really enjoy your work.

Now I want to move on to Chapter 5, the fifth day, where I will give you specific guidelines that will help you develop further your personal power with people. It is a much shorter chapter than the first four, but this does not imply that it is not as important as they are. It is worth reading again and again, for in a way, it serves as a sort of wrap-up and summary of Part I and the first four chapters.

Chapter 5 ✳ *The Fifth Day*

NINETEEN GUIDELINES THAT WILL HELP YOU DEVELOP YOUR PERSONAL POWER

In the first four chapters, I've given you a variety of methods and techniques that will help you develop your own personal powers so you can gain unlimited power with people. I know I've covered a vast array of material, so now I'd like to use this final chapter in Part I as a summary of what has gone before.

The Benefits You Will Gain

1. When you practice the nineteen guidelines that you'll find in this chapter, your personal power with people will become so strong that you'll be able to maintain it at a high level with very little effort whatever.

2. Practice these nineteen guidelines and your life will be filled with joy and happiness. You'll be able to live with yourself. You'll be able to face yourself in the mirror and sleep comfortably every night without any feeling of self-guilt about your relationships with other people.

Now you might wonder if the benefits to be gained are worth all the efforts to be expended. As far as I am concerned, the benefit of achieving unlimited power with people is well worth all the work involved, but you'll have to answer that question for yourself.

One of the best ways to do this is to look around you at some of the successful people you know. I'm sure you will find that they are practicing the techniques you'll find, not only in this chapter, but also in the entire book to gain unlimited power with people.

What kind of person will that individual be? Well, I think you'll find that he is happy, serene, and contented with life. He will be well adjusted and able to get along with almost everyone without discord or friction.

I knew a man very much like that once. Perhaps you know someone just like him or at least you'll know someone who has many of the same character attributes and personal qualities this gentleman had. His name was Charles T. McCampbell.

Charles T. McCampbell was a major in the U.S. Army. I met him back in World War II. Major McCampbell knew his job as an army officer and he knew it well. He conducted himself as a gentleman at all times. I never once saw him lose his temper. This is not to say that he never felt anger, but that he always kept his emotions under tight control, no matter how trying the circumstances or the person might be.

Although he was intensely loyal to his superiors, he had no fear of them. He also stuck up for his own subordinates and was just as loyal to them, too. He was frank and honest; he said what he meant and meant what he said. In all the years that I knew him he never once lied, nor did he ever fail to keep his word. He never abused his privileges as an officer, as some were often prone to do.

The major had a sense of humor. He did not make the mistake of taking himself too seriously. He was kind, decent, and courteous, and he fully respected the rights of others. Although he felt responsible for setting the example for his subordinates to follow, he did not place himself on a pedestal, nor did he become a sanctimonious bore by preaching, sermonizing, or moralizing. He never tried to set up his own standards of right and wrong for others to follow.

He knew that the most reliable way to bring out a person's best was to set high standards for him to attain. I learned this from him quickly for one day he handed me an assignment with the terse command, "Lieutenant, here's a tough job for you to do. I know you can handle it, or I wouldn't give it to you." Without saying another word, he turned sharply, and walked away.

When I looked at the paper in my hand, I nearly panicked. At first glance, it seemed utterly impossible for me to accomplish. But at the same time, it never occurred to me not to try to do the job he'd given me to do. At least I had to try because he'd asked me to, and he'd shown complete confidence in my abilities to do the job.

I remembered the words I'd heard him use so often. "Always do your best," he would say. "You cannot do more—you should not wish to do less." So I set to it and somehow managed to get the job done. After I had completed it successfully, I realized that by setting such high standards for me to attain and by showing complete confidence in me, he got far more out of me than I knew I was even capable of giving myself.

You can get the same results from your people, too, just as Major McCampbell did, no matter what you do—whether you are an army officer, preacher, teacher, business executive, salesman, foreman, supervisor, father, mother, whatever.

Most people settle for less than they are actually capable of doing. If you set a high standard for them to attain, if you show them that you believe wholeheartedly they can do the job, they will give you their absolute best. You'll get far more out of them than they ever realized that they had in them. The major had gained unlimited power with people and he used that power all the time, often without even realizing; it for him using it had become automatic.

After a lot of practice of these unlimited power with people techniques yourself, certain character attributes will grow stronger and stronger within you until your unlimited power with people will become almost automatic, too. Then you can use it to control, to influence, to guide, and to help others without even having to think hard about what you're doing.

All these character attributes are benefits to be gained—not just techniques to be used. For example, if you are kind, decent, and courteous to others, is that only a technique that you are using? Hardly. It is a benefit as well, for you will receive the same kind of treatment in return from those people. I want now to cover these character attributes individually for you.

A person who keeps his or her unlimited power with people at a high level all the time is bound to have most, if not all, of them.

The Nineteen Guidelines for Developing Your Personal Powers

1. Have a strong belief in human rights. Always stand up for the rights of others, even those with whom you disagree. And always remember that you don't have to be disagreeable to disagree with other people.

2. Always have respect for the dignity of every person, no matter who he or she is. Never degrade or attack the dignity of any individual. One of the best ways to practice this principle is to treat every woman like a lady and every man like a gentleman.

I know there are exceptions to this, and that some people don't deserve the title of a lady or a gentleman, but you don't need to point that out to anyone. The person who is not a lady or a gentleman will demonstrate that point quite well and soon be known by her or his conduct.

3. Use the golden rule attitude toward everyone. Time has not dimmed the wisdom of this idea, and it never will.

4. Always show an abiding interest in all aspects of human welfare.

5. Exhibit a willingness to deal with every person as considerately as if he or she were a blood relative.

6. Behave toward new acquaintances as graciously as you do toward old friends and family members.

7. You should never be selfish and self-centered.

Remember, you are not the center of the universe even though at times you might think so. Really, the world does not revolve around you. Always consider other people's desires and talk to them in terms of their interests rather than your own, and you'll have no trouble whatever in using this technique to obtain unlimited power with them.

8. Don't set up your own standards of right and wrong. The longer I live, the more I discover that there's more gray than there is black and white in human behavior. So tolerate and accept the faults and character defects of those around you. Keep in mind that all the things you judge are done by people just like you. So be gracious to them. Make allowances for the weaknesses and frailties of others. Finally, take your own inventory rather than the inventory of others.

9. Keep a healthy, lively, and active curiosity to learn everything you can about how to help others.

10. Make allowances for inexperience. Learning is a slow repetitive process. No matter what your business or profession is, remember that you had to learn by doing. You had to crawl, too, before you were able to walk and then to run.

11. Give ground on unimportant trifles, but always stand fast and firm on principles. You'll find it's always easier to get your way if you let the other person get his way on minor unimportant points that are not crucial to the situation.

12. Make it a point always to help everybody whenever, wherever, and however you can. This does not mean that you are to be a snoopy busybody meddling in other people's business. It simply means what it says. Help the person who needs help whenever you can.

One of the best liked and most respected men I've ever known is Fred Ireland, the manager of a tire and rubber factory in Missouri. When Fred goes through the plant on an inspection tour, he never fails to stop and lend a hand to one of his employees in some way, for example, one who's lifting a heavy roll of crude rubber onto a skid or to anyone else who's having a tough time with his job. Maybe what he does doesn't really lighten the person's load that much, but his people love him and respect him for his concern for their welfare.

13. Look for the inner qualities that make the person rather than by judging by some outside quality that can be extremely misleading.

14. Realize that what you cannot do does not make a task impossible to accomplish.

15. Accept the things that you cannot change, but have the courage to change the things you can. All you need is the wisdom to know the difference.

16. Do not expect a uniformity of opinions or attempt to mold all dispositions alike.

17. Never try to measure the enjoyment of others by your own.

18. Always set the example for others to follow by being honest, dependable, courageous, and decisive.

19. Exhibit such additional character traits as endurance, enthusiasm, initiative, judgment, justice, loyalty, diplomacy, and tact.

If you will practice and follow these nineteen guidelines, these character traits will become deeply ingrained in you. The deeper they become and the stronger they grow, the easier it will be for you to practice these techniques. Your unlimited power with people will become almost automatic with you, and you'll be able to keep it at a high level without even half trying.

Now that you've seen how to gain unlimited power with yourself in Part I, let's move on to Part II, where you'll see how you can gain unlimited power with people.

* PART II *

How to Develop
Your Unlimited Power
With People

In Part I, you saw how to control and discipline yourself so you could gain your own personal powers. In Part II, you will learn how you can use those personal powers of yours to achieve unlimited power, influence, and control over others.

The best way to get ahead in life and get what you want is to use your power to influence and control other people.

Now there will be some who will misunderstand what I have just said. They will equate the word "power" with the word "tyrant" or "bully," probably because they have tried to gain power by using such strong-arm methods in the past, perhaps in their school days. But nothing could be further from the truth. In today's world, the person who gives service, who dedicates his or her whole being to others, and who executes the will of the people in a way that gives them what they want will emerge with the gift of greatness and the reward of true power. Just "getting along with others" is not nearly enough today. You must *give* of yourself if you want to *get* for yourself. In Part II, then, you will learn the following:

1. In Chapter 6, you will learn how to pinpoint the key people who can help you become successful and get what you want.

2. Next, in Chapter 7, you will be shown how to understand, predict, and control the behavior of those key people who can help you achieve your goals.

3. In Chapter 8, you will learn how to use a power play that will always get results for you without fail. In fact, it is a fail-safe technique you can use to get what you want.

4. In Chapter 9, you will learn the magic strategy that will win you unlimited power with people every single time.

5. In Chapter 10, you'll learn how to project an aura of command that will cause others to obey you instantly without hesitation or question.

6. In Chapter 11, you'll learn how to give orders that will always be carried out to the letter.

7. In Chapter 12, you will learn how to use the silent skill to gain unlimited power with people.

8. In Chapter 13, you will learn the delicate art of correcting a person's mistakes without losing your power over him or making an enemy out of him.

9. In Chapter 14, you'll discover the techniques you can use to create an army of loyal followers.

10. In Chapter 15, you will learn how to get people to give their maximum and go all out for you.

11. In Chapter 16, you will see how you can persuade people to your way of thinking as if by magic.

12. In Chapter 17, you will discover the master formula you can use for powerful and persuasive writing and speaking to control people.

13. In Chapter 18, you will learn how to control a person's emotions and turn off his or her anger completely.

14. In Chapter 19, you will learn how to use your unlimited power with people to gain complete control over problem persons.

15. And since you are bound to have some enemies or at least some people who are not friendly to you, in Chapter 20, you will learn how to shore up your own defenses so people will not be able to overpower you.

16. In Chapter 21, you will learn how to use your unlimited people power to succeed in business.

17. And last, but certainly not the least important, you will learn how to hold and increase your power with people year after year after year.

So if you are ready, let's get right into Chapter 6, where I will show you exactly how you can pinpoint the key people who can help you become successful in whatever you choose to do.

Chapter 6 ✳ *The Sixth Day*

HOW TO PINPOINT THE KEY PEOPLE WHO CAN HELP YOU BECOME SUCCESSFUL

Each of us has no fewer than two major goals in life. These are *success* and *happiness*. You've taken the first big step toward gaining both of them when you realize that your getting that success and happiness depends on other people.

Yes, it is a fact. You simply cannot succeed in life without the help of other people. If you want to get ahead in this world and get what you want, you must get other people on your side.

I've had people say to me, "You're a writer. How can this concept apply to you? You work alone; you don't need other people to succeed." How wrong they are. I need other people as much as anyone else does. Unless I had the publisher on my side, you would not be reading this book. And unless I had readers to buy this book, I could not possibly succeed. So, I need people, too, before I can achieve my goals of success and happiness.

You must get people to push for you, to stand up for you, to cheer for you, to vote for you—yes, even to fight for you, to stick with you all the way. And the best way, perhaps the only way, for you to get ahead in life is to *use your personal powers to influence and control certain key individuals, specific persons who can help you achieve success in life*. You must find out *which people can help you the most in getting what you want*.

"Many young executives and managers have the mistaken idea that their success depends entirely upon their own individual efforts," says Charlene Vance, president and chief executive officer of her own management consulting firm. "How wrong they are. The sooner they learn that they need other people on their side to help them get ahead in the business world, just that much sooner will they succeed in doing so."

I agree with Charlene wholeheartedly. The sooner you find out who those key people are who can really help you become successful, just that much sooner will you make a giant leap forward in your efforts to succeed.

Actually, this ought to be your first goal to attain: *Find out who the key people are who can help you the most in your life.* When you do that, you will benefit tremendously, saving both time and energy by *concentrating your efforts on only those key people who can help you achieve your goals of success and happiness.* To devote your attention to anyone else is an absolute waste of your time.

The Benefits You Will Gain

When you pinpoint those key individuals who can help you achieve your goals and become successful, you will realize many benefits. That is exactly what I want to tell you about next: the benefits you will gain when you concentrate your attention on only those key individuals who can help you attain your goals. Here's what some of those benefits are:

1. *You'll be able to control many people through just a few.* You don't need to control everyone to become successful. You can control dozens of people—yes, even hundreds or thousands—through just a few key individuals.

Genghis Khan controlled his far-flung empire through certain key people—his loyal tribal chieftains. The Roman Empire was ruled and controlled the same way: through certain key individuals selected by the emperor. Why did these two fail? Because they were military empires won by armed conquest. As you can see, strong-arm methods never attain lasting success. Modern history also proves that point.

But the basic principle of controlling many people through just a few key individuals is correct. The economic empires of large corporations today—for example, Ford, General Motors, Westinghouse, General Electric, Sony, and Mitsubishi—have thousands of employees. The president and chief executive officer of any of these sprawling economic giants could not possibly control his modern "empire" without the help of key officers and able administrators.

2. *You'll save a vast amount of time when you concentrate your efforts on the right person.* Time is important to all of us. It's a successful salesperson's most valuable asset. He or she will never waste it by giving his or her sales pitch to someone who can't make the buying decision. That's what unsuccessful salespeople do and why they soon find themselves in another line of work. But successful salespeople soon learn to *sell the secretary on seeing the boss. Sell the boss on buying the product.* That's why they are so successful.

Ask any business executive what his or her greatest problem is and you'll almost always be told, "Not enough time in the day to get everything done." That's why they carry a briefcase home each night. And if you are like most of us—and it doesn't matter whether you are a corporate executive, a college student, a teacher, or a clerk—you no doubt have the same problem, too: not enough time to get everything done. But you can solve much of that problem by *concentrating your efforts on the person who can help you get the job done.* Don't waste your valuable time on the person who cannot help you attain your goals.

3. *You'll save much energy and effort when you pinpoint the pivot personality.* This is an especially useful technique to those who work with large groups of people: teachers and preachers, supervisors and foremen, military officers, and industrial and business executives. But its value is not limited to those people alone. If you work with as few as two or three other persons—and it doesn't matter whether it's on your job or with the finance committee in your church—these techniques can be useful to you, too.

Pivot people are always action people. Their personalities demand lots of action. They stagnate and waste their talents in humdrum, routine, monotonous jobs. Learn who the pivot people are in your group so you can use their skills properly; you'll get far better results when you do. Pivot persons are especially important to you when you need action and you need it right now. They can help you get that action when and where you need it for working under pressure comes naturally to them.

4. *When you find the key people who can help you attain your objectives, you will be well over halfway on your road to success.* Russell Conwell, the founder of Temple University in Philadelphia, was also the

author of "Acres of Diamonds,"[1] which was no doubt the most famous speech in the history of the American lecture platform. Although its message is both inspiring and timeless, part of its fame was derived from Dr. Conwell's unique methods of presentation.

Dr. Conwell always arrived in town long before his scheduled speaking time. He would visit the postmaster, the school principal, the mayor, local clergymen, prominent businessmen, and other key people in the town. He won those people to his side long before he stepped on the speaker's platform. They helped him win over the rest of his audience. Not only that, by his visits with the key persons in the town, he knew more about that town than many of its own residents did.

You can do the same, whether you are talking to parents at a PTA meeting, speaking to the Friday night bowling league, attending a meeting of the city council, or addressing the board of directors in a closed conference room meeting. Find the key people and get 'em on your side first; the rest will automatically follow.

5. *When you find the power behind the throne, you can become king or queen yourself.* Key people are often far removed from an official position of authority or responsibility. They will have an aura of influence far out of proportion to their actual position in the organization. They will be the unofficial leaders, the pushers, the instigators, the fifth column (sometimes even the troublemakers, until you learn how to control them), but they will never be out in front in plain view. Their influence always takes place behind the scenes. But you must find them; you must know who they are, for you need them on your side before you can become completely successful.

How to Find the People Who Will Help You Get What You Want

I've already told you not to spend your valuable time and energy on someone who cannot help you get what you want. If you concentrate your attention on the wrong person, all your efforts will be wasted.

---

[1] Russell Conwell, *Acres of Diamonds* (Westwood, NJ: Fleming H. Revell, 1960).

Instead, you should locate the person who can help you, the one who can get the job done for you, the one who can give you the answer to your question, no matter who that person is. Sometimes, you'll find that person in the most unexpected places, just as Robert J. Anderson, the manager of a large textile plant did.

"We were having a huge problem with waste," Mr. Anderson says. "Our profit margin was dropping steadily, and we seemed to have more going out the back door as scrap than we had going out the front door to be sold.

"The production superintendent was raising the devil with all the section supervisors, but he couldn't seem to get any accurate figures from them as to which section was at fault. They were all too busy trying to blame each other for the excessive waste.

"And I couldn't get any straight answers from the people who should've had them either. Then I remembered something I'd heard from a large department store owner one time. 'If you really want to know where your profit is going,' he told me, 'ask the janitor.'

"So I did just that. I called in the night janitor. In a matter of moments, I was able to find out which sections were generating the most waste. Then I was able to solve my problem."

If you want to increase your power with people, then you, too, must do as Bob Anderson did. You must find the right person who knows the answers and who can help you get what you want. When you do that, you'll benefit just as Bob Anderson did.

If you want to pinpoint the people who are really important to you, sit down right now and make up a list of the people in your life who can help you achieve your goals.

When you get through with your list, you'll probably have no more than a dozen or so names on it. You'll no doubt put down the name of your boss and the name of the person he or she works for, too. You could have the names of some of the associates you work with, important customers or clients, your husband or wife, maybe even the preacher or the banker.

And if you have people who work for you, I'm sure that some of their names will be there, too, for a great many times, what your subordinates do or do not do can make you or break you, as Jack Ellsworth, a production supervisor, well knows.

"If you're a production supervisor as I am, you must really know the people who work for you," Jack says. "You must know which ones are the most important to you—which ones are the key individuals you can depend on to get the job done. Those are the people you want to put in your most sensitive spots—your critical positions—so they can watch your most vulnerable areas for you.

"By the same token, you want to know who your potential trouble-makers are so you can keep them away from sensitive jobs where they can cause trouble for you. Those people are also extremely important to you, too, although in a much different way. I've seen the careers of young management people wrecked because they failed to realize this fact."

When you make up your list of names ask yourself these basic questions:

1. *Why* is this person so important to me?
2. *What* can he or she do to *help* me?
3. *How* can he or she help me achieve my goals?
4. *What* can he or she do to *harm* me?
5. *How* could he or she keep me from attaining my goals?
6. *How* can I "use" this person to help me succeed?

How These Key People Can Be of Service to You

One of the best ways you can "use" these individuals who are so important to you is to pick their brains for your own benefit. For instance, chances are your boss didn't get to be the boss just by pure dumb luck. He must have had something on the ball to get where he is.

So ask questions that will give him a chance to impart some of his knowledge to you. And he'll be glad to do that. Remember, the moment you ask a person for his opinion, you've made him feel important, and he can't help but tell you what you want to know.

And the same thing applies to the people who work for you. Pick their brains, too. Just because that person works for you doesn't mean that you're smarter than he is in every area. You can learn from him, too, if you will just ask questions and be courteous and patient enough to listen to his answers.

"Every person I meet is smarter than I am in some way, and I can learn something helpful from him if I will just force my ego to step aside so I can listen to him," says Bruce Hamilton. "Like when our house was being built, I'd go by every day and watch the progress. One morning the foreman said, 'Coming by to inspect again?' 'No,' I said. 'Just to look. I don't know how to inspect for I don't know anything about the construction business. Perhaps you could help me.'

"Well, he jumped at the chance to show off his knowledge to me. He explained every step as construction went along and told me why they were doing everything that they did. I know I have a better built house than I'd have had otherwise for that foreman had to live up to the good reputation I gave him when I asked him to help me."

Nine Characteristics of Take-Charge Persons

In every group of people, you will find certain key individuals who seem naturally to take over. I call them *pivot* people, for the action of the entire group will usually hinge or pivot upon what these key individuals say or do.

You can spot the pivot people easily, for they will always be in the center of the action. They do not stand on the sidelines just looking on. They are not spectators. They insist on getting into the act. Unlike so many people, they do want to get involved.

A pivot person will be the kind who automatically takes charge in some emergency, for instance, an auto accident. He'll send someone to call for an ambulance and for the police. He'll appoint someone else to direct traffic. He'll see to it that the injured people receive first aid.

This kind of person seems to be pushed by an inner urge for action. He has an internal drive to keep things moving along at a fast clip. He is always "chomping at the bit" to get things done. This kind of person will be able to harness his physical drive to solve mental tasks, too. For instance, he will have that natural ability to take a good idea—either his own or someone else's—and ramrod it, promote it, or sell it to the group.

It does not matter what kind of group it is: PTA, city council, school board, church group, employees in a department or section, certain individuals always seem to be able to influence and control the entire group. If you can identify and recognize these key people, you will be able to influence and control the entire group through them.

Although no two pivot people act alike, most of them do have at least one, and sometimes more, of these particular characteristics or tendencies:

1. A pivot person will be the unofficial leader of the group.
2. A pivot person will be a problem solver.
3. A pivot person will be an authoritative figure.
4. A pivot person will possess great drive, stamina, and endurance.
5. A pivot person will be knowledgeable in a broad range of subjects.
6. A pivot person usually has an exceptionally good memory.
7. A pivot person will be an independent and creative thinker.
8. A pivot person will strive constantly to improve the system.
9. A pivot person will often be an "after five o'clock" key person.

Now let me discuss each one of these characteristics of a pivot person in detail.

1. *A PIVOT PERSON WILL BE THE UNOFFICIAL LEADER OF THE GROUP.* This person is part of the unofficial power chart that is found in every organization. He wields an influence that has no relationship at all to his actual position. Though he is not part of the official power line of command or authority, a word from him can often make or break a person or a project.

His power may sometimes be negative rather than positive, as I've just indicated. For example, I have seen longtime employees quietly corner power by getting the authority to initial plans or memos. Even though their initials mean nothing—neither approval nor disapproval—these employees can delay, sometimes even kill, a project by keeping it in their in-box too long. Even though that's negative, not positive, power, it's still power. You need to know who and where that key person is.

2. *A PIVOT PERSON WILL BE A PROBLEM SOLVER.*   A key person will often have a solution for your problem. A great many times the hardest part of solving any problem is simply getting started on it. A key person can help you get that action when you need it most. Often what you need is a supply of suggestions to help you solve your problem, no matter where those ideas come from, or who supplies them to you. A key person will usually have several suggestions to make for solving your problems. His or her ideas may not always be the best, but they will help you get things moving again in a bogged-down situation. And as the old saying goes, "A poor plan carried out enthusiastically is better than a good plan not carried out at all."

3. *A PIVOT PERSON WILL BE AN AUTHORITATIVE FIGURE.*   A pivot person will usually stand out in any group. His manner, his bearing, his way

of speaking all attract attention. He tends to take command of any situation, no matter what it is. Without appearing to force himself on others, a pivot person seems to just naturally assume authority and take over the leadership of the group.

"You can usually spot the pivot person in a group by watching the way the others turn to him for guidance," says Melvin Bryant, a Dallas, Texas, industrial foreman. "For example, a supervisor issues an order, turns his back, and walks away.

"Immediately, all the employees gather around one individual to get his opinion. He speaks; they listen. Then they go back to work and carry out the supervisor's order, but not until they get the unofficial go-ahead from the informal leader of the group."

4. A PIVOT PERSON WILL POSSESS GREAT DRIVE, STAMINA, AND ENDURANCE. A key individual has the endurance, the drive, and the stamina to see things through to the end. He or she is able to stick to a job and finish it when others want to give up. If you are looking for someone to put on a long-term project or a project that has a multiplicity of details, a key person could be just the one you want to carry the job through to its successful completion, especially if the goal to be reached is well worthwhile.

5. A PIVOT PERSON WILL BE KNOWLEDGEABLE IN A BROAD RANGE OF SUBJECTS. One of the best persons to have around in a tough situation will be the one who has a vast range of interests and broad general knowledge—especially when you are looking for new ideas to solve a problem. You see, new ideas usually spring from old ones so the person with this broad range of knowledge has the background and the potential for coming up with them.

6. A PIVOT PERSON USUALLY HAS AN EXCEPTIONALLY GOOD MEMORY. A good memory is important to the acquisition and retention of this broad knowledge. A key individual's good memory can be of great value to you when you need a quick solution to a pressing problem. The kind of person who can remember how a similar problem was solved last year can be invaluable to you in a crisis. A person with a good memory may well be the first one to come up with information or help when you need it in a hurry.

7. A PIVOT PERSON WILL BE AN INDEPENDENT AND CREATIVE THINKER. A key person will be a creative thinker—a true nonconformist. A really creative person will be a wellspring of fresh ideas. He will resist strongly any efforts to restrict and channel his thinking. If his creative urge is strong enough, it will show up in his efforts to get transferred to challenging jobs or, at the least, to acquire additional knowledge of other departments and other people's work. This may well be your first clue to the presence of a pivot person who can help you solve your problems or achieve your goals. Above all, he will never be a "yes person." This is one of the quickest ways you can recognize a creative thinker.

John D. Rockefeller recognized how important a creative thinker was to his organization. One day he stopped at the desk of a busy paper-shuffling junior executive.

After watching this dynamo for a few moments, Mr. Rockefeller put his hand on the young man's shoulder and said, "You shouldn't work so hard. Let your secretary handle all that paperwork. Then you can sit back, put your feet up on the desk, and think up new ways to help Standard Oil make more money. That's what executives are paid for."

And when I see the price of gasoline and oil today, I think this young man must have taken Mr. Rockefeller's advice.

A pivot person will be independent. You can usually spot a pivot person in a group by his or her need for independent action. A great many times, this key individual will be someone who has refused a position of management or supervision—even though he apparently has all the necessary leadership qualifications—simply because he doesn't want to be pinned down by official responsibility. He wants to be free to operate without being hampered by administrative rules and regulations or organizational red tape.

This kind of personality will be found in church groups, too. He will usually classify himself as a rebel or a nonconformist. He'll have ideas and opinions on most subjects. Much of the time his ideas are sound and sensible, but he still wants no part of any lay leadership position in the church. As one fellow told me, "I don't want to be a deacon or an elder. If I were, I could no longer speak my piece. I'd simply have to parrot the party line."

8. A PIVOT PERSON WILL STRIVE CONSTANTLY TO IMPROVE THE SYSTEM. A pivot person can often be recognized by the way he hates the routine way of doing things. He refuses to accept the status quo as being set in concrete and is constantly looking for better ways of doing things. He is the kind of person you want around to help you for he can often solve your problems even before they happen.

9. A PIVOT PERSON WILL OFTEN BE AN "AFTER FIVE O'CLOCK" KEY PERSON. You may not care for this kind of key person—not many managers do—but he does exist, so you ought to know who he is. It will be to your advantage if you do. This person will often have social contacts with top executives. These social connections may have been gained by a long-standing friendship of their spouses or, membership in the same religious, political, or fraternal organization. However this relationship has been formed is not important. But the fact remains that it does exist. This person may not be able to reach your boss at work, but he can surely do it after five o'clock. He can often hurt you as well as help you, so you should know who this key person is so you can guard yourself at all times.

How to Get Your Key People to Cooperate First

In every group you will always find at least one person to whom the other employees look for advice, help, and leadership. The speed of production and quality of workmanship will depend not upon the order from the supervisor in management, but on the order from the informal leader in the ranks of labor.

So if you want to get the best out of your people, if you want to get the entire group to cooperate and work with you, your first job is to find out who those informal leaders are. You'll want to know which people in your organization can help you the most. Do that, and you'll be able to save much time and energy by concentrating your efforts through your management people on only those individuals in labor who can help you achieve your goals.

Once you know who those key individuals are, you can use them as your unofficial communication chain. You can have your managers feel out their groups by taking those key people aside and getting their ideas or opinions first. This doesn't make them the boss or take away any authority from your managers. It simply gets them on your side. The basic rule to follow is this: *Find out who the pivot or key people are and get' em on your side first; the rest will automatically follow.*

Above all, don't lock horns with those key individuals. There's nothing wrong with their having influence in their group as long as they don't misuse their power and try to usurp yours. You'll get much further if you work with these people and use the power they have with their groups to your own advantage.

Let me say, then, that when you pinpoint the key persons who can help you, you'll gain unlimited power with people.

Chapter 7 ✻ *The Seventh Day*

HOW TO FIND THE SECRET MOTIVATORS FOR PREDICTING AND CONTROLLING PEOPLE'S BEHAVIOR

You want to be able to gain unlimited power with people so you can control their attitudes and actions. Then you can enjoy the benefits of having them do what you want them to do.

I know for a fact that you want to do that for two reasons: first, you are reading this book; second, every person I've ever met has this same basic desire for power. Gaining power with people is everyone's goal.

Now getting along with others is an important part of your desire to gain unlimited power with people. The ability to make friends and get along with others is a must if you want to attain unlimited power with them. But that in itself is not enough and here's why.

Although the friendly handshake, the big smile, and the cheerful greeting are all important, they won't get you anywhere *unless you know exactly what the other person wants.*

You'll never gain your objectives or achieve your goals unless you stop thinking of what it is you want from that person and *concentrate entirely on what you can do for him or her.*

To be able to do that, you must get inside a person's mind so you can find out what he really wants. You need to know what actually makes that other person tick. You'll want to discover the *secret motivators* that really turn him on. Only then will you be able to understand why he says what he says, why he does what he does. And only after you understand him completely, will you be able to use that knowledge to gain unlimited power with him.

Now you don't need to be a psychiatrist or a psychologist, nor do you need any sort of advanced degree to be able to understand, predict, and control people's behavior and discover their innermost secret needs and desires. The techniques you will learn, not only in this chapter, but also in the rest of this book, are easy to understand, simple to use, and most important of all, you'll find that they really will work for you.

I have spent my entire life studying applied psychology: why people say the things they say and why they do the things they do. Give me just a few minutes to listen to another person talk, and I can tell you what he really wants out of life for himself even better than he can. With a bit of practice and experience you can soon do the same.

In the lectures and seminars that I give for company and corporation executives, management personnel, and businessmen and women, I show them how they can use this valuable information about a person's deep needs and desires to gain unlimited power with people.

When you gain unlimited power with people, you'll find you can have everything you want. You will become a true leader of people, not merely a persuader or a manipulator, but a leader, pure and simple. Everything you ask, people will now do for you when you use the methods and techniques that I give you here.

The Benefits You Will Gain

1. *You'll gain unlimited power with people.* When you know and understand those secret motivators that cause people to do and say the things they do, when you learn their innermost needs and desires, and when you make the extra effort it takes to help them get what they want, you will gain unlimited power with them. People will always do what you want them to do.

2. *You'll save much time, energy, even money.* Have you ever wondered why some individuals are so successful while others fail so miserably? Or why so many small business ventures fold only a year or so after starting?

The answer is quite simple: *Those who failed didn't determine what people wanted before they started.*

The most successful companies, corporations, and individuals always find out what their customers want before they ever open the front door. They don't waste time, energy, or money in guessing. They benefit by finding out specifically what a person's needs and desires are through psychological studies and marketing surveys.

You, too, can save a tremendous amount of time, energy, and even money by using the same basic procedures. But you won't have to conduct an expensive psychological study or marketing survey to find out what a person's secret needs and desires are. Before you finish this chapter, you will know every one of the secret motivators that controls a person's behavior. You will also learn how you can use those secret motivators to gain unlimited power with people.

3. *You'll be able to influence, control, and gain unlimited power with everyone you meet.* As you study human behavior to perfect your understanding and knowledge of people—and as you discover why people say the things they say and why they act the way they do, and as you learn to analyze their words and actions to find out what their secret hidden motivators are—you'll find that your ability to influence and control every single person with whom you come in contact will continue to improve. Your success in gaining unlimited power with people will be inevitable.

How to Understand Human Behavior

It is easy to understand human behavior when you realize that *people do the things they do because they have certain basic needs and desires that must be met so they can be happy.* Everything a person does is directed at achieving those basic needs and desires. Some of these are purely physical. Others are acquired through the learning processes as an individual goes through life.

Physical Needs. The satisfaction of a physical need can become a specific goal that motivates a person to behave in a certain way. The basic physical needs are those pertaining to one's existence and survival: food, drink, sleep, clothing, shelter, sexual gratification, and other normal body functions.

You will seldom have the opportunity to use a person's physical needs as goals to motivate him except in the specific instance where his basic need has become a want because of *greed.*

I know greed is a harsh word, but I see no point in using some euphemism to describe a drive that most of us have, but don't like to admit. I have found that *when all other human motives fail, you can always depend upon greed.* That is why the flim-flam man and the con artist survive today and always will.

Greed will make a man want a larger house, a bigger car, better food to eat, more expensive clothes, more money than he needs. Let me give you some examples of that. A house with one bathroom would be thought of by most people as a basic need; one with three or four bathrooms would be a desire to many of us. A woman's cloth coat in cold weather would be a requirement; a mink coat would be a desire.

When a person's need becomes a want, it is usually because he is driven by a deep desire for ego-gratification—a feeling of importance or pride—plus a desire for more money and the things that money will buy. We all want to feel more important than someone else whether we will come right out and admit that or not.

For instance, would you rather drive a Ford or a Lincoln? Both are transportation. You'd rather have the Lincoln, right? Why? Because you need it or because it makes you feel more important? Of course, everything is relative. The real feeling of importance comes from being more important than someone else. You can enjoy your Lincoln even more if your neighbor drives a Ford.

Don't feel bad. I'd rather have the Lincoln, too! What's my point in all this? I'm not trying to embarrass anyone. I'm as guilty as the next person. I drive a car too big for my needs, live in a house too large for my requirements, and have more suits and shoes than I can wear in weeks. I eat more and better food than I should; the scales prove that. All I'm trying to bring out is what makes people tick, what turns them on, what makes them do the things they do. I simply want you to understand the nuts and bolts of human behavior so you can use that knowledge to gain unlimited power for yourself with them.

Learned Needs (Desires).   Learned needs are acquired by the person throughout his life as he learns what is valued by other people and the importance of social attitudes. Psychological needs such as the desire for security, social approval, and recognition can be as strong as the more basic physical ones. People will do anything necessary to achieve them.

You can use a person's psychological needs or desires as goals to motivate him far better than you can use the physical needs (except as I have previously indicated) to get what you want from him and gain unlimited power with him. The basic learned needs or desires that every normal person has are these:

1. Financial success: money and the things money will buy
2. Recognition of efforts, reassurance of worth
3. Social or group approval, acceptance by one's peers
4. Ego-gratification, a feeling of importance
5. The desire to win, the desire to be first, the desire to excel
6. A sense of roots, belonging somewhere
7. The opportunity for creative expression
8. The accomplishment or achievement of something worthwhile
9. New experiences
10. A sense of personal power
11. Good health, freedom from sickness and disease, physical comfort
12. Liberty and freedom
13. A sense of self-respect, dignity, and self-esteem
14. Love in all its forms
15. Emotional security

I have not listed these learned needs or desires in any particular order of importance, except for emotional security. I have listed it last because if any of the previous fourteen have not been achieved, a person cannot possibly have emotional security.

The point is, then, that if any single one of them is not fulfilled in his life, the person cannot be completely satisfied and happy. If you do not remember anything else about human nature, keep these basic desires every person has in mind, remembering that everything he does is directed toward their fulfillment. A person's every thought, word, and deed are aimed at achieving those goals. If you help him gain them, he will do whatever you ask him to do, and you'll have unlimited power with him.

Some authorities in the field of psychology consider the desire to win, to be first, or to excel as a part of the desire for a feeling of importance. That may be true to some extent, but I feel the desire to win is important enough to be categorized individually.

There is one other basic desire that a person can have. I have not mentioned it because it can seldom be used to gain unlimited power with people. Not only that, it is a motive that is more commonly encountered in abnormal people rather than normal people, although all of us will have the desire at one time or another in our lives. That motivating force is the *desire for vengeance or revenge, the desire to get even with someone.* This is a motive often used in Western stories where the hero devotes his entire life to getting even with the person who has wronged him or his family in some way. In a normal person, the desire for vengeance is usually short-lived. It does not become an obsession with him as it does in the abnormal individual.

How Sam Crane Used His Knowledge of Human Behavior to Manage More Effectively

"When I went to work for this company years ago, I was a shift supervisor fresh out of college," Sam says. "My boss, a crusty old foreman, believed in pushing people around and using threats to get the job done. He ran the department like an old army drill sergeant. People were scared to death of him and hated him as well. They covered up their mistakes. Morale was bad, production was low, quality was terrible. I vowed then that if I ever attained a position of real authority, I would do exactly the opposite of everything Bill did.

"Finally he left and I became the department foreman. I changed procedures immediately. Instead of yelling at people when they made mistakes, I showed them how to do the job properly. Rather than use harsh criticism, I praised a person for his efforts. Instead of threatening a person with the loss of his job, I helped him improve his work methods so he could speed up production and make more money. My supervisors followed my lead. That department changed almost overnight and became the top one in the company. Where people before fought to stay out of it, they now begged to get in.

"That was a long time ago. I have been rewarded handsomely for my work over the years. I know I could never have attained my position as president of the corporation had I not made the effort to understand our people and help them solve their problems. Actually, I should say that my people helped me get where I am today because I helped them get what they wanted. I have never forgotten that lesson. I still follow the same basic principles in dealing with people today."

If you are a manager or an executive, you should analyze your own operation to determine exactly how you can best satisfy the basic needs and desires of your own people, too. When you do this, I know you will find, just as I have, that *whatever a person is lacking at the moment, he or she has the greatest need and desire for.* It will be your responsibility to find out which specific need or desire is most important to a person at that particular moment of time.

You will need to keep in mind that each person's needs and desires change constantly. They are never static. What he needed most of all yesterday may not be what he needs today. That's why you will want to keep fully informed and up to date on your people's needs and desires at all times.

At this point you might be saying to yourself, "What's so important about my making sure those people get what they want? What about me? What about what I want? Don't I count, too?"

Of course you do, but let me tell you this. I learned a long time ago that *when the person who worked for me got what he wanted, then I always got what I wanted, too.* When I fulfilled his basic needs for recognition and importance, he gave me better quality production with less waste. He cooperated wholeheartedly with me to get the job done. You will find that the same thing will hold true for you, too.

You see, when you give the person who works for you what he wants, then he'll give you what you want. The reverse of this idea is also true. *You will never get what you want unless he gets what he wants first.* This thought brings us quite logically to the next subject.

The Key to Controlling Others

This master key controls *all* human behavior. It is the most important principle in the conduct of human relations. This master key is even more than a principle; *it is a law governing all human conduct.* It is the "number one rule" that you can depend on in dealing with all people. If you want to be successful in management or salesmanship or any other profession or human endeavor for that matter, then find out what a person wants and help him get it.

Does this seem to be too simple to be the number one rule in all human relations? Think about it. If you follow this rule, it will even solve your family problems for you, too. It can be used in any sort of activity in which people are engaged. There is only one sure way to win unlimited power with a person so you can get him to do what you want him to do every time. And that is to find out what he wants and then to make sure that he gets it when he does as you ask him to do.

For instance, does he want recognition for a job well done? Then make sure he gets it; praise his work. Does he want to feel important? Then pay attention to him, make him important by telling him how much you need him, how much you depend on him. Does he want a chance to do something worthwhile? Then offer him the opportunity; give him a challenging job to do. Does he want to feel safe and secure in his job? Then offer him that security. Don't use force or fear or threaten to fire him for every little mistake he makes. When a person fears you, he eventually will hate you. I guarantee it.

When you find out what a person wants and show him how he can get it by doing exactly as you ask, you can rest assured of one thing: he will do exactly as you desire when he knows for sure he will get what he wants. In fact, he will do everything necessary to get what he wants, even if he has to move heaven and earth to get it.

That being so, you will know exactly what his actions and reactions are going to be to your orders and your directives. As long as you make sure he gets what he wants by following your orders, you can accurately predict every single time what he is going to do. You can forecast his response to the letter. And that, my friend, is unlimited power with people.

How to Find Out What a Person Really Wants

"You have only one sure way to find out what a person wants, and that is to ask her questions," says Karen Richards, the owner of a stylish clothing store for women. "Of course, you can't be blunt about it. You must use finesse and subtlety in your questioning techniques. If the person is one of your employees, you can use either formal interviews in your office or informal woman-to-woman chats as you go through your organization on routine inspections or supervisory walks.

"I have always found informal visits with my employees to be better for getting worthwhile information. A person tends to be on guard in a formal interview in an office. She is more likely to give you the answer she thinks you want to hear when she is in your office. But she will be much more candid during an informal visit that 'just happens' to take place out where she works.

"Whichever method you decide on, depending upon your own individual situation, always use your ears, your eyes, and your common sense. You will learn a lot that way. I use the following guidelines in my interviews and my visits to draw a person out and get her to talk about herself and what she wants out of life.

"I am always genuinely interested in my people and their problems. And that is not an act. It is genuine interest on my part.

"Next, I always try to be a good listener. I listen to what she doesn't say as well as to what she does. I've found patience is required at all times to be a good listener.

"Third, I encourage her to talk about herself and I ask her questions to help her get started.

"I always talk in terms of the other person's interests so I can find out what she wants. I never tell her what I want; she could care less about that.

"And, last, I make the other person feel important. I feed her ego and I do it with deep sincerity."

I myself have always used the *five W's* to get specific answers to my questions. This forces me to be precise so I can bring out the answers I need from the person. The five W's I use are *Who? What? When? Where? Why?* I also use *How* to get additional information. By asking a person questions like this, I gain these five benefits:

1. Questions help my listener crystallize his thinking and concentrate his attention where I want it.

2. Questions make a person feel important. When I ask a person for his opinion for his ideas on anything, I feed his ego—I give him that sense of importance he needs so much.

3. When I ask questions, I keep from talking too much myself. My listener has the opportunity to tell me what he thinks and what he wants. My purpose is to get information, not to give it away.

4. Questions keep me out of arguments. By asking questions, I get his idea first. If I disagree with what he says, I don't have to say so. He'll never know what I was actually thinking.

5. When I ask questions, I can find out exactly what a person's desires are. A question is the quickest, most reliable way to find out what a person really wants.

Let me tell you how an insurance saleswoman, Sharon Bruce, uses questions to get results. She kept a record of hundreds of interviews to find out why people bought or failed to buy insurance. She found that in more than 80 percent of cases, the objection raised against buying insurance was not the real reason at all.

Sharon found from her research that a person usually has two distinct reasons for doing anything: a reason that sounds good to the listener and the real one that he keeps hidden all to himself.

Sharon recommends that to find the real reason behind a person's words and actions, you should simply keep on asking him, "Is there any other reason?" or "In addition to that?"

I want to give you two more examples of how people I know used this technique of finding out what people want to increase their sales and make more money for themselves.

My own insurance agent, Russell W., was making an average living using the old-fashioned standard approach of plugging security for the family if the man of the house died.

His secretary, Pamela, who attended some of my lectures, suggested to Russell that he change his sales tactics to offer the prospect the chance to *control and dominate* his family, even after his death, with the proper life insurance program.

Russell called me the other day to tell me how much his business had improved with his new methods. "When I offered a man only security for his family, I was offering him a benefit he could never use for himself," Russell said. "In fact, I was making him think only of his own death with that kind of sales pitch, and he just couldn't handle that idea.

"But by offering him the opportunity to *control and dominate, guide and direct* his family's activities even after he was gone, he saw that he was in a sense still alive. He was not completely wiped out of the picture. My life insurance sales have quadrupled with this new approach, thanks to you and my secretary."

Now, consider my neighbor, Jeffrey N., who found his sales in air conditioning lagging after the energy crunch that began back in the early 1970s. People were willing to give up the physical comfort of air conditioning because of the high cost of electricity.

Jeffrey tried to figure out new customer benefits that he could use to stimulate his sagging sales, but he was at a loss as to how to do it. Then I pointed out to him that with open windows instead of air conditioning, homes were much more susceptible to burglary, so he should offer his prospects the benefits of *safety and emotional security* as well as physical comfort and better health.

So Jeffrey decided to try this new approach. To prove his point, he clipped police reports from local newspapers and pasted them in a sales notebook to show prospective customers the rising crime rate in the community.

Then he would point out to his prospect that with air conditioning, the windows would be closed, the house would be protected, and the person could sleep peacefully all night long knowing his family, his house, and his precious possessions were safe and secure.

"I've sold more air conditioning using your approach, Jim, than I ever did before," Jeffrey told me. "Older people are more concerned with their safety than they are with their wallets, and we do have a lot of senior citizens here in Florida."

Why Accurate Information Is So Important

To gain unlimited power with a person, you must know exactly what he wants so you can help him get it. That's why accurate information about what a person desires is so important to you.

I can best illustrate this point by giving you a specific example with which I am personally familiar. A certain electronics factory was having all sorts of personnel problems. Individual morale and organizational esprit were both at rock bottom. Quality control was turning back nearly 40 percent of production. Absenteeism was running 20 percent above normal. The company's profit margin was being squeezed down to nearly zero.

The company called in a management consulting firm to see if they could find out exactly what was wrong. After talking to a number of employees, the consulting firm made up a questionnaire that listed eight specific basic wants. The firm then asked all the employees to list those eight basic desires in their proper order of importance.

The consulting firm also asked the company executives and management personnel to rate those same items—not in the way they personally felt about them—but in the order they thought their employees would list them.

Shown below are those eight basic wants listed in the order of importance by the employees on the left. Management's listing is also shown on the right side of the chart:

Employee's Rating	Eight Basic Wants or Desires	Management's Rating
1	Credit and recognition for work done	7
2	Interesting and worthwhile work	3
3	Fair pay with salary increases	1
4	Attention and appreciation	5
5	Promotion by merit, not seniority	4
6	Counsel on personal problems	8
7	Good physical working conditions	6
8	Job security	2

The emphasis that employees and employers placed on these items is not the same at all. When management placed its emphasis on what the employees wanted, rather than guessing what they wanted, the company's troubles stopped, almost overnight. That was quite a few years ago. Today, that company is one of the top ten manufacturers of electronics equipment in the United States, with markets all over the world.

My specific reason for giving you this example is to show you that you cannot gain unlimited power with a person until you know exactly what he wants so you can help him get it. Only then will you be able to get what you yourself want.

Summed up in one sentence, the most important point to remember about people is this: *Every normal person wants to know how to be loved, how to win fame and fortune, power, and how to stay healthy.*

If you will keep this thought in mind in dealing with people, you'll never have the slightest bit of trouble in getting them to do what you want them to do as long as you help them gain their goals. You'll be a lot better able to understand human nature and human behavior than the average student (even teacher) of applied psychology ever will be.

Chapter 8 ✳ *The Eighth Day*

THE POWER PLAY THAT NEVER FAILS TO GET RESULTS

We all have certain basic desires that must be fulfilled if we are to be completely happy and satisfied. Of these desires, one stands out above all the rest, for it is much more than a desire, *it is a craving—the craving to be important.* Psychologists say the desire to be important is the strongest drive in human nature. Mark Twain said it this way: "I have been complimented many times and they always embarrass me; I always feel they have not said enough!"

If you don't know how or where to begin in fulfilling a person's basic desires, then here's the place to start. You can always use a person's desire to be important to gain unlimited power with him. This method will work every time on everyone, no exceptions. I have yet to meet the person whose actions I cannot influence or control when I give him that feeling of importance and prestige he needs so much. You can always benefit and gain unlimited power with him when you help him become more important.

The Benefits You Will Gain

1. Each person will go all out to help you gain your goals.
2. You'll gain many true friends.
3. You'll have no enemies.

4. People will admire and respect you.

5. People will always do what you ask them to do; they will give you their full support.

6. You'll win people's hearts as well as their heads.

7. You'll find this master power play works like magic; it literally performs miracles with people for you.

8. *You'll gain unlimited power with people.*

Why People Need to Feel Important

The desire to be important comes from deep within us. Sigmund Freud said everything a person does springs from one of two motives: the sex drive and the *desire to be great.* John Dewey said the deepest urge of all in human nature is the *desire to be important.* Alfred Adler said man wants most of all *to be significant.* William James went even further, for he said, "The deepest principle in human nature is the *craving to be appreciated.*" Discounting the sex drive since it is primarily a physical need, it is readily apparent that *the greatest motivating force in all of us is the desire to be great, the desire to be important.*

I have no degrees in psychology or philosophy, but I agree with these four learned gentlemen. I know from my own experience in working with people that everyone wants attention of some kind. Each person wants to be recognized and be important, no matter who he is or what he does. I have never met anyone who did not want to feel important in some way.

Every person wants the attention of other people whether he wants to admit that or not. He wants to be listened to; he wants to be heard. He has a deep burning desire—yes, even an insatiable craving—to be important, to be recognized and appreciated. In short, *everybody wants to be somebody.*

You think that's not true in your case? Tell me now, have you ever told a joke only to have someone butt in and change the subject right when you were in the middle of your story? How did you feel? You'd probably have liked to strangle him, right? Do you really know why you felt that way? Because he was impolite and interrupted you? No. You felt that way because he deflated your ego; he made you feel small, insignificant, and unimportant. He put himself on center stage and shoved you right out of the spotlight.

Let's say you look at a group picture taken at the annual company picnic. Where do your eyes go first? To yourself, of course. Why? Because you are more interested in yourself than in anyone else. That's not criticism, only a simple statement of fact. We all feel that same way about ourselves. From my point of view, I am the center of everything; the world revolves around me. But from your point of view, you are the center of everything; the world revolves around you. And everyone else feels the same way you and I do.

If people cannot be important in their jobs or at their work, they will make themselves important elsewhere. They will become lay leaders in church; they will hold offices in lodges and fraternal organizations; they will be active in PTA, Red Cross, civic, and community affairs.

I will never forget the janitor in a company I once worked for. He had the most menial job in the plant. His clothes were ragged and dirty. No one paid the slightest bit of attention to him. But when he left the plant at the end of the day, what a metamorphosis! He wore the latest, most fashionable slacks and sports jacket. He was showered, clean shaven, and well groomed. And he drove off in a flashy red foreign sports car!

You would do well, then, to keep the following thoughts in mind when dealing with people:

1. Every person is an egotist. He demands attention, appreciation, and recognition of some sort.

2. Each individual is more interested in himself than in anyone else.

3. Each person's viewpoint is that he is the center of everything. The world revolves around him.

4. Everyone you meet wants to feel important and amount to something.

5. Each person has to be needed in some way by others. He wants to feel indispensable in his job, home, church, or club. He wants to feel that others just can't get along without him.

6. Each person will do everything necessary to gain the attention and recognition he needs so much so he can feel more important.

The Power of Praise

Do you want a person to give you his unswerving loyalty and full support? Do you expect to receive his complete cooperation and willing obedience? Would you like him to have confidence in you and respect you? Then all you need do is *praise him*, not just once, but all the time, over and over and over.

Praise him by telling him what a magnificent job he's doing, how much you need him, how you can't get along without him, how happy you are he's with your organization.

We all hunger for a word of praise. We all need recognition and appreciation. Everybody likes a compliment. No one is immune. As Mark Twain once said, "I could live for two months on one good compliment."

So be generous with your praise. Pass it around freely; the supply is limited only by you. Don't be stingy about passing out bouquets; they cost you nothing. Above all, never act as if you expected something in return for your praise. Don't pay a person a compliment as if you wanted a receipt for it.

Praise is the best way to make a person feel important. Criticism is the quickest way to destroy a person and make you his enemy. If you criticize a person, he will soon hate you. Nothing is more destructive to a person's pride than criticism. Listen to Margaret Nelson, a store manager for Fairfax Fashions, Atlanta, Georgia, as she tells why she uses praise instead of criticism with her employees:

"Some people think it is hard to praise a person sincerely, but I disagree with that," Margaret says. "It's actually very easy to find something to compliment in a person and make her feel more important. All you need do is look for something good about the individual.

"For instance, you can say, 'You really handled that difficult customer skillfully, Jane.' 'That's really a top-notch idea, Fran; I'm so glad you thought of it.' 'I sure appreciate your getting that report out ahead of time, Alice.' 'Thanks for staying late and getting those letters out yesterday, Mary.'

"See how easy it is? It all depends on what you're looking for. If you want to praise a person and make her feel more important, you can always find something to compliment her for. If you want to criticize, you can always find something wrong. But I'd rather use praise than criticism. I've found that it's a much better way to get my employees to do their best for me."

I agree with Margaret. I never criticize anyone, either. I have enough character defects of my own to worry about without taking someone else's inventory. I do make helpful suggestions or show a person how to improve his work methods, but I do not use criticism to do that. I always go out of my way to praise a person, but I am extremely reluctant to find fault.

It would be wise to remember that no one ever criticizes himself for anything, no matter how wrong he might be. He will always find some excuse to justify his actions. If a person will not accept criticism even from himself, then I know he will never accept it from me. However, I do not want to mislead you here. Let me quickly point out that my hesitancy to criticize others does not stop me from taking the necessary corrective or disciplinary action when it is required.

Five Valuable Words That Will Produce the Results You're After

I Am Proud of You are five of the most valuable and powerful words in the English language. You can use them any time on your employees, associates, and friends, or your husband, wife, and children. Just tell them how proud you are of something they did. Be generous with your compliments. They cost you nothing, but they will pay you rich dividends in the form of unlimited power with people.

These five little words will work miracles in human relations for you. You can even use them with your boss. If you feel too self-conscious to say "I'm proud of you" to him or her, then change the words and say, "I'm sure proud to work for you." They'll still produce the same good results you're after.

Does this method work to gain you unlimited power with people? I'll say it does. Listen to what George Whitson, an executive vice president and general manager of a Midwestern radio and television factory has to say about it.

"I've never found any better words to use with my employees than 'I'm proud of you,' " George says. "That's one of the highest compliments you can pay a person.

"When an employee does an exceptionally fine piece of work or turns in a terrific money-saving or cost-cutting idea, just to say 'Thanks' isn't enough. I go to him right out on the production line and in front of all his fellow workers I pat him on the back and say, 'Thanks a lot for what you did, Bill; *I'm really proud of you.*' He'll work even harder for me from then on. So will everyone else. They all want some of that sweet syrup, too."

Why Praise Works Better than Criticism

I want to show you exactly why praise is such a valuable procedure to make a person feel important. I'll also show you why criticism is such a useless method. A team of psychologists from a famous Western university made a detailed study to determine the relative merits of these two techniques.

The team carried out their tests with army recruits at an army basic training center in California. Three thousand young men, still fresh from all walks in civilian life, were tested in their first 48 hours at the reception center before they were sent down to their training units to be indoctrinated by tough army drill sergeants with army customs and procedures. The team tested sixty men a day for ten weeks. Here's how they ran their tests.

Each morning sixty volunteers were divided into six squads of ten men each. The squads were then given the same set of difficult tasks to perform. As each one completed its work, it was judged on its performance. But the results of each squad were reviewed in different ways by the testing team.

Squad 1 was praised in public before all the rest of the squads. The second squad was also praised, but in private with only its own members present. Squad 3 was criticized in private; only its own members were present. Squad 4 was publicly criticized in front of all the other squads. Squad 5 was ridiculed and made fun of in private with only its own members there. But Squad 6 was ridiculed and made fun of in front of all 60 volunteers.

The squads were then given exactly the same work to do again. Their second performance was checked against the first. The second performance results are shown as follows:

Squad No.	Critique Method	% Showing Improvement On The Second Test
1	Public praise	90%
2	Private praise	75
3	Private criticism	49
4	Public criticism	31
5	Private ridicule	19
6	Public ridicule	10

The results are clear. Praise is a much better tool for you to use than either criticism or ridicule when you are trying to get a person to upgrade his performance. When you praise people in public, nine out of ten of them will improve, for you've given them the recognition they need so much. You've made them feel more important in front of other people. Praise in private will not do quite as well as public praise, but three out of four will respond favorably.

However, if you criticize people hoping to get improvement, you will always fail. Even when you criticize in private, only about half the people will improve and do a better job for you. If you criticize people publicly in front of others, less than one-third will show any sign of doing better. No one wants to be disapproved of or have his faults criticized, including me.

So if one of your people asks you to look at his work and let him know where he's making his mistakes, don't be misled. That isn't what he wants at all. He wants you to tell him what a good job he is doing. He wants you to pat him on the back and tell him he's not making any mistakes. He wants to be praised, not criticized. Read between the lines; listen to what he really said. Remember those basic desires every person has. *To be criticized is not one of them.*

Criticism will not help you gain unlimited power with people. In fact, it will do the exact opposite, for criticism will cause the criticized person to do even worse. Criticism destroys his incentive to improve. As Josh Billings, the American humorist, once said, "To be a critic demands more brains than most people have." You cannot criticize a person without deflating his ego and destroying his feeling of importance. Criticism maims and cripples people psychologically. *The best thing you can do about criticism is to forget it!*

Ridicule, either public or private, is a complete waste of time as you can see from the last two figures on the previous chart. However, I do want to take some time here to tell you exactly why ridicule is so useless and will never win you unlimited power with people.

You see, a man will tolerate almost any insult, defeat, or injury and accept it with some semblance of good grace. You can steal his wife, his job, and his money, and although he won't like you for it, he'll probably tolerate it all up to a certain point and still treat you like a civilized human being.

But if you make fun of a person, if you belittle and ridicule him—especially in front of his peers—you'll have made an enemy of him for the rest of your life. He will never forget and he'll never forgive, for you've absolutely devastated his sense of self-respect, dignity, and self-esteem. You've deflated his ego and injured his pride.

You've also taken away the possibility of his being recognized for his efforts by ridiculing him instead of praising him: You have destroyed him in front of his peers and prevented the group from approving of him; you have ruined his desire to accomplish something worthwhile; you have taken away his feeling of emotional security. Can you blame him now for despising you? Look at the amount of harm you've caused just by ridiculing and making fun of him.

How Public Praise Acts as an Energizer

This study by a western university's psychology department confirms something I have known and practiced for many years. *Public praise is the most powerful technique you can use to feed a person's ego and make him feel important.* Praise will most definitely win you unlimited power with that person. Let's dig a little deeper into this technique, and you will find out exactly why praise works so well to get you what you want with other people:

Praise releases energy; praise acts as an energizer. That is exactly why praise works so well for you. To praise means to honor, compliment, pay recognition to, express approval of. If you are praised, what is your own reaction? No doubt the same as mine. You feel thrilled and excited. You are happy that you were able to please someone. Praise increases your enthusiasm; it makes you want to do even better the next time. You work harder than before so you can get more of it. People will do the same for you. Praise brings you unlimited power with them.

Do you see how praise releases energy? Praise makes a person work harder, more efficiently, and with greater enthusiasm. That was proven by Henry Goddard, an American psychologist.

Dr. Goddard performed his experiments when he was research director for New Jersey's Vineland Training School for Retarded Children. Dr. Goddard used an ergograph, a scientific instrument that measures energy and fatigue. When tired children were praised and complimented for their work, the ergograph showed an immediate upward surge of new energy. But when they were criticized and reprimanded, the ergograph readings were immediately lowered.

You don't need an ergograph or any other scientific measuring device to measure the release of new energy in your own employees. Just praise them; you can see the good results for yourself. For instance, when you praise your secretary for her typing skills and abilities, you'll find fewer errors than before in your correspondence. Those letters will also be ready for your signature much sooner than before. Tell your subordinates what good jobs they've done, praise them in front of their fellow workers, and they'll do even better work for you the next time around. This technique will also work with your wife, your husband, children, relatives, friends, anyone. The final proven conclusion is that praise releases new energy in a person. And I'm sure that you can see now how praise will win you unlimited power with people.

Seven Basic Desires That Are Fulfilled by Feeding a Person's Ego

Not only does praise feed a person's ego and fulfill his or her desire to be important, but it also satisfies such other basic desires as

1. Recognition of efforts; reassurance of worth.
2. Social or group approval; acceptance by one's peers.
3. A sense of roots, belonging somewhere.
4. The accomplishment of something worthwhile.
5. A sense of self-esteem, dignity, and self-respect.
6. The desire to win, to be first, to excel.
7. Emotional security.

You can see from this why praise is one of the most powerful techniques you can ever use to get a person to do what you want him to do. You just can't miss when you praise someone for what he's done. It is the quickest, simplest, and least expensive way in the world to win unlimited power with people.

How You Can Inspire Others to Improve

Smart animal trainers know you must praise every single improvement with a kind word of encouragement, a pat on the head, and a bit of food if further progress is to be made. The trainers at Sea World of Florida give their killer whales, their seals, and their dolphins a handful of fish after every trick they do. If we know enough to praise animals for every single improvement they make, we ought to be wise enough to use the same technique on people.

So get in the habit of praising even the slightest improvement in your employees or your subordinates. That will inspire them to keep right on improving. Don't wait until someone does something really outstanding or unusual before you praise him or her. Praise the tiniest bit of progress you can find.

I don't care how long you've been married to your wife, tell her what a wonderful cook she is every single day. I've been married to the same woman for 50 years now, and I never get up from the table without saying, "Thanks a lot, honey; that was a terrific meal." That's why I always eat too well.

The words "thank you" can work magic in human relations when you use them properly. They will always make people glad they did something for you, especially when you use these words sincerely. You can soup them up a bit by saying, "Thanks very much," "Thanks a lot," "Thanks a million," "I sure do appreciate it." Look the person straight in the eye when you thank him. If he's worth being thanked, he's worth being looked at and noticed. Don't be like the checkout clerk in the supermarket who says thank you to the cash register and never sees the customer.

Keep your eyes open and find things to thank people for. Every time you say *Thank you*, you are praising the other person. You're giving him credit for having done something you appreciate. When you let people know how grateful you are for what they've done, when you praise every single improvement they make, no matter how small, they will want to do even more for you. And that, my friend, is unlimited power with people.

So praise the slightest improvement a person makes and praise every improvement he makes. As a famous American billionaire once said, "I am anxious to praise, but loath to find fault. If I like anything, I am always hearty in my approbation and lavish in my praise."

How to Use Praise to Correct Mistakes

Now I want to show you how you can use praise to correct a person's mistakes gracefully so there will be no hard feelings.

The key to this technique is to *praise a person at the same time you are pointing out his error to him.* Here are some examples of, first, the wrong way and, then, the right way to correct a person's mistakes.

WRONG: Miss Jones, you are without a doubt the worst typist I've ever had in my office. I'm sick and tired of your stupid mistakes. Now do this letter over and get it right this time!

RIGHT: Miss Jones, your typing is outstanding. You make very few errors and your work is clean and neat. Your spelling is exceptionally accurate. However, I did find several small mistakes in this letter. They are not big ones, but they do change the exact meaning of what I wanted to say.

WRONG: What the hell is wrong with you, Joe? These measurements of yours are all screwed up again. Of all the idiotic, stupid people I have to work with, I swear you are the worst. Now do the damned job over and get it right this time or else!

RIGHT: Joe, you did outstanding work on this difficult project on extremely short notice. I know you were under a lot of pressure, but I've found one thing here I don't understand. I wonder if you'd mind checking this measurement again for accuracy. It seems to be a little off. If it is, I'm afraid it would throw the whole thing out of whack.

WRONG: Why do you get such low grades in history, dummy? You're either too lazy or too stupid to learn. Which one is it? What's wrong with you? You'd better shape up quick!

RIGHT: Tim, your report card really looks terrific this time. I'm really proud of your work. Your history grade is the only one that's off a little, but I know you can bring that up, too, when I see how well you've done in your other subjects.

Whenever you correct the person instead of the act, you get angry. You automatically use sarcasm and ridicule. Words like *stupid, lazy, dumb,* and *idiot* creep into the conversation. Remember that when the team of university psychologists used ridicule on those army trainees, improvement fell to as low as 10 percent on the second performance.

If you think the language of those wrong statements in the examples I've just given you is too strong, let me tell you that I've heard much worse four-letter words used by managers and supervisors, even by top-level executives. I've heard every cuss word or obscenity that's ever been invented by humankind to criticize and castigate another human being. I've heard everything from "Damn you" to words questioning a man's legitimacy at birth and other derogatory terms about his mother.

So always correct a person's mistakes by using praise. That way, you don't destroy a person's dignity and self-respect. You've let him save face. It takes time, patience, and understanding to use this technique, but if you want to win unlimited power with people, the results are worth the effort.

How Asking for Advice and Help Can Work to Your Advantage

One of the quickest ways to make a person feel more important and win unlimited power with him is simply to ask him for his help or his advice. All you need say is, "What is your opinion on this?" You'll send even the janitor home bragging to his wife that the company president had to come to him for help in solving a problem.

A note of caution here: When you do ask for someone's opinion, listen courteously to the answer. I don't care how outlandish the idea sounds to you, listen to it carefully. Hear the person out to the end. Don't disagree with him as soon as he is finished. Even though you might know his idea won't work, don't tell him so. You'll hurt his pride, deflate his ego, and spoil everything if you do.

When he's finished, thank him sincerely for his help. Tell him you'll give every possible consideration to his idea. You'll find when you do listen to your employees' opinions, they will go all out to think up new and better ways of doing things. This can be extremely profitable and beneficial for you. Listening to people's ideas is a lot like panning gold. You see a lot more sand than gold, but when you do find a nugget, it can be mighty exciting.

Frankly speaking, I do not like a suggestion box. Nor do a lot of top-level executives whom I know. For instance, Paul Kane, Director of Research and Development for Suncoast Solar Energy Technologies in Miami, Florida, also refuses to use one.

"I know most companies use suggestion boxes to get new ideas from employees," Paul says. "We used to have one, but we got rid of it.

It was too impersonal. Besides, a person never knew whether his suggestion was actually read or just thrown away in the trash at the end of the day.

"Now I keep my office door open all the time. Any employee can come in whenever he feels he has a worthwhile idea to contribute. If it's complicated, requiring a lot of sketches or narrative description, he gets every bit of assistance he needs from our office staff. When we first started this program, we got a lot of ideas we couldn't use, but our people soon settled down. Now when someone comes in my office with a new idea, chances are good he has something we can really use."

I've seen Paul's office and when he says he keeps an open door, he really means it. The door has been completely removed and taken away! A former chairman of the board for AT&T also kept an open door. He said it was a major factor in his successful business career.

Keeping an open door is an excellent way to make people feel important. Such a policy lets your employees know you are really interested in them and in what they have to offer. They feel they have access to you, that they can bring you their ideas and their problems, and that you will listen to them. An open door says a lot to your employees about the kind of person you are. It helps you gain unlimited power with them.

Six Ways to Make Someone a Real VIP

It's hard in today's automated and computerized world to keep from being looked at as another piece of office equipment or an extension of some part of the machinery. Even off the job, a person tends to become a nonentity more than ever before since computers depend on numbers rather than names for credit, identification, and billing purposes. Today, people just don't seem to be as important as individuals as they once were, and that makes them hungrier than ever for attention and a feeling of importance.

The desire to be important and the fear of not succeeding at it is such a driving force in everyone you can readily use that fact to your own advantage to gain unlimited power with people. Make every one of your employees or your subordinates a very important person, and they will do whatever you ask them to do. You can make each individual in your organization a real VIP when you use the following techniques:

1. Give your wholehearted attention to the other person. Rejection hurts; attention heals. It's just that simple.

2. Encourage him to talk about himself and his own interests. That shows him how important he is to you.

3. Give each person the special identity he desires by letting him know he's both wanted and needed by you.

4. Remember a person's name. Never degrade it or make fun of it with ethnic jokes. His name is his most important and valuable possession.

5. Never take another person for granted. It is one of the quickest ways to reject a person and lose his friendship, even possibly make him your enemy.

6. Get your mind off of yourself and what you want from that person. You'll get what you want—unlimited power with him—when you give him what he wants: your attention.

The best way I can summarize this chapter for you is to say that if you want to gain unlimited power with every person you deal with, then *make that other person important*. Build him up in every possible way you can think of. One of the best ways of doing that is by the use of praise. Remember that praise releases energy and it acts as an energizer. When you praise a person, he can't help himself. He will automatically do what you ask him to do and that's unlimited power, for you will always get what you want.

Chapter 9 ✳ *The Ninth Day*

HOW TO DEVELOP CONFIDENCE IN YOURSELF AND YOUR OWN ABILITIES

This chapter will help you attain a level of self-confidence greater than any you have ever experienced before. You'll also discover that as your self-confidence increases, it actually becomes self-generating. It will start multiplying of its own accord. Others will recognize your confidence in yourself, and they will trust you. They will gain confidence in you and in your abilities.

To make this magic strategy work for you, you must have confidence in dealing with people as well as confidence in yourself and in your abilities to do your own particular job. If either of these is lacking, you cannot begin to gain unlimited power with people.

The Benefits You Will Gain

1. *When people trust you, they will follow your lead.* When you show by your words and actions that you have absolute confidence in yourself and in your abilities to do your job, people—including your own boss—will trust you and have confidence in you.

If you are, or some day will be, a manager, foreman, supervisor, or executive, remember that your people will always follow your lead. They will adopt for themselves the same measure of confidence you show, not only in yourself, but also in them. Your confidence in their abilities will inspire them to use their full powers to get the job done.

2. *You'll save time, energy, and effort.* When you show confidence in people you'll get far better work out of them. So if you are going to give them a vote of confidence, go all out. You'll be amazed at the extent of their capabilities. This principle will work to solve all sorts of difficult problems. The more confidence you show in people, the more confidence they will have in themselves, and the less time, energy, and effort you'll have to spend in supervising them and their work. That's truly unlimited power with people.

3. *You'll be able to get things done.* When you tackle a tough job with confidence and enthusiasm, you encourage others to do the same. People work best with those in whom they have complete trust and confidence. In fact, when you show such confidence in yourself, you can simply say to your people, "This is what we have to do. Here's how we're going to do it—now let's get right to it!"

4. *You'll become known as a "can-do" person.* When you can get things done this way, you'll become known to your friends, associates, and coworkers and to your boss, as a "can-do" person. Can-do people have complete confidence in themselves and their own abilities. That is precisely why they become known as can-do persons.

Can-do people are always highly sought after in business and industry because they are so few in number. Fred Walker, the personnel director for a large industrial firm, has this to say about can-do people:

"About the finest reputation men or women can make for themselves with us is to have it said that they always get the job done no matter what. They'll become known throughout the company as can-do people. That's about the highest compliment they could receive, for it says everything we need to know."

Two Key Reasons Why a Person May Lack Confidence

1. DEALING WITH OTHERS. The main reason a person lacks confidence in dealing with others is that he does not understand why people do and say the things they do. He does not know what motivates people, what actually turns them on. He simply has not learned any of the reasons behind human behavior, including his own.

But you are in a position to solve this problem quickly. In fact, it should no longer be a problem to you. To gain confidence in yourself and in your own abilities to gain unlimited power with people, you know you must understand human nature and human behavior. When you know why people do and say the things they do, you'll find that you have the answers to their questions and the solutions to their problems. You will feel complete confidence in dealing with people, and they will have full confidence in you.

That is precisely why I gave you that list of fifteen learned needs in Chapter 7, those *secret motivators* that turn people on and the power play that never fails in Chapter 8.

I recommend that you keep them always in mind, not only as you read the rest of this book, but also during every single transaction you have with another person. You'll soon discover that your knowledge and use of them will work magic for you.

2. DEALING WITH HIMSELF OR HERSELF. The main reason a person lacks confidence in himself and his own abilities is that he does not have professional knowledge about the job. *There is no confidence killer more deadly than this one.*

Suppose, for example, you own an expensive European car and you take it to a mechanic who has worked only on American automobiles. He will be hesitant. He doesn't know exactly how or where to start. His every movement will show that he has no confidence in himself and his abilities to repair your car.

But if you take your car to an experienced mechanic who knows and understands foreign automobiles, you will see that he goes about his work with complete confidence in himself. He knows exactly what he is doing.

The more a person knows about his own specialty, the more confidence he has in himself and his abilities to get the job done. There is absolutely no substitute for professional knowledge and expertise in building self-confidence.

How to Be the Expert in Your Chosen Field

If you lack confidence in yourself, other people will also lack confidence in you. So the first step in winning their confidence so you can gain unlimited power with them is to have confidence in yourself. How can you gain that self-confidence so you can win the confidence of others? One of the best ways is to *know your business and keep on knowing it*. In other words you will want to be the authority and expert in your own chosen field.

The person who knows his business, who is the authority and expert in his own field, has complete confidence in himself and his own abilities. This kind of confidence usually comes from extensive study, research, long experience, and plain hard work.

A certain physician I know, a neurologist, Dr. Anna S., is 68 years old. Yet she still spends four to six weeks every year attending lectures and clinics to keep herself up to date with the latest developments in her profession. Is it any wonder that she is regarded as one of this country's top people in the difficult field of neurology?

If you want to be the authority and expert in your own field, no matter what it is, then you will want to do the same. Don't stop studying just because you have graduated from school or already have a degree. You'll never live long enough to know everything there is to know about your chosen profession.

Not only must you retain what you have already learned, but you must also keep up to date with new techniques and procedures so you can be ready for the future. No matter what you do, you will always need to keep on learning, for each new day will bring change.

If you want to retain your position as an authority and an expert in your own field so you can have confidence in yourself and hold the confidence of others so you can gain unlimited power with them, then you must continue your professional education and development. There simply is no other way.

The Magic Strategy; Act as if It's Impossible to Fail

The other day I watched a young relief pitcher come into the game in the ninth inning. His team was only one run ahead. The bases were loaded, there were two outs, and the best batter on the other team was at the plate.

The young man walked onto the field, picked up the ball, and then went behind the pitcher's mound where he stood, eyes closed, talking to himself, psyching himself up for the difficult task that lay before him.

As I watched him, I knew what he was doing. He was using a technique that I have been using for years and that I had taught to him, too. That technique is simply this: *Act as if it were impossible to fail.*

I know of no other method you can use that will give you greater confidence in yourself. Never accept the possibility of failure or defeat in whatever you do. Don't misunderstand me. I do not mean that you should close your eyes to problems and obstacles that could keep you from reaching your goals. But if you will keep the idea of success uppermost in your mind, if you will always act as if it were impossible to fail, you will find that solutions to your problems and ways to overcome your obstacles will soon come to mind.

By the way, in case you're wondering, that young pitcher was successful. He struck out the batter and his team won the game. No matter what you do, you can succeed, too, if you just remember to *act as if it were impossible to fail.*

A successful neighbor of mine, John L., says he never allows the possibility of failure to enter his mind. "I have complete confidence in myself and my own abilities," John says. "I have found from experience that a poor decision carried out with determination and force, vigor, and enthusiasm has a far better chance of succeeding than does the best decision that is carried out in a careless and indifferent manner.

"Of course I make mistakes. Who doesn't? I wouldn't be human if I did not. But that means only that I've met with temporary defeat; it doesn't mean that I've lost everything. I never give up. I'll never fail as long as I keep trying. I will always succeed as long as I act as if it were impossible to fail."

How Persistence Paid Off in Building the Grand Coulee Dam

Our history books are filled with stories of famous people who became successful because they refused to quit. I'm sure you are familiar with many of them, but let me tell you about one you may never have heard. I learned about this one on a trip I made through the Western states one year.

As I stood with other tourists staring in wide-eyed awe at the Grand Coulee, one of the world's largest dams, which is nearly a mile long and almost two football fields high, I wondered how it had been humanly possible to build such a tremendous structure. Then I heard the park guide say, "Had it not been for a young construction engineer who refused to accept defeat, the Grand Coulee Dam would never have been built.

"You see, the engineers working on the project had run up against a seemingly insoluble problem. They had reached a point where their normal construction methods would not work because of deep deposits of constantly shifting sand and mud.

"Tons of it poured into newly excavated areas; it tore out pilings and scaffoldings. All sorts of engineering techniques were tried without success. There seemed to be no answer to their problem, and the situation began to look hopeless. If fact, some of the best engineering minds in the business were just about ready to give up building the dam.

"Then one of the young engineers had an inspiration. 'Let's drive pipes down through all that sand and mud,' he suggested. 'We can circulate a refrigerant through them and freeze the whole mess solid as a rock. When that is done, we won't have to worry about it coming down on top of us while we work.'

"So they tried his idea. In a short time, the unmanageable and shifting wet sand and mud had been frozen into one huge solid block. They could've built a skyscraper on it if they had wanted to.

"The Grand Coulee Dam came into being and millions of people in the Pacific Northwest have benefited because one young engineer refused to accept defeat. Instead, *he acted as if it were impossible to fail*—and complete success was the end result."

So you, too, should act as if it were impossible to fail. You will be amazed at the fantastic results you can get. Your self-confidence will grow until you know you can do anything you set your mind to. You'll become successful far beyond your wildest dreams.

How to Radiate Your Self-confidence to Others

When you believe in yourself and your own abilities, your self-confidence will literally radiate from you. It will be reflected in everything you say and do. You'll glow all over with confidence and enthusiasm. And people are bound to have confidence in you, too. They can't help themselves. You'll find that as their confidence in you grows, so does your power with them grow, too.

What makes a successful doctor, lawyer, plumber, musician, salesperson? Confidence in himself and enthusiasm for what he is doing. Of course, the person has to know his stuff, he has to be the expert and the authority in his own field, as I've already said, but unless he has confidence in himself and enthusiasm for what he is doing, he can fall flat on his face. I've seen top students in school fail miserably in life while average or even poor students became rich and successful. I'm sure you've seen that, too.

It all has to do with confidence in yourself and enthusiasm for what you are doing. Let me give you two examples to show you, first, how a lack of confidence can cause failure, and second, how complete self-confidence can bring about success.

Why Even Smart Doctors Fail Sometimes Even smart doctors can fail because of a lack of confidence in themselves. "I remember when I had a low back problem a few years ago," Bill Lewis told me. "Braces, plasters, and several weeks in traction in the hospital had done me no good at all. So I decided to see a chiropractor.

"Now this doctor was a smart man, no doubt about it. He had graduated from his college magna cum laude. A framed certificate in his office said so. He had also taken a number of postgraduate courses in chiropractic therapy as evidenced by the diplomas and certificates of attendance that I saw.

"But when I asked him if he could help me, he hesitated and said, 'Well, I don't know. . . it all depends on whether yours is a chiropractic case or not. But I'll try. Maybe a couple of treatments will do the trick, and then again, maybe not. I just don't know. I'm not sure. We'll have to wait and see.'

"I left his office in disgust without getting an adjustment. This doctor had no confidence in himself and his own abilities, in spite of all his professional education and book learning, so neither did I.

"But my back still bothered me so I had to do something. A friend of mine said, 'Why don't you see my chiropractor, Dr. Mildred Donovan? She must be good; her office is always packed.'

"Although I was reluctant to go to a woman chiropractor—although I don't know why—I went to this doctor. After nearly two hours of waiting, I finally got to see her. What a difference! It was immediately apparent. She radiated confidence in herself and her own abilities. She bubbled over with enthusiasm. She told me of the people she had helped and the ailments she had cured.

"When I told her about my problem and asked her if she thought she could help me, she stared at me in open-mouthed astonishment. 'Help you?' she asked. 'Of course, I can help you! What in the world do you think I'm here for, anyway?'

"Well, of course I stayed. She cured my backache. How could she not have with the confident attitude she had?"

How You Can Inspire Others to Have Confidence in You   Let me tell you now about still another doctor I know whose confidence in himself inspires his patients to have complete trust and confidence in him, too. Dr. Z. is one the finest clinicians in the state of Florida. He has served as chairman of the Department of Medicine at a famous Miami hospital for many years now.

The hospital administrator told me that the moment Dr. Z. enters the sick room, the patient begins to improve. "The art of healing seems to surround his physical body like an aura," she said. "It is often not his treatment but his physical presence that actually cures the patient."

What better example of how confidence in yourself and your own abilities can inspire others to have confidence in you is there than this?

If you, like Dr. Z., can show by your every word and deed that you are confident of complete success, no matter how hard the task might be, you will always inspire others to feel the same way, too.

Such self-confidence develops the habit of success, even infallibility. With such a reputation, unlimited power with people will be a cinch for you.

The Witness Technique for Gaining People's Confidence

The most important thing a trial lawyer can do in pleading his case in court is to *bring on his witnesses*. Naturally, the judge and jury feel the lawyer is prejudiced in his views. If he is the prosecuting attorney, he sees things far differently from the position of representing the defendant. So most things a lawyer says are not taken at strictly face value. He has to prove his case to win the confidence of his listeners. This he does by calling his witnesses to the stand to verify that what he says is the truth.

You can also use witnesses outside the courtroom to establish the confidence of others in what you say. For instance, one winter when my wife and I were still living in Missouri, we decided to spend January and February in Arizona. We had a travel trailer to live in. I wrote to a dozen different trailer parks in Phoenix and the surrounding area requesting information on their services and facilities.

Eleven of them sent back beautifully printed colored brochures and form letters telling me what they had to offer. The twelfth one sent me a brochure, too, but also enclosed was a personal letter with the names and addresses of people in Missouri who'd spent winters in that park before. Four of those names were people who lived right in my own city of Springfield.

"Please call any of these people," the letter said. "They can tell you, far better than any brochure can, what we can offer you and whether you would enjoy staying with us or not. We look forward to seeing you soon." You know where we spent the winter, of course.

How to Increase Your Self-Confidence and Others' Confidence in You at the Same Time

If you are feeling depressed, if you're making calls on prospects and not making any sales, if you lack faith in yourself and your own abilities, if people have no confidence in you, maybe all you need do to snap yourself out of it is buy a new tie, a new shirt, or a new pair of shoes.

You see, it's important that you look the part. Sometimes that's more than half the battle of winning the confidence of others. How you dress, act, and carry yourself can actually radiate your authority and allow you to gain unlimited power with others.

Jack Stanley, a senior pilot for a leading airline told me this:

"We could fly our planes just as well wearing slacks and sport shirts. And our stewardesses wouldn't have to wear uniforms either.

"But do you realize what would happen to our company if we dressed that way? Why, it would be broke in a year. People would lose confidence in us and in our abilities to do the job. They wouldn't trust us. A uniform for an airplane pilot or a stewardess is part of our image just as is the uniform for the military services. It helps to establish us as authorities and experts in our own field. People trust us and have confidence in us when we look the part."

You should look the part, too. It is a simple and easy, yet extremely valuable, method you can use to increase your unlimited power with people by inspiring them to have complete confidence in you.

Five Practical Tips on How to Win and Hold the Confidence of Others

This is a sort of thumbnail summary of how to win and hold the confidence of others so you can gain unlimited power with them. I know I've covered a lot of material on that subject, but there is no better way to win and hold a person's confidence than to tell him the whole unvarnished truth. By the same token, there is no quicker way to lose a person's confidence than to lie to him. So if you want to gain unlimited power with others, if you want to inspire them to have confidence in you and trust you, then follow these five simple guidelines:

1. *Practice absolute honesty and truthfulness at all times.* I can think of no exception to this rule. Of course, this does not mean that you should intentionally insult a person or hurt his feelings by telling the truth. If you can say nothing good about a person, then do exactly that: say nothing. Just take your own inventory—not someone else's. If you're like I am, that will keep you busy enough. I know I've said this before, but it is worth repeating.

2. *Make your word your bond.* If you want people to have full confidence in you, then your word must be your bond. To make sure you always do keep your word, keep these three simple points in mind:

- Never make a promise you cannot keep.
- Never make a decision you cannot support.
- Never issue an order you can't enforce.

3. *Be accurate and truthful in all your written statements.* You should also keep in mind that your signature on any document or any piece of correspondence is just as important as what you say to a person face to face. When you sign a check, your signature is your certification that you have

enough money in the bank to cover you check. Your signature in your work and in your business should carry the same weight.

4. *Stand for what you believe to be right.* Have the courage of your convictions, no matter what the consequences. Never compromise your standards; never prostitute your principles. If ever you are tempted to compromise, then place honesty, your sense of duty, and personal honor above all else.

5. *Be ready to accept the blame when you are wrong.* If you're wrong, have the courage to say so. Be willing to take the blame if you made the mistake and you know full well you are the one who is really at fault. You'll gain unlimited power with others when you do that.

Chapter 10 ✳ *The Tenth Day*

HOW TO PROJECT A COMPELLING AURA OF COMMAND

One of the best ways to project an aura of command that will cause others to obey you immediately without question is to be decisive in all your actions. The person who can make a decision without waffling is rare indeed. To be able to do that is a hallmark of true leadership. Man or woman, that person will be highly respected by his superiors, his subordinates, and his associates. This is not to say that your decisions should be based on snap judgments or that you should act hastily and rashly. But you should not be hesitant and fearful of making a decision as so many people in high-level positions are.

In the armed services, the commander of any unit, whether a young lieutenant or an old colonel, is referred to as "the old man," that is, if he has earned that title by his decisiveness and his willingness to accept responsibility for his actions. The highest compliment he can receive is when one of his subordinates will say, "Let's go ask the old man about this. He'll know what to do."

Every day a manager or an executive is required to make dozens of decisions. Some are minor and routine. But others demand the greatest skill he can muster, for certain decisions will have long-lasting and far-reaching effects.

The hesitant and indecisive person who procrastinates, who calls a meeting to get a "joint decision" from his subordinates so he can blame them if things go wrong, who farms out the problem to a committee for "more study," or who waits for "further developments" in the situation, is not destined to go far in the ranks of management. That kind of manager will go out of his way to avoid making any sort of decision that might possibly be traced back to him.

This sort of indecisiveness is contagious. It infects the entire organization, causing hesitancy, loss of confidence, and confusion for everyone. Such a manager will never become a top-level executive. He will soon find himself shunted off on a siding in a dead-end position or looking for another job with a different company.

The executive suites of hundreds of companies and corporations are overloaded with so-called managers and executives who are deathly afraid to make decisions about anything more consequential than the time of the morning and afternoon coffee breaks or when to let the secretary go to lunch.

If you want to avoid joining that crowd, you will develop your ability to make sound and timely decisions. Do that and you will project an aura of command that is almost physically touchable. And you will gain unlimited power with people.

I learned a long time ago that when you are in a position of authority, you must be willing to assume the responsibility for making the decisions required by that job. And after you have all the advice and detailed information you can get from others, you must make that final decision by yourself.

I will always be thankful for this one lesson, if I learned nothing else in the army away back when, and that is simply that *you cannot command by committee. You must make the final decision all by yourself.* The same truism applies here.

This chapter will help you not only to improve your decision-making abilities by giving you certain specific techniques to use, but it will also fortify your courage to make those decisions as your skills improve. Constant study, training, planning, and practice will give you the professional competence you need to make sound and timely decisions.

The Benefits You Will Gain

1. *People will have confidence in your skill and abilities.* Your people will have confidence in you when you can make a rapid and accurate

estimate of the situation to arrive at a sound, sensible, and timely decision. To be able to do this, you must gather all the facts, analyze them, make up your mind, and issue your order with complete confidence that you have made the right decision. *Always act as if it were impossible to fail.*

2. *People will always do their best for you* when you demonstrate good judgment and common sense in your decisions. If you're able to reason logically under the most trying of conditions and decide without quibbling what course of action is necessary to take advantage of opportunities as they arise, your people will respect your good judgment and decision-making abilities. They will want to do the best job they can for you.

3. *People will become more positive and decisive in their own actions.* You, as the leader, establish the attitude for your whole organization. When you are positive and decisive in your actions, your people will be positive and decisive in their actions, too. They automatically become a mirror reflection of what you are, what you do, and how you do it.

4. *People will turn to you for advice and help.* When you can make sound and timely decisions, people will be motivated to come to you for advice and help. You will become known as an expert troubleshooter in solving the toughest problems. Such a reputation will enhance your stature throughout your entire organization.

Friends often call me to get advice or neighbors drop by to ask for help in solving some problem so they can make a sound decision. A nuisance? Yes, sometimes that is so, but wow, does it ever build the ego!

5. *You'll rid yourself of frustration.* The inability to make up one's mind is a leading source of frustration, not only in business and management, but also in solving the personal problems in one's life.

But when you use the decision-making techniques that you will learn in this chapter, you'll rid yourself of that frustration. You'll have confidence in yourself and in your own abilities to deal with pressure. Not only that, you'll find that your unlimited power with people will increase tremendously as your decision-making abilities improve.

How to Develop Your Decision-Making Powers

If you want to develop your decision-making powers, you will need both courage and know-how. You must become adept at probing a problem's depths to find its basic cause. You will be required to make a rapid and accurate estimate of the situation so you can arrive at a sound, sensible, and timely decision.

You must be able to use sound logic and reason, common sense, and good judgment under the most trying conditions and decide quickly what action is necessary so you can take advantage of opportunities as they occur. To top off all these requirements, you'll also need foresight so you can predict the actions and reactions that might take place after your decision has been put into effect. When the situation demands a modification in your original plans, prompt action on your part to make the necessary change will build your people's confidence in you as their leader.

Now how exactly can you do all this? How can you put this into practice for yourself? Well, Michael Brown, vice president and general manager of a large industrial company, says here's one way you can develop your powers of decision very quickly:

"Before our division or department managers issue an order to implement a decision, they always ask themselves one final question," Michael says. "And that question is, *'What will happen if...?'*

"As long as each manager in our company does this, just as long as he keeps that phrase uppermost in his mind when he makes his decision or issues his order, the chances of his making a mistake are kept to the minimum.

"Before we established this simple policy, we were constantly finding that today's solutions were often creating tomorrow's problems. Keeping in mind *what will happen if...* helps our managers and supervisors solve a lot of their problems even before they ever happen.

"I never cease to be amazed at the effectiveness of those four small words. We consider them so important we've posted placards and signs all over the place that say in big red letters *"'WHAT WILL HAPPEN IF...'"* so that phrase will be drummed deep into everyone's subconscious mind."

Tips on Setting Priorities

Let me give you a concrete example of how to put your powers of decision making to work so you can gain unlimited power with people. Most managers and executives simply do not have enough time to do all the things they want to do. I assume that you are no exception. So the first thing you need to decide is what is essential that you and you alone must do and what can be done by someone else.

As soon as you know what tasks can be done by someone else, make those assignments and get them off your mind and out of the way. Now you'll be left with those problems that only you can handle. The next thing you must decide is which one to work on first. Let me show you how to handle that problem:

I once knew a manager who created nothing but chaos in his organization simply because he didn't know how to make decisions and establish priorities in the work to be done. Every project to him was a crash. He sent out dozens of red-bordered memos marked "URGENT" to his administrative staff, his division managers, and department foremen every week. But nothing ever got done on time, for *when everything is always marked "URGENT," then "URGENT" becomes "ROUTINE."*

He finally gave up and called me for help in solving his problem. This is the advice I gave him more than ten years ago (He still uses the same system today that I gave him back then.):

"Sam, your problem can be solved when you properly establish priorities," I told him. "Make a list of the most urgent tasks facing you right now. Then give each job a different priority. *No two jobs can have the same number.*

"After you have established your job priorities, then dig right in on priority 1 and stick with it until it is done. Then go to priority 2 and do it the same way. Don't worry if you only finish one or two jobs each day. The point is that this way you'll be making progress where before you were completely stalemated. You'll get things done by taking care of your most urgent problems first. Assign priorities on the work to be done by your subordinates the same way. Teach them the system so they can organize their own internal workload, too.

"In short, Sam, use the *principle of first things first, one thing at a time.* If you can't solve your problems this way, chances are you can't handle them any other way, either. Once you get this system rolling, stick with it. You will clear away the debris on a daily basis one day at a time."

And I'll say the same thing to you, too. Use this system. You will be amazed at how much more work you can get done by using this simple technique. You need to use your power of decision to determine only three things:

1. The work that can be done by others

2. The work that only you can do
3. The priorities in your own work and the work you assign to others

How to Develop the Ability to Plan and Order

Once your decision about what to do has been made, your next step will be to develop a detailed plan to issue an order. A usable plan must be worked out to execute your decision if you are to get the results that you want.

Definite tasks must be assigned to specific individuals. Allocation of supplies, equipment, and facilities must be made. The activity of individuals and groups will need to be coordinated to ensure maximum cooperation. Definite deadlines must be fixed for completion of the intermediate steps. In short, the plan that implements your decision must answer these specific questions:

1. *Why* does this job have to be done?
2. *What* has to be done?
3. *Who* is going to do it?
4. *When* and *where* will it be done?
5. *How* will the job be accomplished?

When your plan has been fully developed, you must issue it as an oral or written order to your subordinates. Your instructions should be so clear that there will be no chance of any misunderstanding. The ability to plan and then issue instructions that get the job done is an essential part of your responsibilities as a leader of people. It is also a must if you are to gain unlimited power with them.

In the next chapter, which is a natural follow-up to this one, I will discuss in complete detail how to issue orders that will always be carried out to the letter.

How to Conquer Fear and Have the Courage to Act Decisively

Let's say you already have the power and the capability you need to make sound and timely decisions. And you have the ability to draw up superb plans and orders based on those decisions of yours. However, you are still a long way from achieving your goals unless you possess this one most important and decisive attribute: *the courage to act.*

The ability to see what needs to be done, the wisdom to draw up magnificent plans and orders to execute your decisions will be of no use to you unless you have the courage to act when action is required.

How do you go about developing this kind of courage? I know of only one way, and that is *do the thing you fear to do so you will have the power to do it.* I consider this concept to be one of the most valuable ideas you can gain, not only from this chapter, but from the entire book, so I want to give you several examples of exactly how others have made this principle work to gain courage themselves. Then you can put this idea into practice for yourself. And I will guarantee you that when you use this concept along with the one of *act as if it were impossible to fail,* you will gain more unlimited power with people than you ever thought possible.

If you do the thing you fear to do, you will gain the power to do it. If you do not do the thing you fear to do, you will never gain the power to do it. It is just that simple. For instance, if you want to be a painter, you must first paint. There is no other way to become an artist. You can dream all day long about how famous and successful you could be as a painter, but until you actually pick up the brush and start painting, you will never gain the power to do it.

If you want to be a writer, then you must write. If you want to be an expert swimmer, then you must swim. The same thing can be said about golf, baseball, skiing, sales, science, medicine, music, management, and on and on. You must make the first move yourself. Until you do that, you will never gain the power to do anything.

So if there do happen to be certain things in your life that you want to do, but you dread or fear to do them, then force yourself to do these things until you no longer fear them. Making a decision and putting it into effect could be only one of the things you fear to do. This concept could improve your life in a great many other ways than gaining unlimited power with people although that is the main point of this book.

When you are no longer afraid to do what you formerly feared to do, then you will have complete control over that fear. That is the real definition of courage: the control of fear. Courage is not the absence of fear, as so many people think. *Courage is the control of fear.* Every battlefield hero, including Congressional Medal of Honor winners, will tell you that.

For instance, speaking in public strikes fear in the heart of nearly everyone at first. I know I nearly panicked the first time I stood up in front of an audience. My throat was dry, my voice was raspy, my palms were sweaty, and my heart was pounding.

But after I spoke the first sentence, I felt better. As I continued to speak, my fears began to fade away. Confidence came back to me, for as soon as I did the thing I feared to do, I gained the power to do it.

Now let me give you a few examples of people who overcame their fears by the same procedure: doing the thing they feared to do so they would gain the power to do it.

HOW MAGGIE SMITH CONQUERED HER FEARS. Maggie Smith, a popular author and lecturer, says she used to suffer untold agonies before every one of her talks. But gradually her fear lessened as she kept on speaking, until she finally completely overpowered it, simply by doing the thing she feared to do. Last year she spoke nearly 150 times, and she said her only regret was that the year was only 365 days long.

The effectiveness of this idea of doing the thing you fear to do is well illustrated by all the letters I've received from people who've heard me speak on the subject and put the formula to work for themselves. Let me quote from just a few.

HOW A SALESMAN PUT THIS IDEA TO WORK FOR HIMSELF. Steven D., an Orlando, Florida, salesman, wrote me to say, "After I heard you talk on how to get rid of your fear of people, I felt I could take on anyone. Yesterday I walked into the office of a really tough purchasing agent—a man I'd always feared and who'd never once given me an order—and before he could say 'No,' I had my samples spread out on his desk. First time I'd ever opened my sample case in his office. And quess what? He gave me one of the biggest orders I've ever received! Why? Because my attitude was positive and confident. I wasn't afraid of him and he knew it. Now I know what you meant when you talked about how to gain unlimited power with people."

HOW A SALES CLERK USED THIS PRINCIPLE SUCCESSFULLY. Sally R., a bashful Atlanta, Georgia, sales clerk, wrote me this:

"I was so afraid of customers I gave them the feeling I was apologizing to them for waiting on them. I was even afraid to come hear your lecture. I thought someone I knew might see me there and laugh at me.

Then I was scared to death to try your idea of doing the thing I feared to do so I would have the power to do it, but I really had no other choice. The sales manager had given me exactly three weeks to get my sales up to par with the other sales personnel or be fired.

"But the moment I did as you said, I found I was suddenly speaking to customers with more assurance. My poise and my self-confidence increased. I began to answer questions with authority. My sales went up nearly 40 percent last month. There's never been another word said about my possible dismissal. In fact, the sales manager told me to start thinking about taking over the management of one of the departments!"

HOMEMAKERS CAN USE THIS CONCEPT, TOO.   Ellen G., a Miami, Florida, housewife, wrote this to me: "I was even afraid to invite my friends in for coffee for fear I wouldn't be able to keep the conversation going. But after listening to you talk at our church last Sunday night, I took the plunge and held a coffee klatsch for half a dozen of my neighbors today. It was a great success. I had no trouble at all in keeping things moving along interesting lines of conversation. Thanks so much for your help."

EVEN ANIMALS AND BIRDS USE THIS PROCEDURE.   Doing the thing you fear to do so you can gain the power to do it is not really man's idea alone. It is a law of nature. For instance, I've watched birds fly, and I always figured it was automatic for them to do so. But that is not true at all. Last year a robin built a nest in the tree just outside my study window. I watched the growth of this little family, from the eggs in the nest until the day that four small heads popped up demanding to be fed. Then, one by one, the mother nudged her babies off into the air when the right time came.

But one little fellow was so afraid he couldn't fly. It took him nearly a week longer than the others. He would peer over the side of the nest and then cringe down in it in abject fear. Finally, the mother had no choice but to force him out of the nest. And when she did, he suddenly flapped his wings and flew awkwardly away.

Now no one had taught him how to fly. Nature had given him the instinct to do it. But he had to fly first before he had the power to do it, for that is also nature's way of doing things. He had to do the thing he feared to do so he could gain the power to do it.

The same thing applies to people. Life will improve for you, too, not only in gaining unlimited power with people, but also in all other areas of your life if you will remember and practice this one simple idea: Do the thing you fear to do and you will have the power to do it. It is just that simple.

Let's say now you have all the prerequisites you need to make those tough decisions. You've developed your powers of decision by using your common sense, logic, reason, and good judgment. You've learned to concentrate on the essentials and establish your priorities. You've developed the ability to plan and look ahead. You know how to announce your decision and not leave anything to chance. You even have the courage to act; you are not afraid to trust your own decisions and move on them. Is this all you need? Perhaps, but I know from experience that certain areas give people trouble in their decision making. So I want to give you a few guidelines you can use to avoid those trouble spots.

Six Guidelines to Help You Make Those Tough Decisions

1. *Plan ahead for any possible emergency.* Always plan ahead for every possible event you can think of that might take place to ruin your plans. Making sound and timely decisions depends mainly upon your having a constant estimate of the situation at all times. Use the phrase I gave you before, *what will happen if...* so you will force yourself to consider everything possible that might go wrong. The manager or executive who fails to use foresight is inviting failure.

2. *Ask your key subordinates for their advice.* Before you make your final decision and issue an order, always ask your subordinates for their opinions, their suggestions, and their advice. Take advantage of their experience and their ideas.

After you've listened to their recommendations, the time for discussion is over. Make your decision and issue your order. From then on, you have the right to expect the full support and wholehearted loyalty of your subordinates to carry out your decision and obey your order.

3. *Know when to announce your decision.* The timing of your announcement is extremely important. Don't leave your subordinate managers out on a limb by not giving them enough time to develop their own plans, reach their own decisions, and issue the necessary orders to do the job for you. Above all, don't surprise your subordinate managers by announcing

your plans and orders to their subordinates. That is their job, not yours, so let them do it.

4. *Encourage continual estimates and continual planning.* No situation is ever static. Mistakes are going to be made; accidents are going to happen. Encourage your subordinates to make their own estimates of the situation and plan on exactly what they would do when that mistake is made or that accident does happen.

5. *Keep people fully informed and up to date.* When you make your sound and timely decisions, don't let all your efforts and time be wasted by failing to let the right people know. Make sure that everyone knows exactly what your decision is and what's going on. If you don't do that, costly errors will crop up simply because you forgot to tell one key person about your decision and your plan for action. Lack of communication causes more mistakes than willful disobedience.

6. *Evaluate the long-range effect of your decisions.* It is not enough to consider only the immediate effects your decision will have. You must be able to predict what the long-range effects are going to be. Remember that a chain reaction of events will be set off when you announce your decision and your subordinates put your plan into action. Don't let today's solution create tomorrow's problem.

Five Common Obstacles to Overcome in Making Decisions

1. THE NEED TO ALWAYS BE RIGHT. Some people can't make up their minds on anything, even such minor matters as buying a suit, a dress, or a pair of shoes or what to cook for dinner because they are so afraid of making a mistake. But no one can be right all the time. Even if you make a mistake, continual planning ahead at all times will keep you from getting too far down the wrong road. The moment you see you've made a wrong decision, back up and start over. For example,

"I was having a hard time getting the trainees fed and back to the training area on time at noon," a young army company commander told me. "So to speed things up, I told the sergeants they would have to give up their reserved mess tables and mix with the trainees to help keep things moving along more rapidly.

"That was a mistake, for it took away some of my sergeants' privileges. Their morale slipped and things immediately got worse instead of better. So I had to swallow my pride, admit I'd goofed, rescind my order, and figure out some other way to solve the problem."

When you refuse to admit you've made a mistake, things will usually get even worse than they were before. To admit you are wrong is not an admission of stupidity. But to refuse stubbornly to change your mind even when you know you're wrong is.

2. CONFUSING OBJECTIVE FACTS AND SUBJECTIVE OPINIONS. Your decisions should be based on hard facts, not on the way you feel about something at the moment. When you don't keep objective facts and subjective opinions separated, you are in for all sorts of trouble.

"Spur-of-the-moment decisions based on emotions have little objective value," Marjorie Seamonds, a local store manager, told me. "Intuition has no place in management as far as I am concerned. For instance, our personnel manager turned down the employment application of a brilliant young man with a degree in business administration just because he smoked a pipe.

"The personnel manager thought the fellow would be too dreamy and not hard-headed and practical enough in business. That makes as much sense as saying a man with a mustache can't be trusted—a favorite idea of my father—or that all red-headed women are supersexed."

3. FAILING TO GET ENOUGH INFORMATION TO REACH A DECISION. Decisions made on insufficient information will often be the wrong ones. Admittedly, there will be times when you can't get all the facts you need. Then you will have to use your past experience, good judgment, and common sense to reach a logical decision. But to shortcut and not get all the facts you need when they are available is inexcusable.

For instance, a man I know, I'll just call him Tom, had a chance to get in on the ground floor of a risky but potentially profitable business deal. He couldn't afford to lose any money, but he was afraid if he asked too many questions or delayed his decision too long, he'd be left out in the cold. So without the proper facts, he said, "I want in!" He lost everything. Why? Because he jumped in without getting enough information on which to reach a sound and sensible decision.

4. FEAR OF WHAT OTHER PEOPLE MIGHT THINK OR SAY.   A lot of people are afraid to speak up because of what they think others might think or say. That's why they hesitate to announce the decisions they've made for fear of criticism. They want others to think well of them.

To desire another person's respect is one of our basic natural desires, but there is a limit. Remember that *you are not responsible for what others might think or say, but only for what you say and do.*

5. FEAR OF COMMITMENT.   To some people a decision is not a choice but a solid brick wall. It makes them feel helpless, powerless to do anything. This fear is closely tied to the fear of failure, which most psychologists say is a businessperson's greatest obstacle to success.

However, if you don't commit yourself and take action, nothing will ever get done. And if you do see you're going down the wrong road, then, as I've said before, back up and start over. Hardly anything is irrevocable except death and taxes. The ability to admit a mistake and change a wrong decision to a right one is one of the hallmarks of a wise, successful, and competent leader of others.

In summary, to develop decisiveness, use these specific techniques:

1. Be positive in all your actions. Don't delay; don't beat around the bush. It takes more energy to fail than it does to succeed.

2. Get the facts, make up your mind, and issue your order with complete confidence that you are right.

3. Recheck the decisions you have made to determine if they were sound and timely.

4. Analyze the decisions made by others. If you do not agree, determine if your reasons for disagreement are sound.

5. Broaden your viewpoint by studying the actions of others and profit from their successes or mistakes.

6. Be willing to accept full responsibility for your decisions.

7. Do the thing you fear to do and you will have the power to do it.

Chapter 11 ✳ *The Eleventh Day*

HOW TO GIVE ORDERS THAT WILL ALWAYS BE CARRIED OUT TO THE LETTER

Giving other people orders and telling them what to do is a subtle art that requires a great deal of skill and expertise. If you want to become highly successful in your chosen profession, you must know how to control and direct people's actions by your orders and commands. Since you cannot use brute force to get people to do what you want them to do, you must learn how to use specific leadership techniques that will command both respect and obedience.

That famous British statesman of the nineteenth century, Disraeli, summed up the idea of controlling the actions of others when he said, "Men govern with words." When you, too, can command words to serve your thoughts and feelings, you are well on your way to commanding people to do your will and to serve your purposes. You will be able to give orders that will always be obeyed and carried out to the letter.

The Benefits You Will Gain

1. *People will respond quickly to orders that are concise, clear, and easy to understand.* Concentrate on a single point; don't scatter your fire. If you overstate your order by adding too many details, you will only create

misunderstanding and confusion. The perfect example of the most concise and clear-cut order of all time can be found in Matthew 9:9 where Jesus simply said, "Follow me." And the Scripture goes on to say that "Matthew arose and followed Him."

2. *People work much better when they know the exact results that you want.* When you keep your instructions simple and to the point, you can emphasize results, not methods. To do this, *use mission-type orders.* A mission-type order tells a person what you want done and when you want it, but it doesn't tell him how to do it. The "how to" is left up to him. A mission-type order opens the door wide so people can use their imagination, initiative, and ingenuity to do the job for you. No matter what your line is, this can lead to a better way of doing things. If you're in business for yourself, improved methods can mean increased profits for you.

3. *You can decentralize and supervise.* When people know exactly what the results are that you want, when they know precisely what their jobs are, you can decentralize authority and supervise their work more effectively. If you are in business or industry, sales, or even in the military services, decentralization of your work and better supervision of your people are two concrete benefits you can enjoy when you make sure people know exactly what their duties are.

4. *You can get rid of mistakes, waste, confusion, and duplication of effort.* When you use clear, concise, and simple orders that are easy to understand, people will know what you want done, and they'll do it right the first time. They'll not have to come back to you time after time for clarification of what you said. Many times a person fails to do a good job for you only because he or she doesn't really understand exactly what you want. *Simplicity is an absolute must if you want to ensure complete compliance with your orders.* This is a hard and fast rule for you to follow.

5. *Simple plans and simple orders are two cornerstones of success.* A certain midwestern university's athletic department has been turning out winning football teams for many years now. Yet the coach tells me that he uses no more than a dozen simple plays. Every single player knows exactly what everyone else is supposed to do on each one of those plays. "A simple play, executed with drill-like precision and speed, is more likely to move the ball and gain the needed yardage than is a detailed and complicated one," he says.

The army uses the same principle. Simplicity is a maxim of war. The best plan will be one that avoids complexities in design, presentation, and execution. Such a plan is better understood by everyone. A simple plan reduces the chances for error, and its simplicity speeds up its execution.

In business, the most profitable companies are those that have simple strategic concepts; clear plans and programs of execution, specific assignment of decision-making responsibilities, simplified administrative procedures without red tape, and simple direct communications. All aspects of the successful business will be kept as simple as possible at all times.

Now that you know some of the outstanding benefits of issuing simple orders, let's take a look at the techniques you can use to gain these benefits.

The First Requirement: Make Sure the Need for an Order Exists

The first requirement in issuing orders is to *make sure the need for an order actually exists*. Certain administrative details in your work become so routine that it's unnecessary to issue any sort of an order about them. For instance, you don't need to give your people an order at the end of each day to come back to work the following morning.

Most of the time, the details of any business or office are handled by some sort of an established and accepted standing operating procedure, whether it's written or not. An order would then be needed only if a change in time or procedure takes place.

For example, if you've left standing instructions with your secretary to bring the morning mail to your desk as soon as it comes in, you shouldn't have to tell her every single day to do that. If you have to keep repeating that order, you need a new secretary! Or if you've left instructions for the night shift supervisor to leave a production report on your desk each morning, then a one-time order should be enough.

Some people make the mistake of thinking they have to issue an order just to prove that they're the boss. That is not necessary. If you're in charge, people already know that. You don't have to issue an order to prove it.

When a foreman or supervisor is new on the job, you'll often see this happen. Once in a while, an executive will go "power mad" and start punching buttons just to see people jump. Young second lieutenants and newly promoted corporals in the army are prone to make that same mistake. But the services are not unique in this respect. I've seen this basic rule violated time and again in business and industry. For example,

"That's an order, damn it!" the young foreman yelled. "Don't talk back to me. They're still on the time clock so get 'em back on their feet. And that's an order!"

I stood with that young foreman, Barry F., watching the change of shifts in his department. It was just short of 7 A.M., the official plant time for punching out on the clock.

Why was I there? Well, I'd been called in as a management consultant by this company, which was in trouble because of its extremely low employee morale. Continual acts of vandalism—even sabotage—had wrecked some expensive items of equipment and had slowed production to the point the company was losing valuable customers because the firm couldn't fill its orders on time. The pressure was on, from the president of the company down through the plant manager to the last supervisor, to get things straightened out. That's why I was there: to help find the problem and solve it.

The day shift had already reported; they stood at their machines waiting to be told about the day's production. They needed only their supervisor's OK to start rolling. The graveyard shift was tired; it was the end of their working day. They had been hard at it since 11 P.M. the night before. Now that they had finished, they were squatting down on their haunches to rest, leaning against the iron railings around the heavy machinery, or sitting on stacks of rubber skids just waiting for the 7 o'clock whistle to blow.

The young foreman called his outgoing shift supervisor over. "Get those lazy bums on their feet!" he snapped. "You know I don't allow anyone to sit down while he's working in my department. I'm not running a damned rest home!"

"But, Barry, my men are all through work," the night supervisor protested. "You know we have a 10-minute changeover period. They're tired and they're simply waiting for the whistle to blow so they can clock out and go home. They're not working now."

"Don't talk back to me!" the foreman yelled. "I'm still the boss in this department. They're still on the clock, so get 'em up on their feet. And that's an order, damn it!"

I'm sure you already know what I recommended in my report to the plant manager.

Now here's how you can determine for yourself whether or not an order is actually required. An order is needed in only four situations:

1. To start some action
2. To correct a mistake in the action or to solve a problem
3. To speed up or slow down the action
4. To stop the action

So if you don't need an order, don't issue one. You make yourself look like a fool when you do. But by the same token, if you do need to issue an order to get the job done, do so at once. Don't be afraid of hurting someone's feelings by telling him what to do. If that's your job, then do it.

The Second Requirement: Know What You Want Before You Issue an Order

The second requirement in issuing orders that will always be obeyed is to *know exactly what you want to accomplish before you issue an order*. It is absolutely essential that you know precisely the results you're after before you tell anyone to do anything. Too many orders grow like a rambling rose, creeping ivy, or the crabgrass in my yard.

Incomplete, vague, and ambiguous orders will get you the same kind of results. If you are not sure of exactly what you want, then no one else will be either. You're not yet ready to issue your order.

To help you determine the results you're after, follow these seven simple guidelines so you can use the same thinking pattern each time you issue an order.

1. *What* exactly is it that I want to get done?
2. *Why* exactly is it necessary to do this job?
3. *When* does the work have to be completed?
4. *Where* is the place for the work to be accomplished?
5. *Who* is the person best fitted to do the job?

6. *How* will the work be done? What tools, equipment, personnel, and facilities are needed?

7. *How much* will it cost to do the work?

By following these seven points, you'll box yourself into a corner and force yourself to answer the relevant questions of *who, what, when, where, why, how,* and *how much*. You are bound to improve your ability to issue orders when you do this, and your skills to make sure the job is understood, supervised, and accomplished will also improve.

Keep in mind that you should always concentrate primarily on *results*, not methods, so you will be able to know exactly what you want before you ever issue an order. Once you know the results you want, just tell your subordinates what it is. Then getting the job done will be no problem at all. You'll gain unlimited power with your people without even half trying.

The Third Requirement: Show How the Person Will Benefit by Doing as You Say

The third requirement in issuing orders that will always be obeyed to the letter is to *let a person know exactly how he or she is going to benefit by carrying out your order*. So before you tell a person what to do, think the situation through thoroughly. Reverse your roles mentally so you can look at your order from his viewpoint. That way, you'll be able to tell him exactly how he will be rewarded by doing as you ask. You must properly motivate him to obey your command. Let me give you a few examples of that.

1. If you complete this work by 2 o'clock, you can leave a couple of hours early and still get paid for it.

2. If you do it this way, you can increase your output and make more money for yourself.

3. Then there's the example of a well-known country and western recording artist and television star. For purposes of illustration, I'll just call him "Sam." A long time ago before he became famous, Sam was playing guitar with a little group in a small California bar. One night the owner said, "Sam, I want you to sing, too. We need more voices." Immediately, Sam said, "But you're paying me just to play the guitar. What do I get if I sing,

too?" To which the boss promptly replied, "You get to keep your job!" You know what Sam did, of course; he sang, for keeping your job is one of the best incentives you can use at certain times.

No matter what your order is, though, your listener always wants to know first exactly what's in it for him. So tell him that. Let him know right away how he's going to benefit by doing as you say. This is especially true if you are going to tell a person how to correct his mistake.

Let a person know how he can fulfill his basic needs and desires when he does as you say. It will be up to you to find out which secret motivator you can use to get him to follow your order to the letter.

Three Techniques for Motivating Others to Follow Your Orders

When you're the boss and an employee has no choice but to carry out your order to keep his job, he'll do as he is told, but he'll do it grudgingly unless you stress the advantages he will gain by doing as you say.

So if you want to get the maximum results from him, not just the minimum, then use these three simple techniques. They can help turn an average employee into a superior one.

1. USE PRAISE, RECOGNITION, REASSURANCE OF WORTH. If you want a person to follow your commands implicitly, then praise him for his work. Tell him what a terrific job he's doing, how much you need him, how you can't get along without him, how happy you are he's your employee.

"Praise is the quickest and most dependable way to make a person feel important," says Carolyn Turner, a highly successful Florida business-woman. "It's also the least expensive for it costs you absolutely nothing to praise a person's work. Praise is one of my favorite motivational tools. I've used it for years now with fantastic results."

If you will remember, credit and recognition for their work was the number one desire of the electronic factory's employees that I told you about earlier. If praise worked for management there and for Carolyn Turner, then it'll work for you, too.

So give the person the praise he needs so much, the importance he craves, the credit and recognition he wants, and he'll always carry out your orders to the letter.

2. *MAKE HIS JOB INTERESTING AND WORTHWHILE.*   Let a person know why his job is so important and how it contributes to the success of the entire group. This, too, feeds his ego and fulfills his basic desire to be somebody, *Everybody wants to be somebody*. When a person understands the purpose behind his job and the crucial part it plays in the larger scheme of things, the greater interest he will have in his work, for you've helped make him *somebody* by making his job important.

3. *OFFER A PERSON EMOTIONAL SECURITY.*   Fred Young, a production supervisor for a tire and rubber company says, "If you constantly threaten a person and cause him to worry about losing his job, demotion, suspension, or a penalty of some sort, you can never get him to work at his full potential. You cannot order a person to do something by using fear or threats and expect to get the best results. *Fear always leads to hate.* When a person fears you, he will eventually hate you. When he hates you, he will never willingly obey your orders and your commands.

As an experiment, now, use these three techniques I've just given you for a few weeks. Use praise instead of criticism. Let people know how important their jobs are. Make them feel like somebody. Offer them emotional security instead of using fear and threats to get what you want. You will get results far beyond your highest expectations. You'll be amazed at the cooperation and support that your people will give you. And you'll gain unlimited power with people with this simple but highly effective technique.

How to Tell if Your Order Was Understood

You can check to see if your order is understood in several ways. You can have your people repeat your oral orders to you. You can have them ask questions if they don't understand. You can ask them questions to see if they really do understand what you want. Let me discuss each one of these separately with you.

1. *Have your oral orders repeated to you.* I can think of absolutely no exception to this rule. The first time you break it, so help me, things will go wrong. If people do not understand your instructions, it's a cinch you won't get the results that you want.

So make this a hard and fast rule to follow. Oh, I know that once in a while a person will become irritated when you ask him to repeat your order. He will think you're insulting his intelligence. There's an easy way around that. All you need say is: "Bob, would you remind repeating what I've just said? I want to double-check myself to make sure I didn't leave anything out or that I didn't give you the wrong information." That will solve that problem at once.

2. *Have them ask you questions when they don't understand.* Normally, if a person doesn't understand what you want, he'll ask you to clarify it for him. But if you are giving instructions to a group, don't assume that everything is understood just because no one asks you a question. Many times, a person will have a question, but he doesn't want to expose his ignorance in front of his peers. If you suspect that is the case, then move on to the third technique, which is to

3. *Ask questions yourself to make sure your order is understood.* For example, you could say, "How do you plan on tackling this problem, Marilyn? What are your own ideas on how to handle this, Dick?"

Or you could use an approach like this:

- "Do you understand why this part goes on last?"
- "Do you see why this small ring goes on first?"
- "Do you know why the temperature has to be kept at a constant 68 degrees?"

How to Use the Mission-Type Order for Achieving Maximum Results from People

If you want to get the maximum results from a person in his work, if you want him to do his best on the job, then tell him *what* you want done and *when* you want it, but *don't tell him how to do it.* Let the person figure that out for himself. That way he will be forced to use his own intelligence and initiative to get the job done. This is called a *mission-type order.*

Mission-type orders develop a sense of responsibility in people. Each person feels that he is really a contributing member of the team. No one is left sitting on the bench.

"Using mission-type orders can bring you all sorts of benefits," says Albert Simmons, a research scientist with a Florida technological institute. "This is especially true in research and development. Our people have to use their imagination and ingenuity to come up with new ideas on how to get the job done. Whenever you use mission-type orders, you open the door wide for people so they can use their initiative to the utmost."

As Albert says, mission-type orders will bring out the resourcefulness of your best people. If people are not stimulated to do a better job for you when you use this kind of order, they are probably not worth their pay.

A mission-type order is one of the most effective ways to weed out inefficient and incompetent employees before they can become a burden to your organization. If a person can't handle this kind of order, he should be replaced with someone who can.

Your use of mission-type orders will bring you unlimited power with people. You can even use them in your own home. Instead of telling your children *what* to do, use this technique, and you won't have to. Let them know what you want, and when you want it, and then let them figure out how to do it themselves. This will develop their initiative, and their ingenuity and teach them how to stand on their own two feet.

How to Disguise Your Orders as Suggestions or Requests

If your people have any initiative, you will get far better results from them with suggestions and requests rather than direct orders. People simply won't react to direct commands unless they're in the military services, and even that's no guarantee, according to a neighbor of mine, a retired army colonel, Robert Williams.

"I spent more than 25 years in the army, and I doubt if I gave more than a dozen direct orders in all that time," Colonel Bob says. "And most of those commands were given to my jeep driver, like 'Please stop here,' 'Turn left,' 'Turn right.'

"Seriously, though, I always got good results by asking a soldier to do something or by suggesting that he try it a certain way. You know there's no law stating that a colonel can't say, 'Why don't you try it this way? What is your opinion, sergeant?' 'Would you be good enough to...,' 'I wish you would...,' 'I desire.'

"I will tell you this much. Disguising your orders as suggestions or requests works far better than yelling at a man to 'Do this!' or 'Do that!' When you yell at a man, you are just inviting him to yell back at you."

A good way you can put this technique into action to gain unlimited power with people is to use it on your children and your husband or your wife. Experiment a little. Pick up some experience around the house, and soon you'll be ready to go out and play the game like an old pro!

Why You Should Always Use the Established Line of Authority

In the armed services, it's called the *chain of command*. In companies and corporations it's usually known as the *organizational line of authority*. No matter what it's called, and regardless of how large or small the group is, it always has a definite fixed chain of command or line of authority through which orders, commands, instructions, and suggestions are channeled. If a group doesn't have that established line of authority, then it's not an organization after all—it's only a bunch of people, in spite of its title.

It is absolutely essential that you use this authority line when you issue your orders. If secondary supervisors are bypassed, they will lose their authority in the eyes of their own subordinates. They could react by becoming recalcitrant leaders of dissident groups and even try to undermine you in an effort to retain their lost status.

To bypass the supervisor below you is not only a violation of good management procedure, but it can also be confusing to an employee, especially if the order you give him disagrees with the one he's received previously from his immediate superior. "No man can serve two masters," Jesus said, and that is as true today as it was when He said it nearly two thousand years ago.

Seven-Point Checklist for Making Sure Orders Are Executed Properly

Here's where so many people go wrong in issuing orders and commands, and why. *They do not supervise the execution of their orders.* Let me give you an example.

You issue an order. Everyone understands. You smile; you are happy. You figure you've done a good job. You go back to your office, have a cup of coffee, and read the morning paper. Everything's all right with the world.

Meanwhile, things are going smoothly. Your orders are being carried out properly and promptly. You might as well go fishing or play a round of golf. Is all this true? No, it's not true at all. Why not? *Because an order without supervision is no order at all.* It's only wishful thinking.

To make sure that the job gets done, and that your order is being followed to the letter, you must personally check the work yourself, for *a person does well only what the boss inspects.* Another way of saying this is: *"Never inspected, always neglected!"*

To inspect a person's work to make sure he is carrying out your orders without harassing him is an art. Oversupervision destroys individual initiative, but undersupervision is just as bad. A good way to supervise and not cause resentment is simply to walk around the work area and look wise. Your presence alone can act as a powerful stimulus to keep a person on his or her toes.

To see and be seen is a supervisory cliche, but it's true and it works, so you really ought to use that technique to make sure your orders are being properly carried out.

You can use the following checklist to inspect and supervise to make sure your people are properly carrying out your orders.

1. *Set aside a specific amount of time for daily inspections.* Always inspect some phase of your operation every day. But don't inspect the same thing at the same time every day. Change things around. Sometimes inspect in the mornings, sometimes in the afternoons. If you have a two- or three-shift operation, do some of your inspecting at night. Don't let anyone home for free!

You'll find that Monday mornings and Friday afternoons are the most critical periods of the week. They're the let-down times when your employees are the most careless and do their worst work. I swear that my last two cars were built in one of those time slots. So bear down on your inspections then more than any other time. The first day of the deer or trout season also falls into that category.

2. *Go over your inspection points before you inspect.* Study up and review your inspection points before you inspect. That way you won't be caught short; your employees won't be able to make a fool of you. You'll always appear to be the expert and in fact, before long you will be. I

recommend you select no fewer than three but no more than eight points to inspect at any one time. By changing these points every day, you will soon be able to cover your entire operation.

3. *Inspect only your selected points.* When you make your inspection—look only at your selected points. *Don't look at anything else. Don't try to be the expert on everything in one day.* You can't do it. Stick to your system and don't let anything distract you. You'll cover everything in good time.

4. *When you inspect, emphasize.* Emphasize the points you have picked for your inspection—not the points your subordinate is trying to emphasize for you. This can become a cat-and-mouse game if you let it get away from you. Just remember who is inspecting and who is being inspected.

5. *Always bypass the chain of authority.* This is an absolute must—no exceptions. No other kind of inspection is ever satisfactory. Don't ask your subordinate managers how they are getting along and how things are. You know the kind of answer you'll get. You must go down to the actual working level so you can see what's going on for yourself. As a matter of courtesy, the manager of that department, section, whatever, should always go with you, but don't ask him questions—ask questions of the people who work for him. That's the only way you'll ever get a straight answer.

6. *Ask questions and more questions.* Remember you are inspecting to gain information, not give it out. So ask questions and listen to the answers. Let your people tell you how they can improve their own performance. They will if you'll just let them. After all, most people do want to do the best job they can.

7. *Recheck the mistakes you find.* An inspection is of no value unless you take the necessary action to correct the mistakes you find. So follow up. Reinspect. Supervise and make sure your corrective orders are carried out. Remember that an order without supervision is the same as no order at all.

Four Benefits of Follow-up Inspections

1. *Inspections give you a personal contact with your people.* It is important to be seen by your subordinates. Even the best worker will get the feeling you don't give a hoot about him if he never sees you. So get out

from behind your desk and out of your office. You establish the mind set for your entire organization by your actions. Don't isolate yourself. Be friendly and approachable if you want to gain unlimited power with people.

2. *Use inspections to keep people fully informed and up to date.* If you handle your inspections properly, you can make them seem to be primarily for your employees' benefit. Let them know you want to keep them fully informed about what's going on, especially in areas that could affect their paychecks, their fringe benefits, their personal welfare. You can make your inspections seem to be secondary by saying, "Oh, by the way, John, I notice you're doing it this way. Is that the best procedure to use?" If his answer is "Yes," follow up with "Why?" If it's "No," your next question would be "Why not?"

3. *Use inspections to improve human relations.* Don't just inspect machines; inspect people. Managers and executives work with people; technicians work with things. You're an executive, not a technician, so use some showmanship during your inspections. Make each inspection a personal visit with your people. Remember their first names. Know everything you can about them, their hobbies, outside interests, and so on. Ask about their wives, their husbands, and their children. When you show a sincere interest in people and in their welfare, it will improve their morale and gain you unlimited power with them.

4. *A person's performance can be improved by inspections.* You can use your inspection as an opportunity to praise and encourage a person in his work. Performance is always improved by praise, not by criticism. Ask for ideas on how to improve work methods and procedures. This always feeds a person's ego. It makes him feel important. Never inspect for the purpose of harassment. Only amateurs do that. Be a professional.

To summarize this chapter quickly,

1. *Make sure the need for an order actually exists.* You don't need to issue an order to prove you're the boss. If you are in charge, people already know that.

2. *Give your orders in a manner that shows you expect immediate compliance.*

3. *Never issue orders you can't enforce.* This point is often violated by inexperienced managers, causing them great embarrassment when they can't back up their orders.

4. *Give clear and complete, correct and concise orders.* People must know exactly what you want done and when. They should not have to guess.

5. *Issue your orders as a lady or a gentleman would, not as a tyrant.* If possible, ask questions or use suggestions instead of giving direct orders. The words in your order say *what has* to be done. The manner in which you issue it influences *how* it will be carried out.

6. *Oral orders must always be repeated to you.* I know of no exception to this important rule. Failure to do this can result in serious errors or grave misunderstandings.

7. *A lack of orders does not relieve you of your leadership responsibilities.* You should keep a complete picture of the situation in mind so you can take the necessary action in any emergency or in the absence of orders from your superior.

8. *Supervise the execution of your orders.* Remember that an order without supervision is no order at all. It is only wishful thinking. This is such an important point—and the one most neglected by executives, supervisors, and managers—you ought to write it down, and slide it under the glass on your desk where you can see it every minute of the day when you are sitting there. It can be a reminder to get up and get out where the work is actually going on.

Chapter 12 ✳ *The Twelfth Day*

LISTENING: THE "SILENT SKILL" FOR GAINING UNLIMITED POWER

Do you want to find out what your employees or your subordinates want? *Then listen to them with an open mind.* Do you want people to do their best for you? *Then let them talk to you about their personal problems, their complaints, their worries, and their fears.* Do you want a person to level with you—to tell you the whole truth? *Then pay attention to him—give him the courtesy of listening to what he has to say.* To listen courteously and attentively is one of the highest compliments you can ever pay a person.

The Benefits You Will Gain

1. *You'll get to know and understand each person better.* What irritates a person can be a key to his personality. If he objects to reasonable rules and regulations, he may be a malcontent and a troublemaker. If you know this about him, you are way ahead of him. If, on the other hand, his complaints are usually justified and not too frequent, he's probably a well-adjusted individual. What genuinely disturbs a person should be taken into consideration in your assessment of his overall value to you.

When you know and understand each person better, you'll not only find out what bothers him, but you will also discover what really turns him on. You can determine where his true interests lie and how he can be motivated to do a better job for you.

2. *Your employees will like you better when you listen.* To listen to others in a sympathetic and understanding manner is without a doubt one of the most effective methods in the world that you can use for getting along with others and tying up their friendship for good.

It's just human nature for people to like you when you listen to them attentively. Let me ask you this: Have you ever disliked a person who listened courteously to your ideas and your opinions? Or put it another way: Have you ever really liked someone who wouldn't listen to you? See what I mean?

3. *People will know you are interested in them.* I know of no faster way to turn a person off than to pay no attention to him or his problems. By the same token, you can turn him on when you show him how interested you really are in him and in what he says. A good way to show your interest is to ask questions like "What did you do then?" "What happened after that?" "What did you say next?"

Even the most reluctant and bashful person will open up and talk when you show your interest in him like that. So concentrate 100 percent on what he is saying. Focus all your attention on him. Listen with all the intensity and awareness that you can command.

4. *You can find out what people really want if you'll listen to them.* People will tell you what they really want if you will just take the time to listen to them. So forget yourself and what you want from them for a change. Concentrate completely on what they want from you and what you can do for them.

Frank Bettger, one of the most successful insurance salesmen this country has ever known, said, "Finding out what people want and helping them get it is the most important secret of salesmanship."

Finding out what people want and helping them get it is also the most effective way to establish good relations with them. When you find out what people want and help them get it, you'll help yourself at the same time when you do. All you have to do to get on the right track is simply *listen to them and to what they say.*

Why Listening to Employee Problems and Complaints Is Your Responsibility

If you're in a management or executive position, you might think you shouldn't have to listen to employee complaints. After all, you tell yourself that you're too busy with your own problems: cutting costs, meeting quotas and deadlines, increasing production, improving quality, attending those never-ending meetings.

Not only that, you say that's why your company has an industrial relations manager, a personnel section to handle gripes, an employee relations counselor—so your people can go to them with their complaints about pay, working conditions, or whatever.

"Not so," says Paul Carlson, the employee relations manager for a huge automobile assembly plant. "Listening to the complaints and gripes of an employee is one of the most important responsibilities every person in a management position has.

"The employee relations department is the company's last line of defense. It's where the last ditch effort is made to satisfy an unhappy employee who's got a beef with the company. If we can't satisfy him, his complaint will probably become a formal grievance to be filed by the union with management.

"Every attempt should be made to take care of a complaint at the lowest possible level. The person's immediate supervisor is most familiar with the problem, and he should try to come up with a satisfactory answer. If he can't, then he should go to his foreman for help in solving his subordinate's problem.

"Here in our plant, when a man comes to our office with a complaint, we want his immediate supervisor to come with him. In fact, when the problem cannot be solved at a lower level, we expect the supervisor to take the initiative in bringing the employee to see us.

"That's what we like to see happen. However, it's not an ironclad rule and it doesn't always work that way. So our door is always open to any employee who has a complaint—with or without his supervisor.

"I can usually tell what's wrong when an employee comes in by himself to see me. His supervisor thinks he's too busy or too important to listen to a person's troubles. When too many people show up from the same department with complaints, I know the real problem doesn't lie with the employees—it's their section chief, foreman, or supervisor who's at fault."

Four Simple Methods for Becoming a Better Listener

One of the quickest and easiest ways to gain unlimited power with people is to listen to their problems with a sympathetic ear. To become a good listener, you will need to learn to *listen with everything you've got, forget yourself, practice patience, be concerned.* Let me discuss each one of those with you now.

1. LEARN TO LISTEN WITH EVERYTHING YOU'VE GOT. I know of no faster way to insult another person or to hurt his feelings than to cut him off when he's trying to tell you something. Ever have someone do that to you? Ever try to tell your boss your side of it only to have him turn his back on you, walk away from you, or tell you to hurry up and get it over with? I've had it happen to me; I'm sure you have, too. You know how deeply it can hurt when other people don't listen to you, so don't be guilty of such conduct yourself.

If you have children, you should realize they feel the same way when you brush them aside, ignore them, refuse to listen to them, or pay no attention to their problems.

Here's what Roy Ellis, a clinical psychologist, says about how important it is to listen to people:

"In our clinic, we find that the counselor most likely to get results is the one who has mastered the art of paying attention to the patient and listening deeply to his problems," Dr. Ellis says. "The reason for this is extremely clear. It matters not whether a person is young or old, happy or sad, rich or poor, each one craves attention. All people want is someone to really listen to what they have to say.

"Recently a couple brought a 15-year-old girl to me. She'd been a runaway from home. Her parents had put her in a juvenile detention center for a week and had threatened to send her to a girls' reformatory until she was 17 unless she straightened out. But the judge of the juvenile court wanted me to talk to them first before he made his final decision.

" 'We give her everything,' her mother complained to me. 'I don't know what's wrong with her; she never listens to anything we tell her.'

"But when I talked to the girl, I heard quite a different story. 'My parents don't care about me,' she said. 'We never do anything together. My mother never looks at me when I talk to her; she just keeps on reading her magazine or watching TV. My father's always nagging at me about money and clothes, but he never listens when I try to explain anything to him. He just says he's not interested and for me not to bother him.'

"I told her parents they should pay some attention to their daughter and start listening to her so they could help her with her problems. Thank God they did that, and things are working out much better for all of them now.

"You see, when you don't listen to someone—you reject them. But when you do listen—you accept them. Rejection hurts; acceptance heals. It's as simple as that."

When you listen to the person with everything you've got, you must put aside your own interests, your own pleasures, and your own preoccupations, at least for the time being. For those few moments of time, you must concentrate your attention 100 percent on the other person and listen deeply to what he is saying. You must listen with all the intensity and awareness that you can command. And to be able to do that, you must—

2. FORGET YOURSELF COMPLETELY. If you are going to use this technique successfully, you must force your ego to step aside and give way to another person's ego instead.

This is hard to do at first for all of us are self-centered most of the time. To me, I am the center of everything; the world revolves around me. But as far as you are concerned, you are the center of everything; the world revolves around you. Almost all of us are constantly seeking to be the center of attraction. Many of our waking moments are spent in trying to gain status of some sort.

But if you want to gain unlimited power with people, that is exactly what you must not do. You will have to train your attention-hungry ego to take a back seat for a change. You'll have to stop trying to be in the spotlight and let it fall on the other person for a while.

Will it pay you dividends to forget yourself long enough to listen to the other person? It most certainly will, says Bert Wheeler, the founder and president of Wheeler's Discount Markets, a Midwest grocery chain.

"I've found that if I can forget myself, my status, and my self-importance long enough to listen to some of my employees, I can pick up a lot of good new ideas," Bert says. "But I can't learn a thing from my people if I'm more concerned about my status, who and what I am, than with what they want to tell me.

"For instance, I can think of all sorts of recommendations I failed to accept in the past just because I thought I was too high and mighty to listen to George, the stockroom clerk, or Sally, the cashier.

"Today, I know better. I've learned that all sorts of good ideas can come from my people who are actually doing the work, because they know more about their jobs than anyone else does. All I need do is forget myself long enough to keep my ears open and listen to them."

3. PRACTICE PATIENCE.   I know it's hard to be patient when you're in a hurry and the other person insists on telling you every single minute detail. A fellow who used to work for me was like that. He nearly drove me up the wall sometimes, and I felt like reaching in his mouth and dragging the words out faster, but by being patient and hanging on until he was through, I was usually amply rewarded, for his ideas were sound and logical. Oh, once in a while I had to listen to some nonsense, but all in all, his good ideas far outweighed his useless ones.

"Sometimes, you can speed up this process by asking the person to give you a brief oral summary and to put all the minute details in writing," says Gordon Freeman, a design engineer. "But that isn't always possible, so if you don't want to run the risk of missing something really important and worthwhile, you'll simply have to develop the patience to hear the person out."

One of the best ways to practice patience is not to criticize and offer snap judgments no matter how pushed you are for time. It's always better to sleep on it first before you offer an opinion, especially if it's one that could destroy the other person's ego, dignity, and self-respect. Useless criticism is not the way to achieve unlimited power with anyone.

A great many times patience is simply a matter of waiting, watching, listening, standing by quietly until the person you are trying to help works out the answer to his or her own problem.

4. BE CONCERNED.   Why is it that Alcoholics Anonymous succeeds in helping people when other more conventional methods fail? Because the people in A.A. learn to listen with everything they've got to the person who needs help. They forget themselves completely in the service of others. They are patient and understanding—they never criticize.

But above all, they are deeply concerned about the welfare of their fellow human being. As a result, they are able to achieve a group people

power that literally works miracles for that person who needs such specialized help.

If you feel you can achieve unlimited power with people at the
expense of the other person, or without being concerned for that individual
and his welfare, let me tell you right now: You are terribly mistaken. Your
unlimited power with people must benefit the other person, too, or it will
not work for you.

So you must be deeply concerned about the other person before you
can expect to gain unlimited power with him. There is no use of listening
to a person, forgetting yourself, or practicing patience unless you really are
concerned about that person and his personal welfare.

To be concerned about the other person is the basic foundation of
all deep and lasting human relationships. It is the heart of all friendship and
a real clue to unlimited power with people.

How to Make the "Silent Skill" Work for You by Asking Questions

1. *Questions will stimulate a person's thinking process.* Whenever
you get right down to specifics by asking *who, what, when, where, why,* and
how, your listener is forced to think so he can give you correct and concrete
answers. This is especially true if the question is directed toward some phase
of his work.

2. *Questions will give your listener a chance to express his or her
own ideas.* You can find out by questions—*and then really listening to
the answers*—what the attitudes of your subordinates are about the plant,
your department, their superiors, their fellow workers. Getting them to
talk about their work first is a good way of getting them to talk about
themselves next.

3. *Asking questions is the only reliable way to get accurate information.* Never dominate a conversation by doing all the talking yourself if you
want to find out where people stand on a certain point. Take a lesson from
the efficiency experts. They always ask painful and pointed questions, and
they listen carefully to the answers. I have yet to hear one answer a single
question—about his progress, at any rate—until it's time for his final report.
So work like an efficiency expert; ask questions and then listen to the
answers. To get information, all you have to do is to insert another question

whenever the person stops talking. Just prime the pump; let him work the handle.

Six Characteristics of Every Good Question

Well-phrased questions are the key to sound questioning techniques. A good question will cover the six following points:

1. *A good question has a specific purpose.* Your questions should be designed for definite purposes. One question might be used to emphasize a major point, another to stimulate thought, and yet another to arouse interest and make your people more alert. If you yourself will ask, "Are there any questions?" you will give your people the opportunity to clear up any misunderstandings and they can voice their own opinions.

2. *A good question is understood by everyone.* Your questions should be phrased in language and terms that are familiar to all your listeners. They must be worded in such a way that people will have no trouble in understanding exactly what you want. If your question creates another question in any of your listeners' minds, it's useless. "Please, tell me exactly what you want me to do" is an age-old plea of employees to their supervisors.

3. *A good question emphasizes only one point.* Avoid asking two questions in one or asking a question in such a way that several other questions are needed to understand the first one or bring out the information that you want. Concentrate on a single point; don't scatter your fire. The words, "This *one* thing I do," are as valid today as when the Apostle Paul wrote them to the Philippians nearly two thousand years ago.

4. *A good question asks for a definite answer.* Don't let your people bluff you or get away with vague answers that tell you nothing. State your question in such a way that a definite and concrete answer will be required. Don't give up until you get the answer you need.

5. *A good question discourages guessing.* Never word your questions in such a way that your listener can guess at an answer and satisfy you. His answer should be based on information and facts, not on imagination and fancy. There will be times when you'll be asking for his candid opinion, but his subjective thinking should be based on objective facts.

6. *The best question always asks "Why?"* The *why* can be spoken or implied, but it should always be there. Too many supervisors are content

with an answer of "yes" or "no," even when that answer tells them nothing. If a person says "Yes," ask him *why*. If he says "No," ask him *why*. If he says that it's always been done this way before, ask him *why*. This three-letter word is one of the most potent question words you can ever use, so use it to your best advantage.

How to Kick a Conversation into Gear

You can get a person to talk freely about himself and his problems if you will follow the pointers I just gave you about questioning techniques. But it is still your responsibility to initiate the conversation. Do that and you won't encounter this problem:

"Too many times a supervisor and his people go around the workplace just staring at each other, " says Arnold Mayfield, an electronics industry foreman. "They act like a couple of strange dogs sniffing at each other, just waiting to see which one will give ground first. Naturally, the subordinate is hesitant to talk unless his boss says something first.

"I've found the best way to break the ice is to ask the person a question, any question; I don't care what it is. Ask him what time it is; that is at least a start. Just ask him something that will get his mouth open for you."

I agree, although it's still much better if you can use specific questions that will keep the person talking and give you information that you want.

How to Listen Between the Lines

A great many times you can learn more by what your subordinate didn't say than by what he did. So learn to listen between the lines. Just because he didn't say that he dislikes his supervisor doesn't mean that he likes him. The speaker doesn't always put everything he's thinking into words. Not only that, watch for the changing tone and volume of his voice. You'll often find a meaning that's in direct contrast to his words. Watch his facial expression, his mannerisms, his gestures, the movements of his hands, his body. To be a good listener will require that you *use your eyes as well as your ears*.

How to Turn an Angry Employee into a Satisfied One by Listening

Listening to a person's complaints is a definite responsibility of a manager or an executive. To be able to do it properly takes a lot of skill and know-how. Martin Harris, a top employee relations man at a large electronics firm, has that skill and know-how, so I want you to hear what he has to say:

"When an angry employee comes through my door with a complaint, I handle him like a VIP," Martin says. "I treat him as if he were the president of the company or a majority stockholder. I have him sit down; I make him comfortable, give him a cup of coffee. I do everything I can to put him at ease.

"After he's settled down, I ask him to tell me his story. I tell him I want to hear it from beginning to end. *I listen to what he says without interrupting him or saying a single word.* That's the first thing he wants—someone who will listen to him—someone who'll lend a sympathetic ear to his problem.

"When he's through, *I tell him I do understand how he feels.* I say that if I were in his position, if the situation were reversed, I would probably feel the same way.

"Now I've already taken a lot of the steam out of him simply by listening to him and then by telling him I understand how he feels. He wasn't prepared for that, so he calms down even more. Instead of finding that I'm his enemy, he suddenly discovers that I'm his friend. He came in prepared to do battle with me, but now he finds he has no one to fight!

"*Next I ask him what he wants me to do about his complaint.* This really floors him because most of the time a manager doesn't *ask* an employee what he can do for him, he always *tells* him what he's going to do.

But we don't run our employee relations program that way. *We don't tell an employee with a complaint what we are going to do for him. Instead, we ask him what he wants us to do for him.*

"I've had men look at me in astonishment and say, 'Gosh, Mr. Harris, I honestly don't know. I hadn't thought about that part. I just wanted someone to listen to my side of the story for a change. You've done that for me, so that's enough. I'm satisfied.'

"Sometimes they will tell me what they expect us to do. Ninety-five times out of a hundred, I find they ask for much less than I'd have offered them. Then when I give them more than they ask, they're really impressed with the generosity and goodwill of management and the company.

"Either way, when they leave my office, they're fully satisfied. You see, in both cases, they supplied themselves with their own answers, so they are bound to be completely satisfied with the end results.

"To tell the truth, my job is extremely easy. All I do is listen. Then I ask what he wants me to do. When he tells me, I help him get what he wants."

Mr. Harris's way of handling his employee relations job sounds a lot like Frank Bettger's method of finding out what people want and helping them get it. You see, this important secret of salesmanship is also one of the secrets of gaining unlimited power with people so you can be a success in any field at all.

One way you can make this method work for you as a manager or as an executive is to set up a proper employee grievance procedure. To help you do this, consider the following guidelines.

Twelve Guidelines For Handling Employee Complaints

1. *Make it easy for people to come to you.* You don't have to be overly chummy, but you shouldn't be cold and distant with your people either. However you do it, you must free your subordinate of any fear that stating his grievance will antagonize you. That's the important point of this technique.

2. *Get rid of red tape.* Don't clutter up your grievance procedure with cumbersome rules and regulations. Keep it plain and simple. You want to get to the problem and its solution in the least possible time. A good way to do this is to keep an open door at all times.

3. *Explain your grievance procedure to everyone.* It does no good to keep an open door for your subordinates unless they know why it's open. So pass the word along, let them know, keep them all informed. State clearly how an employee should present his grievance and what will happen when he does, step by step.

4. *Help a person voice his own complaint.* Sometimes an employee may be unskilled in putting his grievance into words. If he feels that the correction of his problem will depend upon his verbal ability, he may give up before he even starts and bottle up his discontent to become a problem employee.

5. *Always grant a hearing.* No matter how trivial the complaint might seem to you, always grant the employee a hearing so he can air his gripe.

6. *Practice patience.* This is an absolute must if you want to make this grievance procedure work. I know that you're busy and that you have many other things to do. But be patient; hear the person out. If you don't, chances are he'll go to his union with his complaint. The next time you see him, it will no doubt be in a formal arbitration hearing.

7. *Ask him what he wants you to do.* This is how you can turn a complaint into a profitable session for you. This one phrase can do much to oil the rusty relationships between management and labor.

8. *Don't render hasty or biased judgments.* Even though you might be the manager, make your decisions with the wisdom of Solomon, not with the biased viewpoint of management. Nor should you make any hasty or snap judgments. If you need more time to get more facts, do that. A wise decision is more important than a rapid but incorrect one.

9. *Get all the facts.* Sometimes you will need to hear someone else's side of the story. If this is necessary to get all the facts you need to make your decision, do so.

10. *Let him know what your decision is.* Once you have made your decision, let him know what it is. *Tell him yourself.* Call him back into the office if need be. If you pass the word along by some secretary or office clerk, he will know for sure that you weren't really that interested after all.

11. *Double-check your results.* Later on, check back with that employee to make sure the complaint was taken care of to his complete satisfaction. Follow up and he will know you are still interested in him and in his problem. This simple act on your part will gain you much of the unlimited power with people that you want.

12. *Be concerned.* There is not much use of paying attention to a person and listening to his complaints and his problems unless you honestly do care about him, unless you really do want to help him, unless you won't feel right until you do. I can't tell you how to work this technique. It has to come from your heart, from deep inside of you.

Of course, you can't solve all the personal problems of your subordinates just by listening to their complaints. But paying close attention to them while they talk will help them, and it will definitely improve their attitude toward you.

Peter Jansen, an industrial psychologist, feels the same way that I do. "You must pay attention to your employees and their problems if you really want to help them and if you are truly concerned about them," Dr. Jansen says. "I do not mean that you should give them your casual attention either. *To pay means to part with something of value.* In this particular instance, that something of value is your time and your preoccupation with your own interests and desires.

"When you fail to pay attention to your employees and to listen to their complaints, you reject them. Rejection hurts. Attention heals. It's just that simple."

I don't see how I can add anything to what Dr. Jansen has just said, so I'm not going to try. Instead, I'm going to tell you that in the next chapter you'll learn how to correct a person's mistakes without losing your unlimited power with him. That's an extremely valuable technique for you to know, so I want to get right to it.

Chapter 13 ✻ *The Thirteenth Day*

HOW TO CORRECT
A PERSON'S MISTAKES
WITHOUT CRITICIZING

At first glance, you might feel that you don't have to correct the actions of other people, but if you'll take an honest look at your daily activities, you'll soon find that you do. If you are a department manager, a plant superintendent, a businessman or businesswoman, an executive of any sort, even if you have only two or three subordinates, I'm sure that hardly a day goes by that you don't have to call attention to something that someone did wrong. That being so, I know that you can use my *sixteen-step checklist for correcting mistakes* to your advantage.

I do want to make one point clear here. I do not criticize a person when I correct his mistakes. No one wants to be criticized. Criticism is one of our deadliest weapons. It has the power to destroy a person. The best thing you can remember about criticism is: Forget it!

You don't have to criticize or destroy a person when you correct his mistakes. The best way to correct someone is to show him how to do the job properly. You can offer advice, counsel, and guidance in such a way that he will scarcely realize that you are correcting him. The whole purpose of this chapter is to show you how to do that. I want to show you how to correct a person's mistakes without losing your unlimited power with him. You can do that when you learn how to "Say it with flowers!"

The Benefits You Will Gain

1. You'll eliminate certain bad habits and undesirable behavior of people, especially of your employees or subordinates.

2. Your people will do a much better job for you; they won't make the same mistake twice in a row.

3. Individual and group discipline and morale will improve.

4. You'll get far better results from all your subordinates, even those who had no mistakes to correct.

5. Production and performance will improve and profits will increase because things will get done right the first time.

How to Avoid Losing Your Temper When Correcting Others

A great many people are unable to correct a person's mistakes without losing their temper. They are the ones who end up with an upset stomach, ulcers, high blood pressure, and cardiac flutter. Let me give you an example of how that could happen to you.

"I used to run my department like a cop handing out traffic tickets," Tom Snow told me. "I'd been given the idea by a tough old supervisor that I had to keep on a man's tail every minute just to keep him working without slacking off. I thought I wasn't doing my job properly unless I did it that way.

"Well, I ended up in the hospital for three weeks on a sippy diet—a glass of half and half every hour on the hour and nothing but amphogel in between. It didn't take my doctor long to diagnose the cause of my problem either. In less than a week I was trying to run that hospital ward like my department. I was chewing out everyone in sight. When they didn't listen, I got all the madder at them. The madder I got, the more my stomach rumbled and grumbled.

"At my last consultation before I was discharged, my doctor said, 'Tom, you're giving yourself your ulcers. Your employees didn't give them to you. Neither did your boss or your work. Let me give you a little tip. It doesn't matter to the other fellow how much you hate him. It doesn't hurt him one bit. It only hurts you. So ease off, my friend, ease off. Live and let live.'

"I tried it; I had to. That was over four years ago. I haven't had an ulcer attack since. And by the way, I'm no longer a department foreman," he grinned. "I've been promoted."

Sixteen-Step Checklist For Correcting A Person's Mistakes

1. Call attention to a person's mistakes indirectly.

2. Get all the pertinent facts first.

3. If a formal interview is necessary, you pick the time and the place.

4. Never lose your temper when correcting your subordinate's mistakes.

5. Always begin with sincere praise and appreciation.

6. Take your own inventory to help the person see your point.

7. Give your subordinate a chance to talk.

8. Weigh all the facts and evidence carefully without bias or prejudice.

9. If punishment is required, fit it to the mistake and the individual.

10. Let a person pick his own punishment.

11. Emphasize the benefits to be gained.

12. Close your interview with sincere praise and appreciation for the person's work.

13. Praise every improvement no matter how slight.

14. Give your employees a high reputation to live up to.

15. Follow up with a second interview—if necessary.

16. Don't correct a person's mistakes too often.

Now let's get right down to the specifics.

1. CALL ATTENTION TO A PERSON'S MISTAKES INDIRECTLY. The main goal of correcting a person's mistake should be to prevent a recurrence of that mistake. If you can do that by the use of this step alone, no further action is necessary.

When you see that something is wrong, when you see a mistake being made, simply walk over to the group and ask: *"What happened?"* That's all. The rule to remember here is to *leave out all personal remarks.*

Don't pinpoint anyone by name. When you ask, "What happened?" you get rid of personalities completely. *You focus on the mistake itself, and only on the mistake.*

"Here's how I use this technique," says David Wright, an airline safety inspector. I say, 'Funny—we've never had this trouble with this machine before—*what happened?*' 'This is the first accident I've seen like this—*what happened?*' "I've never seen plastic do that before—*what happened?*'

"By asking 'what happened,' I'm not blaming anyone. I'm not hunting for a culprit. I'm simply looking for facts. And it works. Even when the person who is at fault is found, it takes the edge off; it gets rid of the bite. Just compare these two statements: *What happened?* and *Who did it?* You can even feel the difference!"

You can figure out how to use this step in your own operation. The two important words to remember are: *What happened?* Get your people to open up and talk. Get them to tell you what went wrong. With this system, all you need do is listen.

One last point before I leave this step. *Always correct the mistake, not the person.* When you correct the person, you tend to become too personal, and criticism of the individual is bound to creep in. Your goal should be to correct only the mistake so it will not happen again, that's all.

2. GET ALL THE PERTINENT FACTS FIRST. If you can get all the facts together that you need to correct the mistake by asking *what happened*, fine. You should be able to solve your problem then and there. However, sometimes your people won't come right out and give you all the facts you need to correct the mistake, *especially if you are the one who is at fault.*

Sometimes the mistake comes from your poor instructions, improper orders, bad rules, or misassignments. Remember that you can pull some boners, too, but few employees want to tell the boss when he is wrong. To do so could invite devastating retaliation in some cases. But I hope you don't fit into that category.

Consider this view:

"Whenever one of my subordinates has the courage to tell me that I'm wrong and that I made a mistake, I know I have found a person who's capable of accepting much greater responsibility," says Harriet Allison, an executive with a large advertising agency. "So many people are afraid to do that. Of course, it depends on the boss's attitude. I know that, too.

"That's why I have always tried to maintain the policy with my staff of 'Don't tell me what I'd like to hear; *tell me what I have to hear!*'"

3. IF A FORMAL INTERVIEW IS NECESSARY, YOU PICK THE TIME AND THE PLACE. If your problem has been solved by the use of the first two steps, wonderful. You need go no further. But if it has not been corrected, then you need to use this step.

If a formal interview with a person is necessary to correct his or her mistake and solve the problem, then it must be done in *complete privacy.* That is the first requirement of this step.

Your office should be the best place to use, for it in itself will radiate your authority. I know from my own personal experience that if my boss came down to my office to see me, it was usually just an informal visit and chances were that nothing was wrong. But if he called me up to his office, then almost always something was not right.

Some managers think Friday afternoon is the best time for correcting a person's mistakes in a heart-to-heart talk. That way, they won't have to see the person again until Monday morning. I disagree. You run the risk of a person brooding all weekend over what you said and coming back to work the first of the week still unhappy with you. Others prefer Monday morning, but I know from experience that is also a bad time, for no one's really into the swing of things yet for the week.

I personally prefer Tuesday. That way I can let a person know by a wave of the hand, pat on the back, or a cheery "Hello" during the rest of the week that things are OK with us.

4. NEVER LOSE YOUR TEMPER WHEN CORRECTING YOUR SUBORDINATE'S MISTAKES. It's best never to lose your temper with your subordinate or your employee. But above all, never do so in a counseling session. If you do, you will end up with nothing but a raging argument between two angry people. Anger will lead to criticism rather than correction of a mistake. In fact, you probably won't even be able to remember the point of your interview.

If you can't see any good results from your interview except for your temporarily feeling better for having blown off steam, don't do it. You're a human being, not a radiator. Don't let your personal feelings and personal opinions creep into your interview. That's the "Smith, you ought to part your hair on the other side" idea and that's criticism, period.

That kind of correction will go in one ear and out the other, that is, if you're lucky. If your employee remembers any of it, he'll only recall that you lost your temper, that you were sarcastic, or that you chewed him out unmercifully when he didn't really have it coming to him.

A baseball manager or coach has to turn a deaf ear to criticism most of the time. As Casey Stengel once said, "I sure could use a guy who could play every position perfectly, never strike out, or never make an error. Trouble is, I can't get him to put down his hot dog and come out of the stands!"

5. ALWAYS BEGIN WITH SINCERE PRAISE AND APPRECIATION. Don't tear a person apart the moment he comes into your office. Nor should you enumerate all his character defects one after another as if you were checking off a grocery list. No one lives who can take that kind of punishment for very long.

Instead, start out by telling a person how good he is, how much you think of him, what a good job he has done, *all except for this one small point that you want to discuss with him.*

Kind words help to establish a friendly, cooperative atmosphere. Praise and compliments open the other person's mind. Remember Mark Twain saying that he could live for two months on a good compliment. You can use compliments like these to make the person receptive to correction of his mistake.

"Tom, that was certainly a fine progress report you made. You definitely covered all the main points. However, there is just this one thing I want to take up with you."

"Annie, you've done excellent work for me. However, there is one idea for improvement I'd like to discuss with you."

"Hank, I know you're always looking for new ways to improve your work procedures. I've noted one thing you're doing that seems to be causing you a problem, so I'd like to suggest...."

6. TAKE YOUR OWN INVENTORY TO HELP THE PERSON SEE YOUR POINT. A good way to take the sting out of correcting his mistake is to let the person know you are not infallible. Of course, he probably already knows that, but it helps if you let him know that you know it, too. This helps him to accept your comments better than he would otherwise.

You don't have to list all your mistakes for the past ten years to use this technique. Here's how Jerry Ralston, a company supervisor, does it. "I start off by saying, 'John, I've done the same myself before and a lot more times than you have, too,'" Jerry says. "'Here's what I did to correct my mistake.'

"Then I tell him how I managed to do it—which is really an easy way of letting him know what I want him to do—and then I ask him if he'll give it a whirl my way. What else can he say except that he'll give it a try, and he does, too."

I've used the same system myself for many years. It works extremely well with everyone, especially with young people who like to hear that older people make mistakes, too.

7. GIVE YOUR SUBORDINATE A CHANCE TO TALK. If you do this, he will have the opportunity to tell you his side of the story. Most people are extremely anxious to let you know what happened and how. They want to make sure you understand, and the majority of them will talk readily if you will just give them a chance.

If a person does seem reluctant to speak up, ask some leading questions. Keep asking *why, why, why.* When you get all the answers you can, you'll be in a much better position to help him—and yourself, too, for that matter—by taking the appropriate action to keep this same mistake from happening again.

8. WEIGH ALL THE FACTS AND EVIDENCE CAREFULLY WITHOUT BIAS OR PREJUDICE. Before you enter into a formal counseling session, you should have gathered enough information to warrant it. However, more facts may come to light now that weren't available before. It might be that since you've seen your employee's side of the picture, you find that no corrective action is needed. If that is so, *close your interview promptly and pleasantly.*

Handle this properly and your subordinate need never know that he was suspect for some specific mistake. "Whenever I'm in doubt or I'm not sure, I start out this way with the person I've called into my office," says Everett McCall, a security consultant. "I tell him of a problem that's on my mind; then I ask him for his advice or his opinion.

"Like the time we were having a tremendously high rate of small-tool pilferage. I narrowed it down to three or four suspects. I called them in one at a time and talked to them about *my* problem. As an excuse for having the person in my office, I told him I needed his help—I wanted his expert advice on the punishment to be given to the guilty person. I implied throughout the interview that we knew who the thief was. All I wanted was his valuable opinion on what to do with him.

"I talked to each man the same way and asked him to keep our interview confidential. The pilferage stopped. I don't know to this day who was guilty. I really don't care. It might have been one of the people I interviewed, maybe not.

"If not, the company grapevine carried my message to the guilty party. The point is, not only was my problem solved, but some person's job and reputation were saved, too."

9. IF PUNISHMENT IS REQUIRED, FIT IT TO THE MISTAKE AND THE INDIVIDUAL. Before you mete out any punishment for the mistake, weigh all your evidence and facts carefully. It could be that your formal counseling session will be enough and that nothing further will be required.

But if you do decide that something further is in order, remember that *the only purpose of punishment should be to correct*, and nothing more. Don't be vindictive and vengeful about it.

Take our corrective institutions, for example. If one of them has only punishment in mind, a released man is usually interested only in *revenge* and in *getting even with society* for putting him there.

But if the institution is really corrective in its policy, when a prisoner is freed, he's usually ready to become a productive and useful member of society.

These same two methods are found in business and industry. There seems to be no middle ground. When the wrong disciplinary methods are used—when the person feels he's being treated unfairly—the company can have a problem employee on its hands.

I know of a factory that uses *punishment for the sake of punishment*. Management goes far beyond the practice of rules for the sake of rules. And the production workers hate their superiors. Willful destruction of company property is common; theft is a major problem. So is employee turnover. And loyalty is nonexistent. The company could easily double its profits—perhaps even more—if management would only treat the production employees like human beings.

10. LET A PERSON PICK HIS OWN PUNISHMENT. I've found that a good technique to use is to *let the person choose his own punishment*. Ask a person what he thinks you ought to do in his case. You'll be surprised at how many will face the situation realistically and honestly. Ninety-nine out of a hundred will give themselves a more severe sentence than you would have. *Then you can become his benefactor by reducing the punishment you didn't give him*!

For that one person who goes too easy on himself, tell him you're sorry, but that's not quite what you had in mind. Then tell him what his punishment has to be and stick to your guns. Say what you mean and mean what you say. Even though his punishment may be more than he thought he should have, you'll find that he will usually accept it with good grace when the reason why is explained to him. This happens very rarely, however. Most people will give themselves a more severe sentence than you had in mind. Let me give you an example of that technique:

"I had a training company in Fort Riley, Kansas, right after the Vietnam war ended," says Leo Powell, today a corporation executive. "I had a standing rule in the outfit that any trainee who didn't pass his fifth week proficiency test would not be given a weekend pass. Everyone worked hard to pass the test for there were only two weekend passes given during the eight week training cycle.

"Around the first part of the fifth week, a trainee, who was a National Guard sergeant from Wisconsin on active duty for six months, told me his wife was coming down for his weekend pass.

"That's fine,' I said. 'I just hope she doesn't make the trip in vain. Even though you're a sergeant, you are still a trainee and you have to pass the test, too. If you flunk it, no pass!'

"'I'll pass it,' he said, but he didn't. He flunked it cold. So there he was on Friday afternoon with no weekend pass and a wife who'd come all the way from Wisconsin to Kansas sitting in the company area waiting for him to go to town with her.

"I called him into the orderly room. 'You know the company policy,' I said. 'You knew it long before your wife drove down here. What do you want me to do? If I allow you to go to town, then I'll have to give a pass to every other trainee who failed the test, too.

"'I'll tell you what. You get behind my desk and sit in my chair. I'm going to the mess hall and have a cup of coffee. For 15 minutes you are the captain commanding this company, not I. When I come back, you give me your answer. I'll abide by your decision.'

"I didn't get back to the orderly room. In less than 10 minutes he was in the mess hall. 'You're right, Captain,' he said. 'I can't give myself a pass to go into town, wife or no wife!'

"He'd made the right decision. I was proud of him. He and his wife didn't go into town, but they had a ball that weekend anyway. I had them put up in the best guesthouse on the post, and they were special guests of my wife and me at the club.

"I've never forgotten that experience. I still use the same principle today. I'm not quite sure why it works. I'm not a psychologist. I don't know whether the motive that moves a man is pride, a sense of duty, or what, but I know this much: It works; I don't care how or why."

11. EMPHASIZE THE BENEFITS TO BE GAINED.   You'll get much further if you give the person an incentive for wanting to change his actions and correct his mistake than if you were merely to issue him an order to do so.

For instance, Henry Kirkpatrick, the district sales manager of an insurance company, tells me that the secret of keeping his salesmen motivated to work hard is not to preach to them about what the company wants, but to give them an incentive that will make them want to sell more insurance for their own benefit.

"I never tell them they have to do lots of legwork and call on a lot of prospects if they want to work for me," Henry says, "Instead, I tell them that the more calls they make, the more insurance they'll sell, and the greater their income will be."

12. CLOSE YOUR INTERVIEW WITH SINCERE PRAISE AND APPRECIATION FOR THE PERSON'S WORK.   Don't end your counseling session on a sour note. Mix some honey with the vinegar. Correcting a person's mistake should leave him with the idea that he's being helped, not kicked. When you correct a person's mistakes, do it with the thought of being helpful, not with the idea of nagging him.

As Bernard Baruch once said, "There are two things that are bad for the heart—running upstairs and running down people." So give him a pat on the back at the end of your session so you can finish with a friendly warm gesture. His last memory of your meeting should be a good one.

13. PRAISE EVERY IMPROVEMENT NO MATTER HOW SLIGHT.   No person can live on a diet of constant correction of his or her mistakes. If you constantly have to correct one person's errors, either you should get rid of him or you're nagging him and criticizing him, not correcting him.

For example, if you have a son who's still in those tender years of grade school, watch his face the next time he brings his report card to you.

Suppose you look at it and say, "Son, you didn't do well in reading, did you? In fact, that's a pretty miserable grade!" Watch his reaction. His face will drop; no doubt there will be tears in his eyes. To bring the sunshine back into his face, just say, "But your grades went way up in spelling and arithmetic. I'm so proud of you!"

So if you want to get the best performance possible from your subordinates, if you want to gain unlimited power with them, then praise the slightest improvement and praise every improvement they make. As Charles Schwab said, "There is nothing that so kills the ambitions of a man as criticism from his superiors. So I am anxious to praise, but loath to find fault. If I like anything, I am hearty in my approbation and lavish in my praise."

What about you?

14. GIVE YOUR EMPLOYEES A HIGH REPUTATION TO LIVE UP TO. If you practice the technique I just gave you of praising each and every improvement, this step will become automatic. Whenever you praise a person, he will want more of the same. You'll be giving him a high reputation to live up to when you compliment him on his work. If you set a high standard for a person to attain, he'll know when he misses it. You won't have to tell him. But if you set no standard for him—he'll aim at nothing. As Jose Iturbi said, "The only time you realize you have a reputation is when you are not living up to it."

15. FOLLOW UP WITH A SECOND INTERVIEW—IF NECESSARY. If another interview or counseling session is needed to correct the same mistake, harsher methods will be needed. In the first interview, all you should have to do is *plant the seed.* In the second one, it's time to *plow out some weeds.* But if you need still a third interview, then it's high time to *harvest the crop*! And if it takes a fourth one, well then my friend, you just don't have a green thumb!

Three interviews with an employee to correct the same mistake remind me of the couple who'd been happily married for 50 years. In fact, it was said they'd never even had one quarrel. Not one harsh word had been spoken between them. A reporter was interviewing them on their golden wedding anniversary. He asked them for their secret of happiness.

"Well, we left for our honeymoon driving a horse and buggy," the wife said. "Down the road a ways, the horse stumbled. John stopped the horse and said, 'That's once.' Later, the horse stumbled again, and John said, more harshly this time, 'That's twice!'

"Then the horse stumbled the third time, and John said, 'That's three times!' And he pulled out his pistol and shot the horse dead!

"Well, I looked at John for a moment, and I said, 'John, you shouldn't have done that.' But he looked me straight in the eye, blew the smoke from his pistol barrel, and said, '*That's once!*'

"We've never had an argument since that day."

So should be the sequence of your interviews. I have used that story to good effect with my subordinates many times—both in management and labor. Although some people are too young to remember horse and buggy days, it still makes my point crystal clear.

16. DON'T CORRECT A PERSON'S MISTAKES TOO OFTEN. As I said a moment ago, if you have to correct the same person too often, check yourself. Maybe you're carrying a grudge against that individual without even realizing it. If that is the case, you've allowed your emotions to overrule your good judgment.

Chapter 14 ✳ *The Fourteenth Day*

HOW TO BUILD AN ARMY
OF LOYAL FOLLOWERS

If you want to build an army of loyal followers, you must use your unlimited power with people to inspire them and motivate them to do what you want them to do.

This chapter will show you how you can be the leader in all the business, political, social, and neighborhood activities in which you participate. You'll even learn a technique that will motivate your spouse to be your loyal follower, too.

Professional people, like doctors and lawyers, try to convert patients and clients into a permanent loyal army of followers. So do ministers and politicians. Businesspeople, however, need to build two armies of loyal followers: (1) employees, and (2) customers.

Since my experience lies primarily in business and industry rather than politics, religion, medicine, or law, part of this chapter will be used to show you how to gain power with your subordinates or your employees so you can turn them into an army of loyal followers.

It could well be that at this moment in time you are not in the position to concern yourself with building an army of loyal followers, but when that day comes, as I'm sure it will, the information in this chapter will be of inestimable value to you.

Before I discuss how you can use your unlimited power with people to build an army of loyal followers, I want to ask you a few questions that will help you better understand the reasons behind my methods.

Have you ever wondered why the military services are not able to retain their highly skilled personnel? Or why some companies have a constant turnover of their trained people? The answer is simple. *They do not fulfill the basic needs and desires of their people.*

How is it that such highly successful companies as IBM, Procter & Gamble, Eastman Kodak, Xerox, GE, J.C. Penney, and many others are all able to retain the loyal services of their employees for a lifetime? Again, the answer is quite simple. *They do fulfill the needs and desires of their people.*

So if you, then, want to build your own army of loyal followers, do exactly as these top companies and corporations do: *Fulfill each person's needs and desires so he or she will become a loyal and faithful follower of yours.*

Let me emphasize one point for you here. Before you think that the methods used by these big companies are not appropriate for you, let me say that none of them started as big as they are today. Every single one of them began as a small operation. I can remember when 3M was a small, insignificant company almost unknown outside of Minnesota. So how did 3M and the rest of these big companies become so huge and successful? For the sake of emphasis, let me say again that *they made loyal followers out of both their employees and their customers by fulfilling their basic needs and desires.* You can use that same technique to become successful, too, no matter what you do for a living.

Not only will this technique work to make you more successful financially and help you gain even more unlimited power with people, but it will also work to make your home life happier. That alone makes this chapter valuable to you. If you want your spouse to be loyal and faithful to you, then make sure you take care of his or her needs and desires. Then you'll never end up in divorce court wondering how or why you got there.

The Benefits You will Gain

1. People will stick by you when the going gets tough.
2. People will respect you, trust you, and have full confidence in you.

3. People will give you their willing obedience, loyal cooperation, and wholehearted support.

4. People will work together as a team with high spirit and morale—with conviction, purpose, and dedication toward a common goal.

5. You'll make people feel they belong where they are.

6. People will work for you with initiative, ingenuity, and enthusiasm.

7. People will work just as hard as you do to get the job done.

Six Ways to Develop Your Loyalty to Others

If you want people to be loyal to you, then you must give them your loyalty first. If you have someone over you, as almost all of us have, you must set the example for your people to follow by being loyal to your own boss.

Some supervisors and middle-management people try to gain favor with their subordinates by constantly criticizing or making fun of their superiors. This action destroys the confidence and loyalty of their subordinates. To be an effective leader of others so you can gain unlimited power with them, you must be loyal to those above you as well as to those below you.

To develop this special quality that will help you gain an army of loyal followers, follow these six guidelines:

1. Be quick to defend your subordinates from abuse and criticism from your superiors.

2. Never give the slightest hint of disagreement with your superior's orders when relaying his instructions to your subordinates. If you do disagree with his orders, tell him, not them.

3. Do every task assigned to you to the best of your ability. This in itself shows your loyal support to your superior.

4. Never discuss the personal problems of your people with others. If a person tells you something in confidence, then respect that confidence.

5. Stand up for your people when they have been unjustly accused.

6. Never criticize your superiors in front of your subordinates. You cannot expect loyalty from below if you are not loyal to those above you.

How Top Companies Build Their Own Loyal Armies of Followers

A top-line mobile home manufacturer, headquartered in the Midwest, has more than fifty manufacturing and assembly plants in strategic locations throughout the United States. The company president took over that position when he was only in his midtwenties. In only twenty years he has increased annual sales volume from $9.5 million to more than $300 million.

Employees never leave to go somewhere else to work. They are all completely loyal to this company. They do not depend on a union to get higher wages or other benefits for them. Their pay is based on how much *quality* work they can turn out in a day. Morale is high. Each plant has a long list of people waiting to get a job there even though the company is nonunion.

The company builds its mobile homes to order and to individual specifications. Employees work until the day's quota—usually twenty-five to thirty mobile homes for each assembly plant—is filled. Only then is their work done for the day. But this does not mean a necessarily long day. Actually, it can mean a short one, for if they're fast, they can leave early.

Management doesn't have to browbeat their employees to get them to work. Employees police their own ranks. Not only do they get rid of inefficient or lazy people, but they also eliminate those trying to take shortcuts and skip necessary production steps in an attempt to speed up the assembly process and make more money. They know that if quality falls off, they will lose the privilege of quitting early while still getting paid for a full day's work.

Another Midwestern company inaugurated a profit-sharing plan for employees back in the 1930s when many businesses were going bankrupt. The basic concept of their plan was quite simple. *The more money employees made for the company, the more money they made for themselves.* The end result was that all employees worked harder, produced more, and used their initiative and ingenuity to figure out a more efficient and profitable way of doing things.

Instead of concentrating on how to "get" something out of the company, the employees used their brains to think up new ways to make more money for the company and, thus, more money for themselves. In a very real way, everyone was now part of the management team. Some amazing things happened after that profit-sharing plan was put into effect.

- Ordinary, average, working people came up with ideas that would do credit to an inventive genius like Edison.
- Work slowdowns became a thing of the past. All employees knew that the company's ability to pay depended entirely upon their ability to produce.
- The company's sales volume is now over $600 million, an increase of 120 times over the $5 million annual sales in the early 1930s before the profit-sharing plan was started.
- The cost of the manufactured product has been cut more than 50 percent in spite of continued increased costs of raw materials.
- Annual wages for all employees have increased 800 percent, not from union demands or cost of living increases, but solely from employees' productivity.
- Counting bonuses, all employees—including the janitors—now earn more than $25,000 a year.

The company never has to worry about not having loyal employees. A long line of people is waiting to be hired, but there is seldom an opening unless someone retires or dies. Employees never leave the firm for any other reason.

Employees of Japanese firms are especially loyal to their companies. As an assembly-line worker for Sony has said, "Working for Sony is like working for the family."

The same can be said for all Japanese companies, whether they make cars, motorcycles, cameras, calculators, radios, TVs, VCRs, or whatever. Going to work for a Japanese company is like getting married, except that it lasts a lot longer than most marriages do in America.

Employee loyalty to the company stems from the company's loyalty to the employee. Company management pays a great deal of attention to the needs and desires of each individual employee: financial security, need for recognition and status, a feeling of pride and importance in one's work.

Most top companies offer their people *emotional security*. You can do the same, whether you are running a big company or a small two- or three-employee business.

IBM boasts that no one has ever been fired for economic reasons. The company always finds new jobs for displaced employees, retraining them if need be.

Proctor & Gamble people feel that the products they make are the best in the world. They feel they are engaged in an extremely worthwhile work. The high morale accounts for the legendary competitive enthusiasm of the company's sales force.

Eastman Kodak encourages initiative and ingenuity by giving financial rewards for usable ideas. For instance, one employee was paid nearly $7,000 for finding a way to reduce breakage of camera gears. Kodak also likes to promote from within. Not many people ever leave the company.

Xerox has an outstanding benefits plan that pays 100 percent of all hospital costs for employees and their families. There is no limit. They also pay all dental expenses for those who visit their dentist regularly for two years.

The 3M Company offers so many opportunities to its employees that one senior official said, "The company is like a big cake. All you need do is cut as big a slice as you can eat!"

General Electric doesn't fuss much about the chain of command. If an employee has a piece of work to do, he finds the person he needs to work with and goes wherever necessary to get the job done. All he needs to do is keep the right people informed.

J. C. Penney's people seldom leave either. As one clothing buyer said, "Penney takes care of its own. They back you to the hilt on your decisions. It's good to know your head isn't on the chopping block for every single mistake you make."

How to Gain 110 Percent Cooperation from Your People

As you've already seen by the examples I've given you, there is no deep, dark, or hidden mystery about how to win the loyalty and cooperation of other people. It boils down to this: If you want to win the loyalty, cooperation, and support of others, *you must give them your loyalty, cooperation, and support first.*

Successful people know that you must always give before you can get, and when you do, you always get back more than you give away. That's unlimited people power in action.

So if you want cooperation and support from your people, you must give them your cooperation and support first. You can easily tell if you are doing that. If the people who work for you are prompt and cheerful, filled with enthusiasm, enjoy their jobs, and are willing to put in an extra hour or so when it's required, or when you ask them to, you can be sure you're doing the right thing.

But if you are not giving your people your cooperation and support first, you can always tell that quite easily, too. They'll drag into work late, be indifferent about their jobs, and run for the time clock even before the whistle blows. If that's the way your people act, don't ask them for anything extra; you'll never get it.

Remember: You must always give if you want to get, and you always get back exactly what you give away, although the return is usually multiplied many times over.

This idea is so important you should use it in conjunction with every one of the chapters in this book that show you how to gain unlimited power with people. It should be kept in mind in all your daily contacts with other people—your employees, subordinates, associates, coworkers, customers, friends, even your own family—for loyal cooperation with others is a real key to the unlimited power you want.

A Quick and Dependable Way to Get Others to Cooperate

If you want people to cooperate and work with you, then you must be a member of the team, too. You must be willing to share the same hardships, the same discomforts, and the same dangers they do. This is especially true if you work in a modern industrial plant.

If you think today's industrial plants are not dangerous places to work in, you've never been inside a modern steel plant, a textile mill, or a rubber factory. Modern machinery, although highly efficient, can be extremely dangerous. I've seen enough workers with fingers, hands, and even arms missing to know.

I'm not saying you should run a mixing mill, a drill press, or a rubber calendar if that is not your job. But I am saying that if you have an air-conditioned office while your employees work in sweltering heat, then you can cooperate and show your feeling for them by at least getting out there and sweating with them side by side once in a while.

They won't expect you to spend eight hours a day with them that way; that's not your job and they know that. But a simple act of cooperation like this will establish a bond of friendship and respect between you and your subordinates that you'll never be able to gain in any other way.

"I never go through the plant but that I stop and lend a hand somewhere," says Bob Devine, the assistant plant manager of an Ohio rubber and tire factory introduced in an earlier chapter. "For instance, there's always a skid that has layers of rubber stuck to it. It's tough to get a layer of rubber off and into a mixing mill, so whenever I see a millman sweating and tugging away at a stubborn layer of rubber on a skid, I stop and help him with it.

"Maybe it doesn't really help him that much, but we rub elbows, I get my hands dirty, and we both part with a big fat grin for each other. And that's what I stopped for anyway."

Bob's method of lending a helping hand is especially good to use when you're getting out on a new project and people are a little backward about getting started. If you pitch in first, they will cooperate with you and follow your lead.

One small note of caution is in order here: *When the boss gets too involved in the work, he's no longer the boss.* So you might keep that in mind. Before you get in too deep, be sure that you have a graceful way out.

How to Use Teamwork to Build an Army of Loyal Followers

When you train your people as a team, you give each one a sense of being needed and wanted and a feeling that he or she belongs. One of the strongest psychological drives in a person is the desire to belong to and have identification with a group. Give him that identification he needs so much, and you'll motivate him to be loyal to you.

When a person knows that he's wanted, that his work is appreciated, when he knows his efforts are contributing to the achievement of a worthwhile goal, he becomes proud of himself and proud of his group. He'll have a strong sense of team loyalty.

When you promote a strong sense of teamwork in people, they will have a feeling of pride and loyalty. When you can promote a feeling of strong pride and fierce loyalty in every person in your group, your job as a leader will be much easier. When the chips are down, when you need your people to give their best efforts for you, they'll respond and support you as members of a well-trained and loyal team.

Train people to work together as a team, and you'll be better able to reach your goal and accomplish your mission. Teamwork in a big organization is the key to successful accomplishment of the mission. Teamwork should be developed not only within departments, but also between and among them.

Teamwork starts at the top and bottom and goes in both directions simultaneously. To be totally effective, it must spread laterally as well. All your people must work together as one big team for the common good if you want to gain the maximum results.

The Rallying Technique for Winning People's Loyalty

As you've already seen from the examples I've used, my experience lies mainly in business and industry. But I do want to give you another technique you can use to build an army of loyal followers, no matter what you do for a living. Simply said, that highly effective technique is this: *Establish an emotional rallying point for people to gather around.*

One of the best ways to gain loyalty and to get people to cooperate and work together as a team is to give them a goal to attain or a cause to fight for. People will unite solidly behind you if you can establish an emotional rallying point for them. Let me give you several examples of some extremely difficult causes to rally people to.

I have never known of a popular war. If ever there was one, then World War II came the closest to being it. Why? Because the American people were given an emotional rallying point, not by their own leaders, but by the enemy.

Up through December 6, 1941, the American people were noncommittal about the war in Europe and Asia. They couldn't have cared less about either one; they had no interest in foreign affairs. But, when the Japanese attacked Pearl Harbor on December 7, 1941, people's attitudes changed abruptly. No longer was the United States a disinterested bystander.

After the war was over, the Japanese high command said that attacking Pearl Harbor was their greatest mistake. "Our victory at Pearl Harbor was in reality our first defeat, for it awakened a sleeping giant," a high-ranking Japanese admiral said. "Although it was a highly successful maneuver from a military point of view, for our attack crippled the powerful United States Pacific fleet, it was our first in a series of mistakes in underestimating the will of the American people to fight."

Pearl Harbor was the emotional rallying point for the United States in World War II. It marked the beginning of the end of Imperial Japan.

During that same war, the famous Japanese-American regiment, the 442nd, was formed. It became known as the "Go for Broke" unit. The men in the 442nd gave it their all. One battalion was called the Purple Heart Battalion because of its high number of casualties. It was one of the most decorated units in World War II.

You see, these men had an emotional rallying point for they had a cause to fight for. They had to prove to all America that they were not Japanese, but loyal American citizens born in the United States of Japanese parents. And, of course, they did.

Back in the 1930s, a comparatively small religious movement (it had a total of just over 200,000 members in the late 1970s) established an emotional rallying point for its members by erecting a large headquarters building in Independence, Missouri. The building was called the Auditorium. It seats thousands of people and was built primarily by small donations from members in the middle of the worst depression the United States has ever known.

But after it was completed, the church began to stagnate. Today, it does not even retain its natural increase. Why? Because when the Auditorium was finished, so were the people. They no longer had a tangible goal they could shoot for. The church leadership failed to realize that they needed another emotional rallying point around which its members could be gathered.

This last example shows that when the goal you establish for your first emotional rallying point has been reached, you must immediately establish another one. Also, the goal must be tangible, as was the Auditorium.

Intangible goals are impossible for the average person to visualize, for they are too vague and abstract. They do not inspire or stir a person to action. If you disregard either of these two major points, you are only inviting failure.

Apparently, the church leadership I just spoke about has finally realized that they needed to establish a new tangible rallying point for its people, for in the late 1980s they began the construction of a building called the Temple. It is dedicated to world peace, and the members of this church once again are loyally contributing their monies to this new and expensive project.

I did not say that it is easy to establish an emotional rallying point so you can build an army of loyal followers. It is not. But if you put your imagination, initiative, and ingenuity to work, it can be done. The results gained are worth the efforts.

How to Motivate Your Spouse to Be Your Loyal Follower

Since I am a man, I can best approach this from a man's viewpoint. However, the techniques that work to gain a wife's loyalty will work equally as well on the husband. This much I can say with great conviction: *The best method you can use to ensure your spouse's loyalty is to go out of your way to fulfill every one of your spouse's basic needs and desires.*

A great many wives are homemakers and spend the entire day in the house, cleaning, sweeping, dusting, washing clothes, and cooking, but they get no appreciation or recognition from their husbands for what they do.

I know of no quicker way to find yourself in divorce court than to neglect your wife's needs and desires and take her for granted.

You don't have to send her flowers or candy every day to show your wife how much you appreciate her. My method will cost you absolutely nothing and it's even more effective. I know a couple who've been happily married for 50 years now, and the husband doesn't give his wife any presents except on four standard remembrance days: birthday, mother's day, anniversary, and Christmas.

"What's your secret, Tom?" I asked him.

"Very simple, Jim," he said. "First, I pay attention to her all the time. I always let her know by my actions that I'm aware that she's around. I still say 'Please' and 'Thank you' even after all our years together. So does she; sort of builds a mutual respect between us.

"And I never get up from the table without saying, 'Thanks, honey, that was a terrific meal,' or 'Thanks a lot, dear; you are really a wonderful cook.' No wife ever gets tired of hearing that.

"When we pass each other in the house, I reach out and touch her hand gently. Or I bring her a glass of water when she's sitting down watching TV in the evening. Or a cup of tea in the afternoon when she's sewing or knitting. What if she doesn't want it, you say? Are you kidding? She'll drink it anyway just to show her appreciation for my giving her my wholehearted attention."

Little things? Could be, but if you want to maintain a harmonious relationship with your spouse and want him or her to be loyal and faithful to you, then give your spouse your wholehearted attention and loyalty, too.

Try it. You'll like it, and so will your husband or wife. P.S.: My wife does, and that's for sure.

And now I want to move on to a tremendously important chapter in how to gain unlimited power with people and that is how to get people to give their maximum and go all out for you!

Chapter 15 ✳ *The Fifteenth Day*

HOW TO GET OTHERS
TO GIVE THEIR ALL FOR YOU

When you use your unlimited people power properly, everyone will want to do their best for you. They'll want to give it their all. You won't need to threaten, shout, browbeat, or coax them to get things done. Just use the techniques that you'll find in this chapter, and you'll be able to get the maximum from people without having to settle for the bare minimum.

Remember that although all people have the same basic needs and desires, they still differ, one from another, in that *whatever a person is lacking at the moment he has the greatest need and desire for.* Therefore, if you want to get a person to do his best for you, you'll need to know what his most pressing requirement is so you can tailor your approach to fit that need.

When you use your unlimited power with people this way to bring out the best in everyone, you will gain the following benefits.

The Benefits You Will Gain

1. You won't have to accept just the bare minimum performance from them.

2. You'll be able to ask people to give their maximum effort for you.

3. If you're in business for yourself, you'll realize increased profits or increased production.

4. You can look forward to lowered production costs and minimal business expenses.

5. When you can get the best out of people, it will mean increased profit, prestige, promotion, or perhaps all three for you.

6. No matter what you do for a living, your people will want to go all out for you.

Participatory Management: A Powerful Technique for Getting the Job Done

When you are the boss and you have people working for you, you can use one of three ways to get the job done, although you will not necessarily get the same results from all of them.

1. *You can give a person a direct order to do something.* Even when that person is your employee and has no other choice than to obey you, this is normally the least desirable of the three techniques available to you to get the job done, for you will usually get only the minimum results.

2. *You can ask a person to help you do the work, using your already established procedures.* This is better than the first method, but it still leaves a great deal to be desired. This technique is commonly called "cooperation," but that word can be grossly misleading. For instance, management always says it cooperates with labor. What that usually means is that management furnishes the methods while labor supplies the muscles. But that's not real cooperation. That's only giving lip service to the idea.

3. *You can ask a person for his ideas on the best way to get the job done.* This is by far the most desirable method to use. It is called *participatory management.* When you use it, you will gain a person's cooperation and support. He'll give you his maximum efforts and go all out for you.

The participatory management technique is highly effective, for when you ask a person for his opinions and ideas on how to get the job done, you've made him feel important, you've built up his ego, and that's one of the secret motivators that turn people on. I gave you a list of those fifteen secret motivators back in Chapter 7.

Making people feel important is a powerful stimulant and incentive to a person's productivity. As a friend of mine, Joe R., told me, "I was so flattered by having the company president ask for my opinion, I couldn't get my hat on my head for over a week!"

Not only do you make a person feel important when you ask for his ideas and recommendations about how to do something, but you also satisfy these additional learned needs and desires that he has:

1. Recognition of efforts, reassurance of worth
2. Social or group approval, acceptance by his peers
3. The desire to excel, to be the best
4. The feeling of belonging, of being a member of the team
5. The opportunity for creative expression
6. The accomplishment of something worthwhile
7. A sense of personal power
8. A sense of self-esteem and self-respect
9. Emotional security

When you can do all this for a person just by asking for his ideas and opinions, when you ask him to help you figure out a solution to your problem, you know that he will give you the maximum and go all out for you. And that increases your personal unlimited power with people tremendously. After all, that's what you really want.

The participatory management technique doesn't apply just to business or to earning your living. You can use it in your entire life—in everything you do. You can use participatory management in your personal relationships, your church and social activities, civic groups, and school and community affairs. When you ask people to give you their opinions and their ideas, when you ask them to help you, they'll go all out for you and give you their maximum efforts.

For example, one of the best places to use this technique is in your family relationships. Marriage counselors tell me that family problems and divorce rates are much lower with couples who use this technique.

I've also learned from educational authorities that teenagers coming from families who practice this method in the home cause fewer disciplinary problems for their teachers and for other figures of authority. They also get along much better with their fellow students.

It boils down to this: You can best succeed in life—financially, professionally, personally—by getting other people to give you their maximum and go all out for you. Participatory management is the best way you can do that.

So if you want to get to the top, then use this technique in everything you do. It is a real key to your success. Let me give you some concrete examples now of how others use this method successfully to achieve their goal of unlimited power with people.

How to Use Participatory Management in Business

As Jimmy Durante used to say, "Everybody wants to get into the act!" Employees and subordinates are no different. They want to have some say in how things are done, too.

You can make them feel that it's *their* company, department, group, or section, whatever, by giving them a role in the planning, decision making, and formulation of rules and regulations, policies, and procedures. You can use any number of ways to let people participate in the management process. Let me give you an example.

One of the biggest personnel problems in companies and corporations is that executives and administrators at the top make up *all* the rules and regulations for people at the bottom.

But most people—and that definitely includes me—do not like being told what or what not to do. They rebel automatically, and so do I. After all, rules and regulations are restrictions on personal and individual liberties. So people tend to resist those rules or disobey them altogether.

If that's the problem in your group of people, then let me suggest that you use the method Sarah Bates, a personnel manager, recommends. Here is what she says about how her company uses the participatory management technique to get the maximum results from their employees.

"One of the best ways we've found to cooperate and work with our employees is to let them make up their own rules and regulations to govern themselves," Sarah says. "After all, no two departments have the same functions or identical tasks, so it's difficult for top management to work out rules that apply to everyone.

"Not only that, our boss has found that when employees are allowed to set up their own rules for their individual departments, they are usually a lot stricter on themselves than we are. And since those rules are their own, the ones they personally made up, they will be much more likely to follow them than when management tells them what to do or what not to do. It's an excellent way of using participatory management, and we like the results we get.

"Of course, we still reserve the right and authority to review their rules and make changes if necessary with their participation and approval. But our problems with that have been minor and easily resolved."

How to Get Even Problem People to Give You Their Maximum

I, too, have found, just as Sarah has, that one of the best ways to get people to give their maximum and go all out for me is to let them make up the rules and regulations to govern themselves. This is especially true with employees who have a tendency to cause constant disciplinary problems.

I remember one fellow—an especially obstinate and unruly troublemaker—who was so amazed by my asking him for his help and advice in establishing the policies and procedures for his department that he became a completely changed person. Almost overnight he became a model employee and set the example of behavior for others in his department to follow.

Do you know why? *Because he wanted to be important, he wanted recognition, he wanted others to pay attention to him, he wanted to be SOMEBODY.* By feeling important, by being somebody of worth, he was also able to fulfill nine more of his basic learned desires, the ones that I have mentioned earlier in this chapter.

When I gave him what he wanted so much, he went all out for me: He gave me 110 percent, and his actions paved the way for others to follow.

So, if you want your people to give you their maximum, if you want them to cooperate with you, to back you to the hilt, and to go all out for you, then make them feel important. Feed their egos. Give them the attention they crave so much. Ask for their opinions and suggestions, their recommendations and advice. Show them how and why you can't get along without them. Give them a role in the decision-making process.

When you use participatory management with your people this way, you, too, will receive the same big benefits that huge companies and corporations have gained.

How to Use Participatory Management in Your Own Home

As I told you before, participatory management will work for you and your family as well as it does in business and industry. If you've found this technique to be useful in your job, it will work with your spouse and children as well.

Grace Foster, a local clinical psychologist who specializes in marriage counseling, tells me that a lot of husbands are at fault in that they never tell their wives anything about their business, their work, or their plans for the future even though all these directly affect the entire family.

"They never give their wives a chance to make any sort of suggestion," Dr. Foster says. "Yet they complain to me, saying their wives won't cooperate with them in saving money, economizing on household expenses, and so on. A lot of fathers say their children don't cooperate either, but they never ask them for their suggestions or ideas. They only order them around and tell them what to do or what not to do.

"I always recommend to my clients with family problems like these that the husband, the wife, and the children, too, sit down at least once a month for a family conference. At this meeting, problems can be discussed openly, common family goals can be established, and each person can be asked to offer suggestions and recommendations.

"I am always deeply gratified when people with seemingly insoluble problems are able to resolve them when they adopt this family participative management plan. The entire family gets along better. Everyone is much happier when each person is not told what to do or what not to do, but instead is asked for suggestions and recommended solutions to family problems."

I recommend this method wholeheartedly. Although our own children are grown and on their own now, the family conference to get everybody's opinion and then vote on the problem was our standard procedure for many, many years.

I always found that our children would accept parental authority more willingly, even when the decision went against them, when they had the chance to voice their own opinions and make suggestions before the final vote was taken.

As much as possible, let your children make up their own rules of conduct to follow. I know that, just as employees do, they will obey their own rules and regulations much better than those that their parents lay down for them to follow.

Of course, they will need your counsel and advice to help them make their decisions, for after all, you are older, more experienced, and much wiser than they are.

Three Ways to Make a Person Become Emotionally Involved

You will never get the best out of a person unless you appeal to his heart as well as his head. Why is that? *Because the head never hears 'til the heart has listened.*

You see, you can give a person all sorts of logical reasons why he ought to do a job a certain way, but you're only appealing to his intellect. You must make your pitch to his emotional instincts to really get him involved. The more motives you can appeal to, the greater will be your opportunities for success.

How do you appeal to a person's emotions? Easy. You simply show him the benefits he's going to gain when he succeeds in reaching his goal. It's been proven time and again that when a person really wants to succeed at what he's doing, he can do superlative work where before he failed.

Just as, for instance, a D or F student can turn around and make the dean's list when he is properly motivated and when he has a fixed goal and purpose in mind, a dissident malcontent can also become your most dependable worker when he's really inspired. But that will happen only when you appeal to his heart as well as his head, for remember, the head never hears 'til the heart has listened.

If you want a person to give his maximum for you, if you want him to go all out for you, then give him a specific goal to work for, make it possible for him to reach that goal, and make the reward worthwhile when he does achieve it. Here are three techniques you can use to do that:

1. GIVE HIM A SPECIFIC GOAL TO SHOOT FOR.   You will be surprised at how quickly a definite goal, one in black and white, can change a person's attitude from vague generalities to exact and meaningful specifics.

Perhaps one person's goal will be to make more money on the job. Then show him what he has to do to reach that objective. Maybe another person is interested in getting a new and different job. Tell him what he must learn and be capable of doing before he can be considered for it.

If you help a person establish his own goals and then give him every bit of help you can to reach them, you won't have to push him any longer to get him to do his best for you. He'll become his own self-starter.

2. GIVE HIM A GOAL HE CAN REACH.   Don't give a person a goal that's too difficult or too distant for him to reach. Take a student starting out on the long slow grind to become a doctor of medicine, for instance. He'll have to give himself some intermediate goals so he can pace himself for the long haul, or he might not make it. First, he'll need to make his goal his bachelor's degree; then on to medical school; after that, his internship; finally, his own private practice as a physician or surgeon. And if he wants to specialize, it will take still more education to realize that goal.

No matter what the person's goal is, cutting it up into intermediate steps will make it more attainable for him. For instance, my daughter wanted to be able to type without errors at a speed of 75 words a minute.

"Teresa, give yourself a goal of 50, then 55, then 60, and so on," I told her. "If you don't, you'll get too discouraged and quit long before you reach your final goal."

3. MAKE THE REWARD EXCITING AND WORTHWHILE.   A person will never be able to reach the final goal unless the reward is exciting and worthwhile. Attainment of the goal must give the person a reward that will fulfill one or more of his basic needs and desires. For example, you say to a woman, "Sue, if you do a better job, I'll see that you're rewarded for it."

Now this statement by itself is not enough to get Sue to do her best for you. She cannot see the reward clearly. She must be able to visualize how she can gain certain concrete benefits from that promised reward. She'll need to know if the reward she gains is worth all the effort she's going to expend.

So it's up to you to tell her how she will benefit. For example, she'll earn more money, she'll have increased importance, prestige, and status, her coworkers will respect her even more. That way you make her reward exciting and worthwhile, so she will do her best to reach the goal you've set for her.

How to Transform a Thankless Job into a Worthwhile One

No matter what a person does for a living, you can get him to do a better job and establish some worthwhile goals if he will just get his eyes off the ground. Let me give you one of the best examples I've ever seen of making the most of a so-called menial job.

Tom Gannon was once a night janitor at a large food plant in the Midwest where I also worked as a night supervisor years ago. All he could see ahead for himself was a long row of sleepless nights, year after year. "All I know how to do is sweep and scrub floors," he told me one night. "I don't have any college education like you do. You can get ahead; I can't. I'm in a dead-end job."

"Then why don't you take what you know and go into the janitorial business for yourself, Tom," I said. "There are a lot of big department stores and other businesses in town that would gladly pay for a dependable regular cleaning service."

Today Tom has the custodial contracts for many of the big stores and factories in that same Midwestern city. He also has a residential division in his company that provides a regular monthly maintenance service for homes and apartment buildings. Tom transformed a thankless job into a profitable business simply by looking up at the stars instead of down at the dirt on his feet.

Eight Guidelines for Emphasizing Skill and Results—Not Rules

You should be interested in results—not rules and regulations if you want to get the maximum from your people and have them go all out for you. As long as the job is done and done well, you should not be concerned with the methods used.

It's a proven fact that when you emphasize skill and results rather than rules and regulations, when you give a person the responsibility and the authority to do the job, he can be up to ten times as effective as others in getting his work done. Here are eight proven techniques you can use to emphasize skill and results, not rules.

1. *Have complete confidence in the person.* Let him know you expect him to do his best, not just for you, *but for himself.* Nearly everyone tends to perform as closely as possible to what is expected of him. When your people know that you expect them to do a superior job, and that you have every confidence in their ability to deliver, that's what they will usually give you.

2. *Don't dominate a person or oversupervise him.* Your subordinates will like to know that you are available for advice and counsel when they need you. However, they will resent oversupervision and harassment. Individual initiative is best developed when they can use their imagination in developing their own methods and techniques to do their jobs.

3. *Throw down a challenge.* A challenge will bring out the best, even in the most average person. Nothing motivates a person more than to find out that he is better than he thought or to prove to others he can do a better job than they thought he could. This method will also help you discover your best people so they can be pinpointed for future more important responsibilities.

4. *Besides financial security, offer a person emotional security.* This could take the form of approval, recognition of efforts, self-respect, and self-reliance. When a person succeeds in completing a difficult task, he will have achieved much more than just a monetary reward. He'll gain recognition from others for a job well done, and he'll have increased confidence in himself and in his own abilities.

5. *Encourage him to set some personal goals of his own.* I've already shown you how to make a person want to give his maximum and go all out for you by setting certain goals for him to attain. But he must be able to visualize his own personal goals. These personal goals are extremely important, for if he can achieve them, the attainment of your goals will be much easier to realize.

6. *Let a person be himself.* Unless long hair and beards are safety factors in a man's work, they should have no bearing on a man's job security or his promotion status. My father-in-law used to say, "You can't trust a man who wears a mustache," so of course I immediately grew one.

If you can, have a flexible work schedule for your people. For instance, employees at some plants I've visited as a management consultant came to work any time between 6:30 and 8:30 A.M. They left when they had completed an eight-hour workday. This system proved to be highly effective and satisfactory to everyone. I know that this system is not possible for all, but if you can use it, then I recommend it highly.

7. *Let the person tell you how and where he needs to improve.* No matter how good you are in your ability to find a person's mistakes, remember that criticism does not help a person to give his maximum for you. To get a person to evaluate himself critically, call him in once in a while and tell him about his good points. Praise him. Then ask him to tell you about his weak points and how he plans to correct them.

8. *Always use praise and encouragement.* You reward a person when you praise and encourage him and when you show him how much you appreciate his efforts for you. Everyone thrives on praise and appreciation. Praising in public is especially beneficial, for public praise increases a person's prestige and status, it raises his morale, and it strengthens his self-confidence. Public recognition of a person's efforts is one of the best ways to gain unlimited power with people.

How to Use the Buffer Technique to Increase Your Power with People

The buffer technique is one of the best methods you can use to get people to give you their maximum and go all out for you. Let me give you an example to show you how well it works.

A company controller, Max R., was having all sorts of trouble with his subordinates. Late payrolls were an especially sore point with him for they were a recurring problem.

When one of the department heads would take him to task for this, he would snap back, "That's not my fault. I don't make up the damned payrolls myself." He would then pass the blame down to one of his payroll clerks. That individual would catch it from both Max and the complaining department head.

"Max, you're taking the wrong approach to solving this problem," I told him one day. "As long as you pass the blame down to someone else, you're going to have this difficulty. You are never going to solve your problem this way.

"But just as soon as you accept the responsibility for the mistakes of your subordinates and act as a buffer between them and those complaining department heads, you'll find that your people will give you the maximum and go all out for you. They'll get the job done right and on time. If you protect them, they will protect you."

Although Max was doubtful about this solution to his problem, he decided to try it, more or less as a last resort. Naturally, this technique worked, just as I knew it would.

You see, I learned a long time ago that you must always accept complete responsibility and take the blame for the failures of those who work for you if you want them to give their maximum and go all out for you.

When you do that, you'll find that your people will go all out to keep mistakes from happening. *When you keep them out of trouble, you'll discover that they are anxious to keep you out of trouble, too.* The buffer technique, when properly used, will help increase your unlimited power with people tremendously.

The buffer technique should be used to help you accept the responsibility for the actions of your subordinates, not to cover up for them. For example, it would be a mistake on your part to use this technique to hide an employee's alcoholism. You would only make his drinking problem worse. The best way you can help an alcoholic employee would be to put him in touch with someone who understands alcoholism, say, an Alcoholics Anonymous member.

And now I want to move on to an exciting and interesting chapter that will help you greatly increase your unlimited power with people. That chapter is how to persuade people to your way of thinking as if by magic.

Chapter 16 ✳ *The Sixteenth Day*

HOW TO PERSUADE PEOPLE TO YOUR WAY OF THINKING AS IF BY MAGIC

I have met one manager after another who has told me he knew he should try to use persuasion to get the job done. He has said that he knew better than to use force, threats, fear, or intimidation. Yet, time after time he has found himself threatening people with demotion, dismissal, transfer to the boondocks, suspension, and loss of privileges simply because he was at wit's end as to what else to do.

As one industrial manager from Pennsylvania told me, "I know I shouldn't use threats or try to instill fear in a person, but sometimes, so help me, I get so mad and frustrated, I reach the end of my rope. I find myself barking and yelling at people. I realize that's no good, but I'm under so much pressure I run out of patience. I just don't know anything else to do!"

Why does an experienced manager or executive like this use threats trying to scare people into doing a better job? Because of frustration, anger, worry, impatience, lack of time, harassment, and pressure. Besides, executives and managers have certain fears, too. They're human beings just like the rest of us.

If you've been using force or threats or fear hoping to get the job done, use the methods you'll find here to persuade people to your way of thinking.

The Benefits You Will Gain

1. You'll no longer need to use fear or threats vainly trying to persuade people to do things your way.

2. You'll not waste your time in fruitless arguments.

3. You'll greatly strengthen your powers of persuasion.

4. People will do as you ask them to do. They'll carry out your orders and directives with conviction and enthusiasm.

5. You'll be better able to attain your goals.

6. You'll gain a new feeling of self-confidence and personal power.

7. And above all, you'll gain unlimited power with people.

Why Fear, Force, Threats, and Intimidation Are Not Effective Persuaders

None of these methods—fear, force, threats, intimidation—will work or get the lasting results you want. Not only that, none of these will bring you the unlimited power with people that you're after.

For example, take the manager who tries to scare an employee into doing what he wants him to do by threatening him with the loss of his job, demotion, a fine, suspension, transfer, or loss of privileges. What will his results be? I can guarantee you that he will find himself running scared, too, for that manager will have problems of low morale, insubordination, absenteeism, inferior quality, low production, increased waste, pilferage, perhaps even sabotage.

For this reason, the use of threats, fear, or force leads to more problems than most managers or executives can handle because *fear always leads to hate.* The person who is afraid of the boss soon hates him and will do everything possible to discredit or destroy him.

If you think for a moment that does not happen, listen to what Walter Gardner, a Kansas City, Missouri, management consultant, has to say about fear and hate:

"I personally saw a factory in the heart of the Ozarks country of Missouri nearly go bankrupt because the plant manager, production superintendent, department foremen, and shift supervisors all tried to control the labor force by using threats and attempting to fill people with fear.

"But Ozarks mountain people are just as stubborn as our famous Missouri mules. Lead them, and they'll follow you anywhere you go; they'll do whatever you ask them to do. But mistreat them, threaten them, use force, and they'll balk every time. You can't drive them anywhere.

"That plant, which employed 1,500 people, survived only because of a wholesale dismissal of management personnel from the top to the bottom by the corporation's Chicago headquarters and a complete change of company policy and procedures based on my recommendations."

Please don't make the same mistake of using fear or force to gain unlimited power with people. You'll always fail in the long run. Lead people, and they'll follow you gladly. Push them, and they'll strike back. Only slaves or prisoners can be ruled by fear or force, and they will rebel at the first chance.

I have selected seven techniques for you to use to win people to your way of thinking. Each one follows the other in a logical sequence. I know there are still other techniques you can use, but I also know from long experience that these seven are the best ones you can use to get the results you want, and to help you gain unlimited power with people.

How to Make It Easy for a Person to Change His or Her Mind

The first thing to remember about a person whose ideas or work methods you want to change is that every human being is a creature of habit. He doesn't like to change. He prefers things exactly as they are. He's used to them that way, and he's comfortable with them. A person doesn't want his routine upset. You'll always encounter resistance to new ideas, novel methods, and different ways of doing things. To reduce that resistance, *make it easy for the person to change.*

Why do people do things a certain way or follow a certain set routine? For two reasons: first, because it's a habit and, second, *because they feel it is beneficial to them to do it that way.* Whether the advantages gained are imaginary or real makes no difference. As long as a person thinks he will benefit by doing things a certain way, that's the way he'll do them. If a person believes that raw cabbage juice will cure his ulcers, he'll drink raw cabbage juice, no matter how bad it tastes.

Take my own father, for instance. For years he suffered with chronic indigestion. He always took two teaspoons of bicarbonate of soda after every meal to help his heartburn, never realizing that he was making his gastric juices too alkaline and thus was causing his own bad digestion.

Nothing his doctor could say would convince my father otherwise, because he was so sure that baking soda benefited him. It was not until he took a three-week fishing trip to Canada and he forgot to pack his baking soda that he found he was better off without it. Why did the doctor fail to convince my father? Because, in spite of all his vast professional knowledge, he didn't understand human nature well enough. He failed to offer my father a bigger benefit than the baking soda did.

That's what you must do if you want a person to change his way of thinking. If you want him to change his work habits, for example, then you must *offer him a bigger and better benefit than the one he's now receiving when he makes the change you're asking him to make.* Let him know how he'll gain one or more of his basic desires when he does as you ask. For instance, show him how this change will increase his production, how a greater output will mean more money for him. Let him see how this increased production will give him a feeling of accomplishment. Show him how achievement of this desire will make him feel proud; it will give him a feeling of being more important. Three big benefits will be gained from just one small change.

"I used to try and drive my people to greater efforts by using threats," Keith McMillan, an Iowa gypsum plant manager, wrote me to say. "For example, if John was holding up production on the assembly line because he was too slow, I'd yell at him and threaten him with dismissal for inefficiency. But that never helped one bit. If anything, it slowed him down even more.

"Then I got a copy of your book, *The 22 Biggest Mistakes Managers Make and How to Correct Them,*[1] and realized what I was doing wrong. Nowadays I say, 'John, if you do it this way, you can make more money for yourself by increasing production.' He'll make the change I want immediately, for I've shown him how to get what he wants: *more money.* That incentive alone motivates him to change faster than all my threats could do."

That's the quickest, surest way of persuading a person to change. *Show him how he will benefit when he does as you ask.* If you can't come

---

[1] James K. Van Fleet, *The 22 Biggest Mistakes Managers Make and How to Correct Them* (West Nyack, NY: Parker, 1973).

up with any benefits for him, keep digging until you can. Don't ask him to change anything until you do.

When you are asking a person to alter some improper work method or correct some bad habit, the implication is that he's wrong and you're right. Don't stress that point. Don't make him lose face or feel embarrassed. Let him retain his dignity and self-respect for that's one of his basic desires, too. He'll be able to do that as long as you stress the benefits he's going to gain by doing as you ask. That makes it easy for him to change his way of thinking. You'll gain your goal of unlimited power with people when he does.

Sell the Benefits, Not the Features

Have you ever seen a TV commercial that says, "*Our* goal is to sell umpteen cars this month. Come in and see *us* today. Help *us* make *our* goal. *We want to sell you a car.*" What's your reaction to all this? Same as mine, I'm sure. I'm not the least bit interested in how many cars that dealer sells. I don't give a hoot how many sales records he beats. I couldn't care less about his goals. It doesn't matter to me what he wants. *I want him to tell me how I'll benefit* by buying one of his cars. *I want to know what's in it for me. I'm only interested in what I want*, not what he wants.

To gain unlimited power with your people, you must be a salesperson as well as a manager. What are you selling? Yourself, your ideas, your methods, your procedures. If you want your subordinates to discard their old ideas for your new ones, don't use the style of that TV car sales commercial. Your people don't give a hang about what you want, what your goals are, what records you want to beat. They want to know what's in it for them. Show them how they'll benefit by accepting your ideas. People don't like to give up their old ideas unless they're sure they will be better off by doing so.

Use the Sears, Roebuck sales approach. *Sell the benefits, not the features*, of your new method. Sears always plugs the benefits the prospective customer will gain, over and over again. It never sells features or tells the customer what Sears wants. What's the difference between a benefit and a feature? Simple. The squelch control on a CB radio is a *feature*. Since it gets rid of static and background noise so you can hear the other party better, that's a *benefit* the feature gives you.

Use Features Only to Sell Benefits.   Sears teaches its salespeople to offer the customer such benefits as comfort and convenience; safety and security; a feeling of importance and pride of ownership; a material gain; or a savings of money, time, and effort. But before a salesperson can offer any benefit, he must know which feature offers that specific benefit. That's why Sears sales personnel must know the product inside out. They must know everything there is to know about it. If they don't, they won't be working for Sears very long. Sears must be doing something right. They're one of the biggest, most successful retailers in the entire world.

You, too, have a fistful of benefits you can sell: the attainment of those basic desires every person has that I've told you about before. Show a person how he can gain those basic desires by accepting your ideas; you'll win him over to your way of thinking as if by magic. He'll do what you want him to do every single time, and that's unlimited power with people.

Everybody's Interested in What's in It for Them.   That is always the person's primary concern. Everyone wants to know what he's going to get when he does as the boss asks him to do.

So make sure the person needs the specific benefit you're offering. If he doesn't need it at that particular time, your efforts will be wasted. As Elmer Wheeler, one of America's greatest salesmen of all time, said, "Don't try to sell a person an empty box." If you're offering a benefit he doesn't need right then, you're doing exactly that; you're offering him an empty box. He won't be interested. You must offer him something worthwhile that he really wants at that point in time.

Let me tell you about one more benefit you can consider that I haven't discussed before. You can always appeal to a person's sense of *laziness.* Now you can't call it that right to his face. Like those topnotch Sears salespeople, you must disguise it and call it comfort, convenience, saving of effort, time, energy, efficiency, or any other appropriate euphemism that fits. But you can be sure of this: *Every single person is as lazy as he dares to be and still get by.* Appeal to that sense of laziness in your employee, but call it something else to disguise it. If it saves him time, energy, and effort, he'll buy your idea at once for he wants to do his job the easiest way possible. I'll admit that I'm susceptible, too. I don't believe in standing up if I can sit down or in sitting down if I can lie down. How about you?

How to Ask Questions to Overcome a Person's Resistance

When a person offers resistance and objects to your idea, don't get angry about it. You can't change his mind by talking louder or faster or by using threats just because he doesn't happen to see things your way immediately.

To overcome his resistance, find out exactly why he doesn't agree with you. Smoke his objection out into the open. You can't overcome it until you know exactly what it is. The information you need to win him over to your way of thinking is locked up tight in his head. The only way you'll ever get it out is to ask him questions.

Start with Questions That Are Easy to Answer. Always start with questions that are easy to answer. Then your listener will relax and feel completely at ease when he talks with you. People enjoy giving answers they are sure of for it builds their confidence. It gives them a chance to show you how much they really know. That makes them feel more important.

If you begin with hard questions your listener can't answer, you make him feel ill at ease. He'll become nervous and withdrawn. You've injured his pride by exposing his ignorance. When you press even harder to get an answer, he'll become sullen and morose. He'll withdraw completely in a hard shell of silence. You'll get no agreement or understanding between the two of you that way.

So not only should your questions be easy to answer, but they should also be phrased properly to let you retain control of the situation. Poorly worded questions actually discourage answers. They can confuse, even antagonize your listener. To correctly phrase your questions, I recommend using these basic guidelines. I have found them to be extremely helpful.

I know I have already covered some points about questioning techniques in Chapter 12. However, here I want to amplify and expand the information I gave you before. Not only that, your questions here are used for a far different purpose than they were in Chapter 12, Listening: The "Silent Skill" for Gaining Unlimited Power.

1. YOUR QUESTION SHOULD HAVE A SPECIFIC PURPOSE. Your goal is to get your listener to accept your new proposition or point of view. Ask questions that will lead your listener straight to your goal. You can use a variety of questions to do that. For instance, one question might be used to arouse your listener's interest and make him more alert and attentive. Another one can be used to stimulate thought. Still another to emphasize a major point. You can also use a question to check your listener's immediate understanding while a similar one can be used later on to check his retention.

   2. YOUR QUESTION SHOULD BE EASILY UNDERSTOOD.   A question that's easily understood is not necessarily the same as a question that's easy to answer. A hard question can be much easier to answer if you keep it short and simple. Don't ask complicated or long-winded questions that require a lot of explanation and clarification. You'll only confuse the issue. By the same token, avoid vague abstract language and government-style gobble-dygook. Instead, use clear, concise, plain, and simple one- and two-syllable words so your listener will know immediately what you want and exactly what you mean.

   3. A GOOD QUESTION EMPHASIZES ONLY ONE POINT.   The best question covers only one point and asks for only one answer. Don't combine two or three questions in one sentence. If your question requires more than one answer, break it down into two or three separate questions.

   4. ASK A QUESTION THAT REQUIRES A DEFINITE SPECIFIC ANSWER. A vague and indefinite question gives you a vague and indefinite answer. That's no help to you at all. Word your question so a definite and specific answer is required. Don't give up until you get the answer you need.

   Along that line, remember that a person generally has two reasons for doing anything: one that sounds good and a *real* one. The best way to drag the real reason out of a person is to keep asking these two little questions:

   "*Why?*" and "*In addition to that...?*"

   5. A GOOD QUESTION WILL DISCOURAGE GUESSING.   Don't ask questions that can be answered with "Yes" or "No" unless you follow them with "Why?" or "Why not?" This kind of question makes your listener explain his answer. You want answers that are based on facts, not fancy.

   When you ask questions, listen carefully to the answers. Don't interrupt; you wound a person's ego and make him feel unimportant when you do. That could cause him to have a mental block to what you say when you present your viewpoint. He will not be willing to pay attention or listen to you if you won't pay attention to him first. If you want to win unlimited power with him, be courteous enough to listen to his ideas.

How to Explore the Other Person's Position for Weaknesses

Suppose you want an employee to change the way he does a certain job. You suggest the new method, but your employee isn't convinced that he should change. He feels the old way is better. Since you're the boss, you could put your foot down and tell him to change his work methods or else. But if you do it that way, you'll get nothing more than the bare minimum from him from then on. Persuasion is always better than force, even when you're the boss. Your benefits will be far greater, and they'll last a lot longer.

Your goal is to get him to discard his old idea and accept your new one. He won't do that until he's thoroughly convinced that the new methods you want him to use are not only better than the old ones but that they are also more beneficial to him. To help your employee become more receptive to your idea, lead him on an objective fact-finding survey of his own position so you can pinpoint and expose its weaknesses.

When you do find a weakness, use it to persuade him to your point of view. When he sees the weakness in his own argument for himself, he'll become more open and receptive to your proposition. When you want to persuade someone to your viewpoint, it's better to let him talk first. Let him try to justify his own position. You already know you have a stronger case than he has, so weaknesses are bound to show up as he talks. You can use these to penetrate his defenses, but it's best to let him discover them for himself.

How can you get him to discuss his viewpoint? Ask him leading questions to guide his thinking as I showed you just a few moments ago. To give you an even better idea of how this works, let's listen to Shirley Bennett, director of industrial relations for a large corporation.

"If a new plan or idea of mine meets resistance from an employee, I always go out of my way to hear the person out," Mrs. Bennett says. "What he says will usually give me a hint as to how to proceed, for he will almost always expose the weaknesses in his argument while he's talking. In fact, he'll see them for himself, which helps tremendously.

"I ask him to go over his main objections to my plan several times. I seek more information by asking him if there's anything else he wants to add. I ask lots of questions so I can get every possible fact he feels is important and relevant to the case.

"Before I state my side, I show him I'm deeply interested in his viewpoint. I let him do most of the talking in the beginning, but I never let him take charge of the conversation. I retain control by asking the questions; he will eventually exhaust himself from answering them. Then I can take over.

"If you want to make sure of winning him over to your way of thinking, let him discover the weaknesses in his own position for himself. That way he will be more willing to accept your point of view."

You can do the same. If you let your employee state his position first, you get his ideas out in the open where you can probe them for weaknesses. The moment he realizes he has some holes in his argument, he'll be much more willing to accept your viewpoint.

If by some strange chance, his old method is better than your new one, you can keep the old one and throw your new one away. Either way, you'll still win.

How to Know When a Person Is Ready to Accept Your Idea

The best idea in the world, presented to a person at the wrong time, will fail. You need to know when he's ready to accept your new concept. You'll also want to be able to tell when the individual is not ready, so you won't move too rapidly to take your objective. Here are three red warning flags that will let you know when he is *not* ready.

1. He asks unnecessary questions. When a person asks a question, the answer to which was readily apparent in what you just told him, you know he's not yet interested in what you're saying. He's not listening to you carefully. Had he been, his question would not have been necessary.

2. He returns to a question that has already been answered. This shows he's still at point A while you're way ahead of him at Point D. You have no choice but to start over, preferably with a completely different approach.

3. He changes the subject abruptly or presents ideas completely counter to yours. If he changes the subject abruptly, he may have something pressing on his mind, and he can't wait to tell you about it. If it's a personal problem, bear with him. Hear him out and get back to your subject as soon as you can. If he is presenting ideas completely counter to yours, he may be so ego hungry he can't wait to show you how smart he is. Let him explain his position thoroughly. Ask him questions about it. As soon as you've exhausted his point, get back to yours and start over again.

How will you know when he is ready to accept your new idea? One or both of two ways. One signal comes when he makes statements filled with self-doubt. The other occurs when he shows interest by asking relevant questions himself. Let's take a look at the first clue, expression of self-doubt.

"This is the way I look at it, but I could be wrong on a point or two."

"Of course, I'm willing to change if I find I'm wrong."

"To tell the truth, I've never looked at it this way."

"Maybe I could be in error on this one small point."

"Well, I'm not alone; we all make mistakes sometimes."

When you hear expressions of doubt like these, you know it's time to launch your attack. Your listener is now receptive to change; he's ready to listen and be persuaded to your point of view.

The second clue can be detected when he asks you logical relevant questions. When you hear the question words *who, when, what, where, why,* and *how,* that's a sure sign the person is interested in what you are saying. You know he's almost ready to change his mind. He's asking for more information so he can make a rational decision that is favorable to you but at the same time allows him to save face. Another sure sign that he is ready to change his mind is when he wants to know the benefits that he will gain. If you hear questions like these, it's time to move in and consolidate your position.

"*Why* do you want me to do it this way?"

"*Who* will benefit by this new procedure?"

"*What's in it for me* if I do it your new way?"

"*How will I be helped* by your new system?"

"*What benefits do I get* out of this?"

"*Where will I gain* from your new methods?"

The Key to Persuading Others

Let's say you want to make certain changes in a person's work methods or you want him to accept a new idea. But the individual happens to be one of those strong-minded persons who finds it hard to accept any suggestion from others no matter how good it is. He thinks the only worthwhile ideas are his. How do you go about getting this fellow to do things your way or make the changes you want?

You let him think the new project was all his very own idea. You plant the seed; you let *him* harvest the crop. Will it work? I'll say it will. I've used it for years. But don't take my word for it alone. Here's what Kelly Ryan, assistant manager for a large Missouri electronics manufacturer, says:

"I've found the best way to make any change in work methods or plant procedure is to let the other person think it was all his own idea," Kelly says. "I let him take all the credit for the change. I compliment him on his initiative and foresight. He becomes convinced he thought it all up in the first place. We both win. He feels more important and secure in his job. I get a more efficient operation. I've yet to meet the person who isn't susceptible to this approach.

"Take our production super, for instance. Last Friday I said to him, 'Jack, I believe we could speed up production if we moved the number 3 cutting machine over there and added two more motor winding stations. Wish you'd let me know how you feel about that.'

"Yesterday he came to my office and said, 'Kelly, this weekend *I had the most wonderful idea.* If we move the number 3 cutting machine to here and add two more motor winding stations, we can cut down on a lot of wasted motion on the assembly line and speed up our motor production at least 5 to 10 percent. Shall we try it?'

"That's exactly the change I wanted to be made. This way is better than telling an employee what to do. People don't like to be told how to do their jobs. They like to do things their own way. This suggestion method works every time. I get what I want. The employee gets the credit for the idea, so we're both happy."

The only special requirement for this technique is time and patience. Take it easy, don't rush. Give the person time to absorb your idea so that it will become *his.* Remember: Your job is to plant the seed, let *him* harvest the crop. Give it a chance to take root and grow. Your benefits will be enormous when you do. You'll gain unlimited power with people without even trying hard.

Now it's time for us to move on to a new and exciting chapter: The Master Formula for Powerful and Persuasive Writing and Speaking. If you are one of the silent majority who has a real fear of public speaking, this next chapter will help you. Or if you feel paralyzed when you pick up a pen or sit down at the typewriter, you'll gain some real help in that area, too. When you've finished that chapter, you'll feel like a professional in both speaking and writing. And remember: You can't possibly gain unlimited power with people if you can't handle yourself properly in the spoken and written language.

Chapter 17 ✸ *The Seventeenth Day*

THE MASTER FORMULA
FOR POWERFUL WRITING
AND SPEAKING

After more than 35 years as a consultant in business management and human relations, I have found that a person's success depends as much on the ability to talk and write as it does upon the professional and technical know-how to do the job.

All other things being equal, advancement and promotion will invariably go to the person who has mastered the art of self-expression, both in speaking and writing, while his colleague, who attaches little or no importance to what can be achieved with the use of language, will be marked for mediocrity or failure. I cannot repeat too often what Disraeli said: "Men govern with words."

The more capable you become in expressing yourself clearly and precisely to others so there will absolutely be no chance of misunderstanding, the more successful you will become in mastering people and controlling their actions.

The Benefits You Will Gain

1. You'll develop a winning and positive outgoing and powerful personality.

2. You'll gain greater self-confidence, inner security, and peace of mind.

3. You'll gain the ability to think clearly and to express yourself precisely and correctly.

4. There'll be a genuine meeting of the minds in your communication with others.

5. You'll develop your unlimited power with people so they will always do what you want them to do.

6. You'll achieve your purposes. Goals can be reached, missions accomplished, objectives attained.

7. Your boss will take notice of you and recognize your talents.

8. You'll succeed, for promotion and advancement will come your way as a matter of course.

Language: The Magic Key to Winning Unlimited Power with People

A well-known psychologist made a detailed study of hundreds of successful men and women to determine the main reasons for their success. She found that all these people had one thing in common: *their skill in using words.* She also discovered that *their earning power was closely linked to their word skills.*

You, too, can expect your own earnings to increase when you improve your skills in the use of language to deal with people, just as an engineer at Harris Corporation in Melbourne, Florida, found: "My last promotion—I happened to see the promotional package—was at least 85 percent related to my speaking ability," Robert O. says.

If you want to gain unlimited power with people in your profession, your social activities, and in your community, you must learn how to use words that will command both respect and obedience for you.

When you can command words to serve your thoughts and feelings, you are on your way to commanding people to do your will and serve your purposes.

To gain unlimited power with people, you must first master both the spoken and written language. You may not realize right now how important language is, but if you analyze your day's activities, you'll find that no less than 75 percent of it is spent in oral or written communication. You'll be explaining, persuading, advising, ordering, influencing, and asking and answering questions. In short, you will spend most of your time putting your proposals across to others, including your own family, so you can gain unlimited power with people and get them to do what you want them to do.

How to Become a Better Speaker

How to Develop Your Own Distinctive Talking Style

Some years ago, I met a young insurance salesman, Gary Davis, in his company's regional office in St. Louis. Gary was 5 feet 4 inches tall. He was an ordinary-looking person except for one thing. He had a fiery red beard, and this was long before beards were in fashion. "Why?" I asked him.

"To attract attention," Gary said. "I want to make sure that people remember me. You wear a mustache for the same reason, don't you?"

I had to admit that he was right. People remember me as "that fellow with the salt and pepper mustache." If it were not for that, most of them wouldn't recall the slightly overweight, rather short, middle-aged man with thinning hair who wore glasses. That description fits most American men over 50. But people do remember the man with the "distinguished-looking" mustache.

By the way, that young insurance salesman is now a division manager and vice president of his company. Somebody topside kept him in mind. He still sports that flaming red beard, too.

My point is that you need to be distinctive in some way to be both *noticed and remembered*. Generally speaking, a salt and pepper mustache or a crimson beard is not enough. That will help you to get *noticed*. But unless you happen to have some of the charisma of a Paul Newman or Oprah Winfrey, developing your own style of talking is one of the best ways you can be *remembered*.

It's also one of the most profitable. When I was a boy growing up in Iowa, the Keokuk Hotel in Sigourney was the most popular spot for miles around with traveling salesmen. They drove out of their way to stay there. Why? Because the owner, "Happy" Weller, was always cheerful and smiling. He had a good word for everybody. I never heard him say an unkind thing about anyone in all the years I knew him. Hap Weller had his own distinctive style, and he became successful and well-to-do because of that.

The style of your talking, the way you converse with others, makes a vital contribution to your reputation and your success. If you talk down to your subordinates, they will resent you. If you are too deferential to your superiors, they may consider you weak and spineless, incapable of accepting further and higher responsibilities. Your talking style is not only a matter of the words you use, but also your way of using them, as well as your attitude and bearing.

Be Yourself When You Talk

Don't try to imitate someone else or be something you're not. Too often, people try to copy the style of others who are "supposed" to be successful or in the know. That's why government writers are usually wrong. It's good to learn from others, but don't try to copy another person's style or manner of talking. People will always know. You'll be like the alcoholic who can't hide his sins. People can always smell them. The best person you can be when you talk is yourself. Develop a style that is distinctively yours, not someone else's.

For instance, I was born and raised on an Iowa farm. I made my home in the Midwest for a great part of my life. I still have that flat Midwestern way of speaking. I've never tried to change it. Why should I? If you have a *genuine* Southern accent, don't try to get rid of it. As long as people understand you, leave it alone. The same goes for the long Texas drawl of the Southwest or the clipped abrupt New England way of speaking.

A longtime friend of mine, Dale Dunlap, says flatly that any success he has is due to his ability to talk with people. Dale, a top-level executive with a Midwestern electronics company, has a distinctive style all his own. He is gentlemanly, cordial, and sincere. He never tries to be anyone except himself, and he knows who he is.

As Dale told me, "A lot of people in our company are better electrical engineers than I am. I attribute whatever success I have attained to my ability to put myself and my ideas across to people.

"So many people feel they need to put on an act or wear a false face when they're talking with others. Some try to be overly friendly, sometimes even servile. Others are too dynamic; they come across too strong, like a TV commercial. Still others try to act tough. The trouble is, none of these people are ever themselves, so they just don't register with others.

"But I'm always me. What you see is what you get. Whether you like what I am or not, you'll always know it's the real me talking with you, not some phony. Right or wrong, I'll always be honest with you."

Eight Guidelines for Speaking in a Forceful, Positive, and Convincing Manner

Force makes your speech positive and convincing. It gives vigor and strength to what you say. Force creates movement; it makes things happen; it brings your words to life.

How can you be forceful but not overbearing when you talk? *Use lots of short active verbs that denote or imply movement.* Verbs such as *break, cut, drive, drop, kick, pull, push, stir, strike, tear,* and the like will bring life to what you say. Verbs like this impel people to do things.

Another way to be forceful, positive, and convincing is to *be clear and precise when you talk.* Give your listener only one idea at a time to digest. When you come to the end of one idea, stop. Pause. Take a breath. Then go on to your next thought. Don't link one idea to the next with endless connectives like *and, but, for,* or *nor.* Even the most difficult technical explanation can be made plain and clear to your listener if you present your information one step at a time.

It is impossible to be forceful, positive, and convincing when you use vague and abstract words and long-winded sentences. Try saying this sentence out loud with power and conviction as if you were actually talking to one of your subordinates:

> It is directed that you take immediate appropriate action to accomplish the correction of your financial records, and that you transmit a directive to your branch offices with the view to having them make a similar correction of their own.

Now say it loud this way. Note the difference in the positive tone of force you can put in your voice:

Straighten up your records right now. Tell your branch offices to do the same thing.

Eight guidelines you can use to be forceful, positive, and convincing when you talk are these:

1. Use active verbs of motion to create *force.*

2. Use small easy-to-understand words to make what you say *positive.*

3. Give your listener one idea at a time to be *convincing.* Too many ideas at once confuse and muddle your listener.

4. Specify; use illustrations and examples.

5. Be direct. Don't beat around the bush.

6. If you don't know, say so. Don't try to bluff.

7. Avoid all pompous and pretentious, vague and abstract words.

8. Don't insult your listener by talking down to him or her.

Power Words Convince Your Listener to Take Action

Another way to be forceful, positive, and convincing when you talk is to use *power words.* By carefully observing people, you can learn which words are the most effective in creating a favorable reaction in your listener's mind. But that takes time, so let me give you a head start.

For example, some words cause people to think rationally using logic and reason. Other words cause people to react emotionally. Let me give you a specific example:

A sharp real estate agent will tell the owner he will be glad to sell his *house.* He doesn't use the word *home* when talking with the owner. Home is an emotional word, and the seller can become reluctant to part with his *home* even though he is perfectly willing to get rid of his *house.* By the same token, that smart real estate agent will never sell the buyer just a *house.* He always offers him a *home.*

These two words represent two entirely different ideas for the same object. A house is not a home, it's only a house. It's made of bricks, wood, and concrete. It's a very nonemotional idea. But a home is where your heart is, where your family lives, where your kids grew up. It is an extremely emotional *power word.*

Emotional words are power words, and people are ruled more by emotion than by logic and reason. Salespeople always like to use emotional words because they cause people to buy. A top salesperson will never ask a person what he *thinks* about a product. Instead, he'll always ask the potential buyer how he *feels* about it.

Think is a nonemotional word that requires a person to use logic and reason. But *feel* is an emotional word that goes straight to the listener's heart. If you'll remember I told you before, *the head never hears 'til the heart has listened.* That one statement tells you more about the human psyche than all the books on applied psychology ever will.

Another point about power words worth mentioning is this: You should learn which words turn your boss on and which ones turn him off, for no matter what they are, they are power words, too.

Everyone has certain likes and dislikes when it comes to language, so you would be wise to use the "pet" words your boss likes to hear. People like to hear their favorite words and phrases played back to them. Emulation of a person is still one of the highest forms of praise when it is subtly done.

How to Give a Successful Speech

Get Your Material Together.   The first thing you need to do is to gather the material you need for your talk. No doubt you will need to do some reading and note taking to bring yourself completely up to date on your subject.

Make Up an Outline.   After you've gathered your material it's time to organize it. If you don't, you could sound like the speaker I once heard at a convention in Miami. He rambled and wandered for ten minutes or so without coming to any point whatever. His audience grew nervous and restless. Sensing this, he stopped and said, "Please be patient with me. When I get through talking here, I'm going to say something." Only his sense of humor saved the day for him. You might not be so lucky.

The best way to organize your material is to make up an outline for your talk. In my own experience, I have found the following one to be extremely useful.

1. The opening
2. Benefits to be gained
3. Techniques to be used
4. Examples of people who've succeeded by using these techniques
5. Conclusion

The opening sets the theme of your talk. It is used to gain the immediate attention of your listeners. You can use any of the following methods to do that:

- A startling statement of fact
- An unusual anecdote
- A strong example
- An authoritative quotation
- An arresting question

The benefits to be gained are stressed next to keep your listeners interested and to show them how your talk will be helpful to them.

Techniques to be used tell your listeners how they can gain the benefits you've offered them or told them about.

Examples of others who've succeeded should be given to prove that the techniques you've offered really do work. They must be relative to your topic or the theme of your subject. To lend them authenticity, you should be specific about names, occupations, dates, and places.

Your *conclusion* can be an appeal for action of some sort or a summary of your talk. This will depend primarily on whether your talk is made to persuade or inform your audience.

Ten Proven Tips for Putting Power into Everything You Say

1. *Speak with the voice of authority.* To do this, you must know your stuff. The more you know about your subject, the better off you'll be when you talk with people.

2. *Use simple words and short sentences.* It's the simple things that last longest and wear best. The simplest writing is always the best because

it's easiest to understand. The same can be said about speech and conversation.

3. *Use concrete and specific words and phrases.* The absolute master of this art was Jesus. The words He used and the order He gave were simple, concise, to the point, and easy to understand when He said, "Follow me."

4. *Avoid needless words and useless information.* The person who talks too much usually says very little. Don't clutter your listener's mind with trivia and worthless details. As my minister says, "Most preachers say more than they have to talk about. I'd rather quit before I'm through to keep from boring my listeners." Smart man. No wonder his church is always full.

5. *Be direct and to the point.* This idea is fundamental if you want to achieve unlimited power with people in everything you say. If you concentrate on a single point, you won't scatter your fire. You'll be able to zero in on your target.

6. *Don't exaggerate.* Not only should you never exaggerate or stretch the truth, but you would also be wise to understate your case. Then you need have no fear of any repercussions.

7. *Don't talk down to your listeners.* Even though you might be the authority on your subject, that's no reason to talk down to your listeners. I've never met a person yet who didn't know more than I knew in some subject.

8. *Be diplomatic and tactful.* Tact is the ability to say the right thing at just the right time and place without offending anyone. You especially need to be tactful and diplomatic when you're dealing with difficult persons or touchy subjects. As easy way to do that is to treat every woman like a lady and every man like a gentleman.

9. *Present the proposition that is best for your listener, not the one that is best for you.* Do this and no one will ever be able to cut the ground out from under you. Your defenses will be impenetrable.

10. *Answer all questions frankly and openly.* If you've followed the guidance I gave you in the first nine tips, you'll have no trouble at all with this one.

How to Become a Better Writer

Write the Same Way You Talk

Many people do not write the same way they talk. They use pompous words and stilted phrases that they would never use in a conversation in an effort to impress their reader.

The best way to avoid this unnatural style of writing is simply to write the same way you talk. If people understand you when you talk, then they will be able to understand you when you *talk on paper*. After all, that should be your main purpose—to be understood—not to dazzle or impress your reader with your knowledge and education.

A good way to write as you talk is to forget "business English." Use the same words you would use in your home or talking over the fence to your neighbor. If you use such terms as *okay, no sweat, good deal, horse of a different color* when you talk, then do the same when you write. Use colloquial English whenever you want to. It's a good way to keep from writing formal and pompous letters.

The third way to write as you talk is to *use contractions*. There's nothing wrong with using *don't* for *do not* and *won't* for *will not*.

Six Guidelines for Writing Superior Letters, Directives, and Reports

1. KNOW PRECISELY WHAT IT IS YOU WANT TO GET DONE.   A lot of people fire off letters without having a clear-cut idea of what it is they want to get done. I'm sure you've been on the receiving end of letters like that. When you finish reading them, you don't know what it was the writer actually wanted from you.

If you know your purpose in writing, if the objective you want to gain is clear in your mind, then your letter will be clear and easy to understand. But if your objective in writing is vague and abstract, then your writing will be vague and abstract, too. So before you start any letter, you should know exactly why you're writing it. Figure out what it is you want to say.

Writing, just as speaking, can normally be divided into three major categories:

1. *To order or command* someone to do something
2. *To inform* someone of something
3. *To persuade* someone to do something

All three types of letters will be concerned with *who, what, when, where, why,* and *how*, but the emphasis will be different in each case depending on its purpose.

A letter directing action tells *what* has to be done. An informative letter tells a person *how* to do something. A persuasive letter explains *why* some action should be taken.

These purposes can often overlap, as when you make an order or a directive more palatable by explaining the *how* and the *why* as well as the *what*. If you were writing a persuasive memo to your boss asking him to approve some new office procedure, you would emphasize *why* it should be used; that is, you would *stress the benefits to be gained*, as well as explain *how* the new system would work.

So even though you might have some overlapping in your letters, keeping these three basic purposes in mind will help you find clear explanations or convincing reasons to back up your arguments so you can gain the specific objectives you want.

2. KNOW WHO YOUR READER IS GOING TO BE.   Who is going to read your letter? A person with a college degree or one with an eighth grade education? You'll get your point across far better when you use words and ideas that your reader can easily understand. Whether that person reads you loud and clear depends on his training and knowledge, not on yours.

"A lot of directives here at the plant are written at college levels of comprehension," says Barbara Sheridan, the business office manager and executive secretary for a large chemical plant. "The writer forgets that people of modest education must read them. It's my responsibility to get everyone to keep their memos simple enough for everyone to understand."

3. ESTABLISH THE PROPER FOUNDATION.   Masterful and powerful letters are based on proper preparation—the selection, analysis, and organization of your ideas.

Many people write ineffective letters because they start writing before they're actually ready to do so. They don't do the necessary homework first. That's why those letters aren't satisfactory and they don't get the desired results.

So before you pick up a pen or sit down at the word processor or typewriter, think your problem through thoroughly. Get the answers to *who, what, when, where, why,* and *how* first. Then you can start on the actual job of writing.

4. IDENTIFY AND PINPOINT YOUR MAIN IDEAS. Successful writers of powerful and masterful correspondence know that deciding what to leave out is just as important as what to put in, if not more so. Words, ideas, and facts that are not essential to the understanding of your main idea only hide and weaken it.

It doesn't matter whether your writing is based on personal knowledge, reading and research, or both. The problem you face is usually having too much material rather than not enough.

So preparing to write is a process of defining, sifting, and discarding until you have only one clear goal in mind and the main ideas necessary to reach it.

5. WRITE FROM AN OUTLINE. Any piece of writing, no matter what it is, can be done logically and quickly if you use an outline. An outline makes your writing plan easy to see and helps you keep your specific goal in mind. But it is worthless unless you stick to it and work from it. This is not to say that you should not change your outline here and there if better ideas come to you. Your outline should be a working sketch, not a final blueprint.

6. REVIEW YOUR WRITING FOR OBJECTIVITY. Unless you are writing a chatty personal family letter or a love letter, chances are you won't have a finished product the first time. When you have completed your first draft, review and revise your work.

As you do, concentrate on the objectivity of your writing. Business letters in particular should be objective, whether they are informative, persuasive, or directive. When you present a decision or a recommendation to your boss, he will assume your letter or your memo is based on careful thinking.

The Four S Formula for Writing Successfully

The four S's stand for *shortness, simplicity, strength,* and *sincerity.* Here are the rules for their use.

1. *How to ensure shortness in your writing*

    a. Don't repeat what was said in a letter you answer.

    b. Leave out unnecessary words and useless information.

    c. Shorten your prepositional phrases.

    d. Don't use nouns and adjectives made from verbs.

    e. Don't qualify your statements with irrelevant *if's.*

2. *How to gain simplicity in your writing*

    a. Know your subject so well you can talk about it naturally and confidently.

    b. Use short words, concise sentences, and compact paragraphs.

    c. Keep closely related parts of your sentences together.

    d. Tie your thoughts together logically so your reader can follow you without getting lost.

3. *How to give your writing strength*

    a. Use concrete and specific words: the names of people, places, and things.

    b. Use short active verbs.

    c. Give the answer first; then explain if necessary.

    d. Don't hedge by being vague and abstract.

    e. Get rid of all empty, dead, and useless words.

4. *How to achieve sincerity in your writing*

    a. Be yourself; don't try to be someone else.

    b. Always tell the truth.

    c. Admit your mistakes.

    d. Don't write down to your reader.

Five Fundamental Tips to Help You as You Write

1. *Use personal words (I, me, you, we, us)*. They make your reader feel more comfortable. Don't say "This writer believes" or "It is the opinion of the undersigned." Instead, say, "I believe" or "It is my opinion." I've never been able to understand why a TV commentator or a writer will say, "*This reporter* has been told" when all he really means is "*I've* been told."

2. *Use specific words*. Don't say machine if you mean *bulldozer, mimeograph, typewriter*. Why say *personnel* if you mean *John* and *Mary* in the accounting department? If you know who did it or who it is, say so. Don't blame it on *them*. *They* said it or *they* did it has always been one of my pet peeves.

3. *Don't exaggerate*. Avoid words or phrases that overstate what you actually did. People know better. Why say you made an exhaustive search if you looked through only one file? *Tried but failed* is more believable than *a strenuous effort was made without tangible results*. Most people interpret that last remark to mean nothing at all was done.

4. *Don't use pointer words in your writing*. Pointer words like *herein, herewith, enclosed herewith, hereunder, attached hereto* are unnecessary, old-fashioned, and out of date. Don't use them.

5. *Crutch words cripple your writing*. Don't use crutch words like *very, such, same* in these ways. Rather than say it's *very* hot, say *It's hotter than the hinges of Hades*. That says it more expressively than *very*. *Such* is useless in this sentence: Mailmen, *as such*, walk many miles a day. *Same* is awkward in this sentence: The new procedure will not be used until the manager approves *same*. What's wrong with using *it*?

And now on to the next chapter, How to Control a Person's Emotions and Turn Off His Anger Immediately. As you can see from its title, it is loaded with information that will help you gain your goal of unlimited power with people.

Chapter 18 ✳ *The Eighteenth Day*

HOW TO CONTROL
A PERSON'S EMOTIONS
AND TURN OFF HIS ANGER
IMMEDIATELY

If a person is angry with you, or if he views you with suspicion and mistrust, it will usually be for one of several reasons. It could be because of something you've said or done. It might also be because of something he *thinks* you've said or done. But either way, you'll need to take some sort of corrective action to resolve this problem, even if you are not at fault.

At times, a person will take out his anger at the system, for instance, the company or corporation, the government, even society as a whole on you only because you happen to be the closest or most convenient target. Or, some people's imaginations work overtime. They have the idea that everybody in the whole world is against them or out to get them.

But no matter what the cause of a person's anger, you'll want to turn it off immediately so you can restore normal friendly relationships. You can do that with the techniques that you'll learn in this chapter.

The Benefits You Will Gain

1. When you use the first technique that I'll give you, you'll be able to use your unlimited power with people to assume immediate control of the person's attitudes and actions and the situation as well.

2. When you use the *white magic* technique, you will not only turn off a person's anger immediately, but you will also convert him into your faithful friend and loyal supporter.

3. Another technique you will learn will show you how to change a belligerent neighbor into a true friend.

4. The *fact-finder* technique will not only stop an angry person dead in his tracks and create a friend for you, but it can also be used to improve business relationships and make more money for yourself.

5. You can use the *power play that never fails* to turn a recalcitrant, stubborn, mean, dissatisfied person into a cooperative and friendly individual.

6. The last technique you'll learn will take some special effort on your part, but it will be worth it, for you can turn anger and bitterness into love and friendship when you use it.

How to Quickly Take Control of a Person's Emotions and Actions

When two people meet, one will automatically become the leader and assume control of the conversation or the situation. The other person will become the follower. You can always take control if you will simply remember that *everybody in the world is waiting for someone to take the responsibility and tell him what to do*. So let that someone be you. You will find that this amazing strategy will put even total strangers under your control instantly.

All you need do is take the initiative, and you will immediately have the momentum on your side. If you adopt a positive attitude and act as if the other person is going to do what you want him to do, you'll find that in more than 95 percent of the time he will carry out your request or your command without any hesitation or question. In less than 5 percent of cases, all he will need is a little extra push.

Remember, too, that *other people will always accept you at your own appraisal of yourself.* You are more responsible for how people accept you than anyone else. A lot of people worry about what other persons think of them. You can rid yourself of that fear if you will simply remember that *you are not responsible for what other people think of you. You are responsible only for what you think of yourself.* People form their opinions of you based upon the opinion you have of yourself.

If you act like a nobody and put yourself down, people will treat you like a nobody and put you down, too. But if you act like a somebody with authority, people will treat you the same way. It is a truism that a person can have whatever allowances or liberties he takes without opposition. Take the place and attitude of a leader, seize control, and others will immediately acquiesce to you.

How You Can Control the Attitudes and Actions of Others

When you study physics or chemistry, you find that positive attracts negative, like goes with unlike, acid neutralizes alkali. But this doesn't hold true when you're learning how to master and control others with your unlimited people power. When you're dealing with human beings, just the exact opposite is true. Let me show you precisely what I mean by the following:

- Be kind to others; they will be kind to you.
- Be mean to others; they will be mean to you.
- Be courteous to others; they will be courteous to you.
- Be rude to others; they will be rude to you.
- Be friendly to others; they will be friendly to you.
- Be hostile toward others; they will be hostile toward you.
- Smile at others; they will smile back at you.
- Frown at others; they will frown at you.

Just as I told you in the previous technique, whenever two people are involved in a relationship, one will be the leader, the other will become the follower. If you assume the position of leadership, as you should, the attitudes and emotions of others will depend entirely on your attitude and emotions. The power you have over others and your ability to master and control their emotions and actions is enormous.

In dealing with others, then, you will always see your own attitude reflected back to you in the other person's behavior. It is almost as if you were looking at yourself in a mirror. When you smile, the person in the mirror smiles back at you. When you frown, the person in that mirror frowns back at you. Let me give you a simple example of what I mean by that.

Take my granddaughter, Leah, for example. When I smile at her, she's happy, and she smiles too. But if I frown the least little bit or if I act irritated and impatient about something, she gets a worried look on her face, and says, "Are you mad at me, grandpa?"

Then I'll smile back at her and reply, "No, of course I'm not mad at you. Are mad at me?"

A look of relief and joy comes into her face, and she says, "Nope, I'm not mad either. I'm happy!"

So you see, you don't have to say a single word to influence another person's attitudes or actions. Smiles and frowns are both contagious. It's all up to you how you want to infect the other person. His attitudes and actions will depend entirely upon your attitude and your actions.

The "White Magic" Technique for Offsetting Anger and Hard Feelings

Oliver Wendell Holmes, one of the most distinguished Supreme Court justices our country has ever known, said in effect, "To be able to listen to others in a sympathetic and understanding manner is the most effective method you can use to get along with people and tie up their friendships for good." This famous justice went on to say that few people knew how to practice the "white magic" of being a good listener.

I know that I have already given you one chapter about how to use the silent skill of listening, but this ability is also required if you want to control a person's emotions and turn off his anger immediately.

Listening to the other person can make you rich in dollars, rich in friends, and rich in the satisfaction of worthwhile accomplishment and happiness.

You see, one of the highest compliments you can pay another person is simply to listen to him. By your patient attention you are saying to him, "You are really worth listening to." You increase his self-esteem, for every person likes to think that he has something important to say.

On the other hand, one of the most deflating things you can do to the other fellow's sense of pride and ego is to brush him off before hearing what he wants to tell you. Always remember: People like to be paid attention to; they want to be heard.

Have you ever heard a wife say of her husband, "He never hears a word I say. I could tell him that the dishwasher blew up, the washing machine stopped working, and the clothes dryer fell apart, and all he would say would be, 'Is that so?' and go right on reading his evening paper." Maybe you have never heard this, but I have, and so have a great many marriage counselors.

Have you ever heard an employee say, "I try to like my boss, but she never listens to me. If I go to her with a problem and want her advice, she interrupts, gives me a pat on the back, and tries to get rid of me even before she knows what I'm talking about." Maybe you haven't heard those words either, but in my work as a management consultant, I've heard them over and over, hundreds and hundreds of times.

What about your children? Even though I don't know them personally, I could tell you what a lot of them are saying about you right now. "My dad and mom don't understand me at all. I try to tell them how I really feel about things, what my problems are, but they just won't listen to me. They're too busy to listen, I guess. They either treat me like a baby and brush off my problems as not being important, or else they are so anxious to tell me how I ought to feel about things, they never know how I feel. How can they? They never listen to me at all." Juvenile court judges hear that same story every day of the week.

If you really want to control a person's emotions with your unlimited people power, then you must listen to find out what people want so you can help them get it. Do that and the dividends you'll gain are enormous.

How to Defuse Tense Situations

If your neighbor gets angry with you, you can do one of two things. You can get mad and fight back, or you can do exactly the opposite, take steps to appease his anger.

Now if you fight back and try to retaliate—which is exactly what the other person expects and wants you to do—you will lose complete control of the situation and only make things worse. You will accomplish nothing if you lose your temper, too. In fact, the inability to control one's temper indicates a definite lack of self-discipline. And if a person cannot master and control himself, he most certainly cannot expect to master and control others.

What happens, then, if you don't fight back? Does this mean that you lose and that the other person will automatically win? Of course not. In fact, the only time you can be really sure of winning is when you don't lose your temper and retaliate. *It always takes at least two people to make a fight.* When you refuse to become angry, the other person's anger has to burn itself out. Let me give you a specific example:

"I have a next-door neighbor with a short fuse who flies off the handle for almost any reason at all," Roger S. told me. "It used to be before I wised up that when he came over raising the devil about something with me, I'd get mad, yell back, and we'd get nowhere. We always ended up in a shouting match until I learned how to control him.

"Now when he gets mad at me—which doesn't happen very often any more because he knows he can't win—I simply remain calm and quiet instead of flying off the handle, too. When I refuse to fight back, he realizes that he might as well cuss out a tree or a shrub, so he throws in the sponge and gives up."

So take a tip from Roger's example. The best way to turn off your neighbor's anger immediately is not to lose your temper, too, but to respond in a kind and friendly manner. Just say nothing until he's drained himself emotionally. Then answer him quietly and softly, for as the Bible says, "A soft answer turneth away wrath," and that is ever so true. If you use a quiet soft tone of voice, it will not only calm the other person down, but it will also keep you from getting angry as well.

When you refuse to fight back, when you hold your temper in check and speak softly, the angry person quickly realizes that he is the only one yelling. This embarrasses him and makes him feel like a fool. He will suddenly become extremely self-conscious and anxious to get the situation back to normal as soon as possible.

You can use this psychology to master and control the angry person and calm his emotions until he becomes rational and reasonable again. So, when you find yourself in a tense situation with an angry neighbor—or

anyone else, for that matter, subordinate, employee, wife, husband, whom-
ever—stay cool and calm. Deliberately lower your voice and keep it down.
This will motivate the angry individual to lower his own voice. As long as
he speaks softly, he cannot remain angry and high-strung for very long.

The "Fact-Finder" Technique for Stopping an Angry Person in His Tracks

When a person is angry with you, it will usually be for one of several
reasons. It could be because of something you have actually said or done.
It could also be because of something he *thinks* you've said or done. Or it
could be that he thinks you haven't done something that you should have.
And sometimes he will take out his anger on you, even though he is upset
with someone else.

No matter what the cause of his anger, and no matter who the person
is—employee, customer, client, business associate, or friend—it's up to you
to find out what the problem is so you can correct it and restore friendly
relationships with him immediately.

The best way to do this is to use the *fact-finder* technique. In other
words, play detective and go after all the facts in the case. Ask questions of
what, who, when, where, why, and *how* until you discover what he's angry
about.

Find out *why* the person is angry, *what* made him mad in the first
place, are *you* the one who is responsible for his anger, if not, *who* is, *when*
did it happen, *where, how*? Ask *what* you can do to set things straight after
you have found out *what* is wrong.

I always use this technique to find the reason behind a person's
anger if it is not readily apparent. Even when I think I have all the answers,
to make absolutely certain, I will ask one more question: "Is there any other
reason for you to be upset about this?" Let me show you by an example now
how well this technique can work for you.

Arthur Harper, a young salesman for a vitamin products company,
attended one of my seminars. He told me about a big account with a large
health clinic that his company had lost and had not been able to regain. I
suggested that he go back to call on them again and use the fact-finder
technique to determine out exactly what had gone wrong. About a month
later, I received this letter from him:

"As you suggested, I went back and requested an interview with the chief administrative officer of the clinic. Our conversation went like this:

"'Dr. Brown, my company would like to know exactly *why* we have lost your valuable business. We feel sure you must have had a good reason for leaving us because no one makes a better product or sells it more economically than we do. We must have been guilty of some mistake, and we would like to know what it was so we will not make the same mistake again with someone else. Will you please help me and tell me what we did wrong?'

"His answer was, 'I simply decided to try a different company. I'm perfectly happy with their service and their products and I have no desire to change.'

"'Dr. Brown, isn't there some specific reason that you left us?' I asked. 'In addition to what you've just told me, isn't there some other reason?'

"After a long silence while looking out the window, he finally turned to look me straight in the eye and said, 'Well, if you must know, your company president promised me a special extra 5 percent discount on our purchases because of the large volume of business we did with you. But when I received your company's monthly bill, it was for the full amount. There was no extra 5 percent discount.

"'So I had our bookkeeping section call your accounting department to find out why. They told us that your company never gave extra discounts to anyone, no matter who they were or how much they bought. So I figured I'd been lied to just to get our business, so I quit your company and went somewhere else. I don't want to discuss the matter any further.'

"Well, I knew there had to be a mistake somewhere so I asked Dr. Brown if I could call my office collect right then so I could find out where the error was. When I talked to the company president, the mistake was discovered immediately. He had simply forgotten to tell the accounting department about the special 5 percent discount that was to be given to Dr. Brown's health clinic.

"I then asked our president to speak to Dr. Brown immediately so this misunderstanding could be cleared up. He did so, and as a result, we regained the biggest account our company has, all because I used your fact-finder technique and refused to give up until I had all the answers."

The Power Play That Never Fails
to Turn Off Anger

This is the best technique you can use with a person who's angry because he feels slighted, overlooked, or left out. Basically, this person's problem is that he wants attention and he will do almost anything that's necessary to get it. Lack of attention destroys his ego and makes him feel unimportant and unwanted.

If you will remember, the desire to be important is a deep craving in every one of us. The best way, then, to handle the person who feels overlooked and left out is to use your unlimited power with people to make him feel important by paying attention to him. One of the best ways to do this is to ask him for his help, his opinions, and his advice. This procedure will turn off a person's anger immediately and change his attitude completely around from negative to positive. Let me give you a concrete example now of this technique:

A friend of mine, Harold Miller, a department foreman, was having all sorts of morale problems with one of his employees. "Jack's a heck of a good man," Harold told me, "and I don't want to lose him. The problem is, Jack was passed over for promotion to supervisor a couple of months ago and he's been mad about it ever since then. He's a good man where he is, but he has reached the top level of his ability. Can you give me some ideas on how to handle him, Jim?"

"Give him a job where he's noticed by others so he can gain back a feeling of importance again, even if the job is only temporary or part-time work," I said. "For example, put him in charge of reviewing the safety regulations or inventory procedures for your department. Tell him you want his recommendations because you value his opinion highly in view of his long and faithful service with the company. Pay him extra if you can for this special work.

"If that isn't feasible, figure out some other special project for him to do that carries extra responsibility and high visibility. Some sort of troubleshooting job would be perfect for him. Just make sure it's the kind of work that makes him feel important and that will cause other employees to take notice of him, too."

Did this technique work for Harold Miller? Of course it did. When Jack got the feeling of importance he needed so much, his anger evaporated, and the situation returned to normal almost immediately. Once Jack's bruised ego was healed, he forgot all about the supervisory position that he'd missed out on.

This technique will work for you, too. All you need to do is to pay attention to the angry person who feels slighted or overlooked. *Making a person feel important is a power play that never fails.* It will work every time on everyone; no exceptions, period.

The Power of Apologizing—Even When You're Not at Fault

To say you're sorry, even when you're wrong, seems to come hard to most people. It's hard to apologize. But when you are wrong, you ought to admit it quickly. I know of no faster or better way to turn off a person's anger and win a true friend than to apologize to the individual whose feelings you've hurt.

I once had occasion to write to a lawyer with whom I was extremely unhappy. I felt that the fee he'd charged me was far too high, and I told him so in no uncertain terms. I guess I got carried away even more than I realized for my letter became more caustic than I'd meant it to be.

He called me to tell me, also in no uncertain terms, what he thought about both me and my remarks. He was really angry and he laid it on me hot and heavy. When he finally paused for breath, I cut in and said, "Phil, I'm truly sorry I wrote that letter in such haste. I should never have done it. I apologize for what I said. You have a perfect right to be upset. Please forgive me."

He was quiet for several moments and then he said, "That's all right, Jim. I admire you for having the courage to say when you're wrong and apologize. Maybe my fee was too high, so I guess I owe you an apology, too. I'll send you a new bill that's not as much as the first one. Let's be friends and start all over, okay?"

So you see, to admit your mistake promptly when you're wrong and apologize to the person you've hurt can immediately turn his anger into a lasting friendship. But you can go further than that for even better results.

All you need to do is say you're sorry even when you are not at fault. When you're not in the wrong, you can afford to be big about things. If just saying you're sorry will restore peace in the family or restore friendly relationships between two people, then say it so you can get on with the more important business of enjoying each other's companionship rather than worrying and fretting about who's right and who's wrong.

The next chapter, How to Gain Complete Control over Problem Persons, is a natural follow-up to this one. It will show you how to use your unlimited power with people to its fullest extent. Controlling the behavior of problem people will test your abilities to the maximum.

Chapter 19 ✳ *The Nineteenth Day*

HOW TO GAIN COMPLETE
CONTROL OVER PROBLEM
PERSONS

Problem people require special methods and take extra attention because they are potential or actual troublemakers. They can wreck good friendly relationships and create havoc in any group by their actions.

Every factory or store, department or section, group or organization has a certain percentage of problem people. They can be found in every neighborhood or community. If they are allowed to go their own willful way unchecked, they could cause a great deal of harm or damage to you.

Right now you might not have any subordinates under you, and therefore, no problem people to bother you. However, the best time to learn how to handle problem people is before you have them working for you, not afterward.

Not only that, the information in this chapter can help you from being bullied by a domineering fellow worker. I know that he or she can be a definite problem to you. Then there's where you live to consider. If you have a problem person in your neighborhood—and what residential community doesn't have at least one or two—you can use some of the techniques in this chapter to take care of him or her, too.

Statistically speaking, one hundred people can be categorized this way:

Group A: Five persons will be self-motivating.

Group B: Ten must be challenged to develop their full potential.

Group C: Seventy must be stimulated by competent leadership to do their best.

Group D: *Ten are difficult to handle, present constant problems to you, and require extra effort on your part.*

Group E: Five are completely incorrigible.

Out of every one hundred persons, the unlimited power with people techniques you have learned in the previous chapters will easily handle the eighty-five people listed in groups A, B, and C. The five found in group E are completely incorrigible and can usually be found in jails, reformatories, and penitentiaries. They are beyond the scope of this book since I have not covered the field of abnormal psychology.

This chapter is devoted to the people in Group D—the ten out of every hundred who are difficult to handle, give you problems, and require extra effort on your part to get the job done.

Is it worth all that extra effort to handle a problem person? I think so, and so does Carl Franklin, the director of personnel management for a large Southeastern utility company.

"Every time I'm inclined to give up on a person and say to hell with it all, I remember a fellow named Warren Roland," Mr. Franklin says.

"I was in the army then, a training company commander at Fort Riley, Kansas," Mr. Franklin goes on to say. "Private Warren Roland was transferred to my unit. He'd been in the army twenty-one weeks and still hadn't finished his first eight weeks of basic training. He'd been AWOL or in the stockade most of that time.

"When he came to my company, I made our status extremely clear to him. 'I don't care what you've done before,' I told him. 'All that matters is what you do for me now. If you'll soldier for me, I'll back you up all the way. Your past will be wiped completely clean. It's all up to you.'

"Warren ended up as the company's honor graduate. He wasn't a bad person at all. He'd just gotten off on the wrong foot, and everybody expected the worst from him, so they treated him that way. I started him off with a clean slate. I held no prejudice against him for his past mistakes. All that counted as far as I was concerned was what he did for me. I gave him the chance to succeed, and succeed he did.

"So every time I'm tempted to give up on someone here, I remember Warren Roland, and I try to give the person another chance. I know I can't win 'em all, but I'm going to get as many as I can."

Sometimes the opportunity to prove himself is all the problem person needs. At other times, it will take something more. That's why I've included other techniques you can use to reach that difficult individual.

The Benefits You Will Gain

1. *You'll convert a problem person into a satisfied worker.* If this problem person works for you, you'll want to do something positive to protect your investment of time, money, and training. If you don't, you'll end up as the military services do, replacing a person every two or three years. Few companies can afford a personnel turnover like that, for they cannot train skilled replacements at taxpayers' expense as the armed forces do.

2. *You can establish cordial relationships with those around you.* You can use the techniques in this chapter to influence a difficult boss to give you a raise, promotion and authority, status, and prestige. Or you can establish harmonious and friendly relationships with a recalcitrant and sullen co-worker. You can even transform that grouchy and irritable next-door neighbor into a friendly human being by making an extra effort with him.

3. *You'll have a feeling of tremendous self-accomplishment.* Learning how to master and control difficult or problem people is almost like taking a postgraduate course in applied psychology or human relations. You'll learn new and exciting techniques to master and control the problem person with your unlimited power with people.

4. *You'll broaden beyond measure your abilities to master and control all kinds of people.* You can use the techniques in this chapter to put tough bosses, stubborn authorities, obstinate customers and clients, and any other problem people in their proper places. In fact, you'll develop a sixth sense that will help you scare off a nasty person before he can cause trouble for you. As you progress in your ability to master and control the behavior of problem persons, you will develop the skills to get things done through people that you never dreamed possible before.

How to Identify and Isolate Problem People

It is important, first, that you know how to determine whether a person actually is or is not a real problem to you. Lots of people will disagree on this basic point. Some will say that a nonconformist, an offbeat individual who speaks, thinks, or acts differently than the majority of people do is a problem person. A lot of people tend to classify an individual with long hair or a beard as a problem person.

Members of an unorthodox religious group are often regarded as being out of step with society. Mormons were once looked at that way. But today they are considered to be a respectable denomination. Today, the born-again Christian is thought to be a bit odd. But in a few years, he, too, will no doubt lose that tag of nonconformity.

So you see, a person could fit into any of these categories and still not be a problem to you or to anyone else. As Thoreau once said, "If a man does not keep pace with his companions, perhaps it is because he hears a different drummer. Let him step to the music which he hears, however measured or far away."

No matter what other people say about a person, you need answer only one question to determine whether he's a problem to you or not. *Is this person causing you damage or harm in some way?* If he is, then he's a problem to you, and you should do something to correct this situation. But if he is not causing you tangible harm or damage, *no matter what his appearance, dress, or personal behavior*, then you don't have a problem person on your hands, after all, so you need do absolutely nothing.

Don't let personal dislikes or prejudices about red hair, short skirts, pipe-smoking, or beards and mustaches mislead you. If you do, you are trying to judge all people by your own standards of right and wrong.

When you understand this simple concept of what a problem person is, you're actually much better informed in this business of handling problem people than are a lot of personnel managers or industrial relations people who make this a full-time job.

How to Keep a Potential Problem Person from Becoming a Problem

A great many times you can keep an unhappy worker from becoming a problem person simply by sitting down with him and helping to analyze his job in detail. Mismatches between a person's needs and capabilities and the demands of his work may explain his dissatisfaction. The following four questions can serve as a guide to help you and your employee evaluate his job and his attitude toward it.

1. *Is the person expecting too much from his job?* Many times, a young, inexperienced worker expects a lot more intrinsic reward from his job than he gets. An older employee tends to be more satisfied with his work, sometimes because he's moved into a more fulfilling position or because he doesn't look for all of life's joys and pleasures to be found only in his work.

2. *Is the job too demanding for the employee?* Perhaps the job is beyond the capabilities of the worker. It presents more challenges than he can handle. As an end result, he will feel frustrated and insecure. If this is so, you must either help him develop his abilities to do the job, or move him to one that is less demanding.

3. *Does the job demand too little of the person?* This is just as frustrating to a person as being overworked for it leads to boredom. It also invites problems from other employees who view the individual with envy, jealousy, and suspicion.

4. *Is the job taking him where he wants to go?* If a person's goal is to make a lot of money, he definitely won't be satisfied in a dead-end job that offers no opportunity for promotion or financial reward. You can best help this type of individual by letting him know how and where he needs to improve so he can be better qualified for promotion to the next higher position.

How a Problem Person Can Create Trouble for You on the Job

When you know exactly what to look for, it is very easy to identify the problem person who works for you. To cause you harm or damage on the job, he must be hurting your production, your sales, or your profit. All you need do is ask yourself three simple questions. If you cannot answer *yes* to at least one of them, then he's not a problem; you'll have to look elsewhere.

1. *Is his job performance below your standards?* Is the person's work below the accepted norm in either quality or quantity? Does he produce fewer units than he should in an average workday? Does he have more work rejected by quality control than anyone else? Does he always have fewer sales than other salespeople at the end of the week? *Does this individual fail in some specific way to measure up to the reasonable performance standards you've set and that all others are able to meet?* If he does, then he's costing you money, and you definitely have a problem person on your hands.

2. *Does he interfere with the performance of others?* Is this person a constant source of irritation, annoyance, or interference? Do you usually find him at the bottom of employee disturbances? Does he keep other people from doing their best work? Does the quality or the quantity of his work slow down or prevent other sections or groups from functioning properly? Does he cause some of his coworkers to lose incentive pay by his careless actions? If so, then this person is a definite problem, not only to you, but to others as well.

3. *Does he cause harm to the group as a whole?* The reputation or good name of any group can be damaged even if only one of its members is a chronic source of trouble. He can keep the rest of his group on edge or in a constant turmoil by what he says or does. For instance, if one member of a professional athletic team gets out of line, he gives the entire team a morale problem. One troublesome sales representative can give the entire company a bad name. If any of your people have constantly caused you to get complaints, have orders canceled, or lose good customers by carelessness, indifference, or sloppy work, you have a problem person to take care of.

To sum up this section quickly on how to decide whether a person is actually causing you trouble, ask yourself these three questions:

1. Is his job performance below your established standards?
2. Does he interfere with the work of others?
3. Does he cause harm or trouble for the group as a whole?

If you answer *yes* to any of these questions, you have a problem person on your hands.

Seven Common Employee Problems
and How They Were Resolved

Problem 1: "I once had a problem employee I'll just call Bill," Doug Ellison, a Midwestern industrial plant manager, told me. "Bill was a constant critic of management. Whenever he was told to do something, he always wanted to do it the opposite way. If there was an argument or disagreement of some sort, Bill was sure to be in on it. And he worked overtime to get in the last word. He demanded the attention of management, it seemed, and he always got it. He fulfilled all three requirements that constitute a problem person. He was underperforming in his job, constantly interfering with the work of others, and harming the members of his team by causing them loss of incentive pay because of lowered production."

ANALYSIS: "Well, I was at wit's end until I met you, Jim," Doug went on to say. "Then I sat down and analyzed Bill's problem and determined he was simply going out of his way to attract attention to himself. Bill had an ego problem and he needed to feel important, not only to himself, but also to others. The next question was how could I give him that feeling of importance that he needed so much?"

SOLUTION: "I decided to follow your advice, Jim. I gave Bill the responsibility of heading up the employee safety team for his section. It became his job to establish safety rules and regulations and to work out emergency rescue procedures with the plant safety officer in case of an industrial accident in his section. He was also to inspect daily to see that the safety rules he had established were being followed. We gave him the full authority to do that. Wonder of wonders, it worked. Bill's desire for importance was fulfilled. People were actually listening to what he said when he talked. His ego was gratified and now everyone's happy."

Problem 2: "I hired an ex-army major as a supervisor in the mill department," Joel Galloway, a cereal factory division manager, said. "But his manner was too much like that of an army drill sergeant. He issued orders right and left in a loud demanding voice and was extremely impatient and critical of the work of everyone. Yet I knew he had a lot of potential management ability, and I didn't want to let him go unless I absolutely had to."

ANALYSIS: "It was comparatively simple to analyze Tom's problem. He was simply too authoritarian as a result of his many years in the armed forces."

SOLUTION: "I didn't have much trouble in getting Tom to see my point. His brisk and curt military bearing was not caused by a compulsive desire for power, but simply resulted from his army training. When he spoke, he expected people to listen and not ask questions. He now realizes that his subordinates can have some good ideas, too, so he listens to them and cooperates with them without being permissive. He's still strong and firm, no doubt about that, but in such a way that he is well accepted by all his people. They like him and respect him a great deal."

Problem 3: "Neal S. was promoted to section supervisor from the labor force and retained in the same department so we could use his technical skills and experience to the maximum," Elston Richards, a division manager in a North Carolina furniture manufacturing company said. "Neal wanted to succeed in his new job, but he was also anxious to keep his friendships intact with his former coworkers and associates so they wouldn't think he was putting on airs and lording it over them. Trouble was, he became too permissive and let his former buddies run over the top of him. He overlooked their mistakes. Absenteeism rose, quality went down, accidents increased, soon the section was a complete disaster area."

ANALYSIS: "I was at fault for waiting too long before I took action to correct the problem. When I did, I pointed out to Neal that his problem was his normal desire to keep the friendship of his former coworkers and that as a result, he was being too permissive with them and letting them get away with murder."

SOLUTION: "It was almost too late, but Neal asserted his authority and natural leadership ability, and within thirty days things were back to normal. I realize now I made a mistake in keeping Neal in the same department when he was promoted. It is now a standing rule in our company that when a man from the labor force is promoted to a position in management, he must be moved to a different department."

Let me give you now some personal examples from my own experience in management:

Problem 4:   The alcoholic is always a problem. He'll come to work late, do a poor job, and call in sick several days a week. No one knows why he drinks the way he does. He doesn't understand himself either.

ANALYSIS: Not every alcoholic is a total loss or destined to become a gutter bum. Alcoholics come in all shapes and sizes. Some are doctors, lawyers, farmers, plumbers, male, and female. Alcoholism plays no favorites and makes no exceptions. Many alcoholics can be salvaged. Not all end up on skid row.

SOLUTION: The only solution I've ever found to be successful is to contact a member of Alcoholics Anonymous. Have him or her get in touch with the problem person and talk with him. Chances are you have a recovered alcoholic working for you right now and you don't even know it. Tell the employee what you're going to do and let him know *it's either A.A. or his job.* The point is you've offered him a way out, but you can go no further than that. He has to solve his own problem. You can't do that for him.

Problem 5:   Gladys K., a programmer in a data processing organization, changed almost overnight from a pleasant hard-working employee to a sullen, resentful, and insubordinate person.

ANALYSIS: A little digging and some personnel work showed that a new male employee who was also a programmer was hired at about the same time Gladys's personality changed. Further investigation revealed that the new employee was being paid more than Gladys simply because he was a man. They were both doing the same work.

SOLUTION: Since it was impossible to lower the new man's salary without losing him, the only fair thing to do was to raise Gladys's salary up to equal his. When this was done, the problem was solved. Gladys became her own pleasant self again.

Problem 6:   Joe was not doing his job properly. Quality control turned back 75 percent of his production. Yet Joe was a hard worker. He was serious and sincere about his work and seemed to be trying hard to do a good job.

ANALYSIS: Joe had been given this job only a few weeks before. He had never received the proper training to do the work. His supervisor had assumed that Joe knew how to do the job, but that assumption was in error.

SOLUTION: Joe was given further training and instruction until he was properly qualified to do the job.

Problem 7:   Jerry was a constant source of irritation to his supervisor. There seemed to be a definite personality clash between them. He was a good worker and his supervisor was also a good employee. The company didn't want to lose either of them.

ANALYSIS: Sometimes people do clash without any logical or visible reason. If the friction between an employee and his supervisor cannot be ironed out peacefully, then you should transfer the employee to a new department. I must admit that I, too, have met a few people in my time that I wouldn't care to work with or for. Nor would I care to have them as my next-door neighbor.

SOLUTION: In this instance, Jerry was transferred to a different department. He gets along well with his new supervisor and is doing an excellent job.

How Some Bosses Create Employee Problems

When you are trying to find the solution to a person's problem, you should always keep one thought in mind. And that is: *You should never allow his problem to become your problem.* Show the person how to carry his load, but don't carry it for him. It's easy to become too sympathetic and soft when a person cries on your shoulder about his sick mother, his bedridden wife, the broken-down car, and so on, but you must establish a firm line somewhere. We all have personal problems to resolve, and we have to take care of them and work at the same time. Your problem person will have to do the same thing. This is not to say you shouldn't help the person. You should, but don't let him take advantage of you.

Many times I've been called in as a management consultant to find out what was wrong with the labor force only to determine that the boss himself was the cause of his problems. I want to give you a list now of the most common gripes people have told me about their bosses so you can avoid making those same mistakes if and when you are in charge.

I'm just going to list these complaints for you. I'm not going to give you any solutions as I just did for the previous problems. By now you've received enough information about how to use your unlimited power with people to formulate your own solutions to these problems.

1. "My boss treats me like a piece of office equipment. He makes me feel stupid in front of others. He has absolutely no knowledge whatever of human relationships."

2. "He's always making promises to get people to do things for him, but then he never keeps his word."

3. "My boss isn't fair. He plays favorites and they're the ones who get the promotions, pay raises, and special privileges. With him it isn't what you know, but who you are that counts."

4. "She never says thanks or gives a compliment to anyone. It would be nice to hear her say just once in a while what a good job I've done for her."

5. "He's really disorganized. He tells you something one day and then denies he ever said it the next day. You never know which way you're going with him."

6. "He always passes the buck to someone else when he makes a mistake. He wants all the credit when the job is done right, but he won't accept any of the blame when things go wrong."

7. "He discriminates against older people and women."

8. "My boss doesn't have the courage to stand for what he knows to be right. He waffles all over the place trying to compromise and please everybody."

9. "He doesn't tell the truth. You can't trust what he says."

10. "He's two-faced. Tells me what a good job I'm doing, and then tells others I'm the worst secretary he's ever had!"

Why You Can't Win Them All

No matter how hard you try, you are not going to be able to salvage every problem employee. A small percentage of people seem to be constitutionally incapable of working with others, obeying orders, accepting discipline from a higher authority, or even disciplining themselves.

Perhaps they are not at fault. I do not know. I am not a psychiatrist. Not only that, the study of abnormal psychology is beyond the scope of this book. From a management point of view, the important thing for you to do is to identify the incorrigible employee as quickly as possible so you can get rid of him before he contaminates and ruins the rest of your people.

Many of these incorrigibles seem to have been born that way. They are by their very nature unable to grasp and develop a manner of living that demands simple honesty. Unfortunately, this small segment of humanity seems destined for the gutter or prison, and nothing on earth you or I can do will stop them.

The answer, then, to this kind of problem person? There is none as far as you or I as managers or executives are concerned. You are not a social worker and neither am I. You can't win 'em all, and this is one of those you cannot win. Since you are not running a rehabilitation center or a rest home, you really have no choice in the matter. If the individual is a member of your management team, *fire him*. If he's a member of organized labor, you'll have to do the same thing. It might just take a little longer, that's all.

And now I want to leave the work area to discuss the problem of the neighborhood gossip and the grouchy neighbor who might live next door to you so I can show you how to use your unlimited people power to handle them.

How to Handle Gossip

Every neighborhood has at least one motormouth who is a potential or an actual troublemaker. A neighborhood gossip tries to demean people by spreading lies and rumors that will blacken a person's good name and reputation or cut down his accomplishments or abilities.

Most people in the neighborhood know the gossip for what he or she really is. But sometimes they can't help but wonder if what's being said is true or not. If someone tells you some juicy tidbit about Hank or Vicki or Michele behind their backs, rest assured that you yourself are not immune from this kind of slander. That same person will talk to them behind your back, too.

You can deal with this neighborhood gossip best by telling him that you are not interested in what he's saying and refuse to listen. Tell him to take his garbage elsewhere, preferably to the trash dump. If that doesn't work, then use the *silent treatment*. Don't speak to that person at all at any time.

Whether you run into the person at social activities, in business, at church, or in the supermarket, put yourself above him, Don't even say "Hello" to him. Ignore him utterly and completely. Nothing stills a rumor-monger's evil tongue more quickly than your refusal to talk with him or even listen to him. If no one will listen, how can he spread gossip and rumors?

We had a neighborhood gossip who was squelched by our ignoring her completely. Three of us made a solemn pact never to speak to her again. Soon our avoidance of her spread through the entire neighborhood until she was completely isolated from the whole community. How effective is this technique? It will work much better than trying to fight back. Yesterday I saw a "For Sale" sign go up in front of her house.

How to Befriend a Grouch

It could be that some of the problem people in your life are your boss, the person who works beside you, a business competitor, or a grouchy neighbor. Just ask yourself the test question (Is this person causing me harm or damage in some way?) before you decide whether the other individual is a problem to you or not.

Let's suppose it's a grouchy neighbor who's giving you fits. Don't try to get even with him. That will only make things worse. Instead, try to find out what's wrong if you can and try to help the person solve his problem. If you can't find out what's bothering him, give of yourself and help him any way you can. Let me give you a personal example of that point.

Once there were two neighbors, Jim and George, who could not get along with each other. Jim and his wife had three growing children. George and Elaine were childless, and they demanded absolute peace and quiet, even throughout the daytime, an impossibility in the summertime when there are three healthy active children and their friends playing in the backyard.

There were other problems as well, most of them, though, having to do with noise. Jim's wife even gave up playing the piano, for if the windows were open, the moment she did, the phone would ring. Or if Jim made a little too much noise in his garage workshop on weekends, the same thing would happen.

Jim was deeply hurt and disturbed, for he had never run into a situation like this before, and he was at a loss as to how to handle it. Time and again he tried to establish a friendly and cordial relationship with George, but he couldn't seem to break through that hard shell of enmity so he finally gave up. Even when their lawn mowers nearly rubbed wheels along their backyard battle lines, they never spoke to each other.

Then one summer George and Elaine went on vacation. At first, Jim didn't even realize they were gone. But one evening after he'd mowed his yard, he saw how high George's grass was. It was an open invitation to a burglar for it was a sure sign that no one was home.

"A sudden thought came to me," Jim said. *"Don't try to love your neighbor, just help him.* I looked at that high grass again and my mind rebelled. Help George? After the way he's treated me? No way! No dice; nothing doing."

But the next morning the same thought persisted in Jim's mind. It refused to go away, so he finally gave up and mowed George's lawn.

A day later, George and Elaine came back. Within the hour George was knocking at Jim's door. When Jim opened it, George said belligerently, "Did you mow my yard? I've asked everybody in the whole neighborhood. Jack says you did. I don't believe it. Did you?"

"Yes, George, I did," Jim said. "Why, is something wrong?"

"No, nothing's wrong," George said. He turned and walked away. Then he stopped, turned around, and with a great deal of effort, said "Thanks."

So the ice was broken for Jim and George. Months of bitter silence was gone. Oh, they aren't playing golf or bridge together, and their wives don't have coffee together in the morning nor do they borrow salt and sugar yet. But definite progress is being made.

Love your neighbor? Could be, but as far as I'm concerned, it works better if you spell *love* H-E-L-P! How can I be so sure of that? That's easy. *I'm Jim*!

There is simply not enough time or space to cover every problem situation with each person such as your boss, your coworker, your competitor, and so on, but this principle can be used to gain unlimited people power with them almost every time.

Just remember: Don't try to love a person—just *help* him solve his problem. Do that, and out of that small beginning can grow a lasting friendship and a mutual understanding.

And now let's get on to Chapter 20, How to Build Up Your Defenses and Keep People From Overpowering You. Although it would be wonderful if everyone in the world were your friend, that is not always true. Especially in the competitive business world or the company where everyone is scrambling to get to the top, you must protect your flanks from attack. The next chapter will show you exactly how to use your unlimited power with people to do that.

Chapter 20 ✳ *The Twentieth Day*

HOW TO BUILD UP YOUR DEFENSES AND KEEP PEOPLE FROM OVERPOWERING YOU

The best way to gain unlimited power with people is by filling a person's needs and desires and doing it better than anyone else can. There is absolutely no better way of getting other people to do what you want them to do, and that's for sure. The only thing is, though, sometimes you can get so absorbed in doing that in your campaign to gain unlimited power with people, you forget that other people are trying to gain power with them, too. In their attempt to do that, they will often try to undercut you. So you need to shore up your own defenses and keep other people from trying to overpower you.

The main people you need to be concerned about are those who try to get what they want from another person without fulfilling that person's needs. They give back nothing for what they get. And since they normally have no real personal power of their own, they try to get what they want by using the position or status of others. In other words, they are parasites; they try to get something for nothing.

I'm sure you've met people like this at times. Perhaps you've had lunch with one of them and been deeply embarrassed at the way he delights in making a false show of importance, the way he keeps a waitress on the run just for the apparent satisfaction of it. Then there's the golfer who treats his caddy or the bartender at the club the same way. Or the person who pretends to have the ear of the old man, or the inside track with the front office, so everyone will be extra nice to him or her.

Of course, people usually do handle that type with kid gloves. Who knows; he might really have an in or he could well be a spy for the boss. Then there's always the one who wields his company's name and his expense account like a club of authority. He never seems to work for anybody; he always *associated* with them.

If people like these get just half the chance, you'll suddenly find that you've become their waitress, their golf caddy, their servant. Since they have no real power to sustain themselves, they will use any means they can to protect their position. Plenty of people can get injured in their struggle to maintain their parasitic power. So in this chapter, I want to show you how to shore up your own defenses, so they will not be able to take advantage of you and win power over you.

The Benefits You Will Gain

1. *You'll retain control of the situation.* You'll retain complete control of the situation, not only in name, but also in fact. Agency or borrowed power evaporates when the agency is gone. Real personal power has staying power. No one can take it from you. A real estate salesman has power to sell a client's house until the owner terminates his contract with that agency. Then the agent's borrowed power disappears.

I once knew an army lieutenant in a reserve outfit called to active duty during the Korean conflict. He had sergeants and corporals—his superiors in civilian life—running around like mad to do his will until he went back to his job as an elevator operator in a hotel after the war was over. His power was lost as he went through the gate at the separation center, for he carried it only in his silver bars. He had no real personal power to fall back on in civilian life.

Since your unlimited power with people is based on an understanding of what they need and want, your power will continue without pause. You will always retain full control of the situation because of your knowledge of the real source of your power.

You can turn off his play for power at will and gain more personal power and stature for yourself by forcing the person out into the open. Nothing succeeds like success, and nothing defeats like defeat. The smallest crisis will force the person who's using borrowed power to get by to run back to his source for reinforcement, since he has no authority or power of his own.

You'll run into this kind of person in all professions and occupations. He's the freeloader, the user of borrowed power, and the one you really have to watch out for. He can hurt you badly if you don't know how to recognize him for what he is so you can handle him properly.

2. *You'll know how to defend yourself.* When you understand how people use agency or borrowed power to gain their ends, you'll know how to defend yourself. Many people often defer to those with borrowed power, primarily because of their fear that they will lose position or status if they do not. But when the situation changes, as it always will, those with borrowed power are the first to go. When their source of power disappears, so do they.

So don't ingratiate or prostrate yourself to them. To do so is but to feed the dragon. The end result can be disastrous for you: a complete loss of your unlimited people power.

How to Control People Who Use "Borrowed Power" to Get Ahead

Since the person who uses "borrowed or counterfeit power" trying to achieve his ends will be your greatest problem, I want to discuss him first and at some length.

The person who uses borrowed power trying to influence and direct the actions of others has no real personal power of his own. Borrowed power is agency power. In other words, it belongs to another person or to the organization itself. And even though that person can use this agency power to his advantage, the power does not come from him at all.

For example, in the military services, people who use borrowed power to get what they want will usually be generals, aides and high-ranking officers' wives. In business and industry, it can be the boss's secretary, the doctor's nurse, or a lawyer's receptionist, a brother-in-law, a nephew, or some other relative.

Now if you happen to be an officer's wife, a general's aide, a boss's secretary, a doctor's nurse, or a lawyer's receptionist, and you don't fall into that category, don't get upset. My point is that I have seen this type in these categories. If the shoe doesn't fit you, then don't try to wear it.

You can easily identify people with agency or borrowed power this way. They have nothing to offer to get what they're after. They always try to get what they want without fulfilling another person's needs. Since they have no real personal power to gain their goals, they have to use the position or status of others who do have that power. In short, they are parasites. They always try to get something for nothing, often by using veiled threats.

Another ploy that people with borrowed power will try to use is to issue an order they are not authorized to give. The recipient of such an order will attempt to carry it out and then end up in a peck of trouble when he does. This is often exactly what the person with borrowed power wants to have happen.

You can usually recognize at once whether an order is legitimate or not by what you hear. If you hear phrases like, "This is what the boss wants," "This is what the boss asked for," "This is what the general manager told me to tell you," watch out. In the end, if something goes wrong, it will only be your word against his.

The best way to keep this from happening to you is to follow this one simple rule: *Never take orders from anyone outside of your power line of authority.*

Let me give you an example of how this could create a problem for you. Taking orders from someone who has no authority to give that order can be a source of tremendous friction in business, industry, the armed services, church, school, you name it. Wherever people are, you can have this problem because the person using borrowed power always tries to take over.

This play for power often takes place in factories where department foremen are vying with each other for position. I personally saw this happen in a rubber factory where automobile V-belts and industrial belts were built.

Belt building demands for rubber often outstripped the mill department's production capacity before new calendars and mixing mills were installed. Bob C., the foreman in charge of industrial belt production, used to make sure his department would have plenty of material on hand for the night shift to the detriment of other departments who also needed the rubber. Bob would go back to the plant after supper, go to the supervisor in the mill department, and tell him that production orders had been changed and that he was to shift all production to the stripping and sheeting he needed

in his belt department until 11:00 P.M. Then he was to shift back to his
regular production schedule.

So the young supervisor would follow the foreman's orders. After
all, he figured a department head like Bob C. was higher than a supervisor
and he ought to know what was going on. The point he failed to consider
was that he was not under Bob C.'s jurisdiction; he was not in Bob C.'s
chain of command. *And since Bob C. was not his superior, he therefore had
no authority to give orders to anyone in the mill department.*

It took several months, a lot of chewing-out, and hard feelings
between department heads before matters got straightened out properly.
When they did, the production superintendent had posted an organizational
command line chart in all departments, in the cafeteria, all rest areas, every
vacant wall he could find, and issued strict instructions that failure to follow
this chain of authority line to the letter would result in immediate dismissal,
no matter who the guilty party was.

To conclude this concept, then, let me say this: If your boss tells
you to do it, then do it. If *his* boss tells you to do it, then do it, but be sure
your immediate superior knows about the order. But if you're in personnel,
and someone in purchasing or sales or engineering tells you to do it, forget
it. Tell him to issue his order through the proper command channels if he
wants it to be carried out.

Always be courteous, of course, but refuse to do his bidding. As
soon as you stand your ground, the person using borrowed power will leave
you alone. Give in and you'll be under his thumb forever. Remember that
when the present power structure changes, people with borrowed power will
be the first to go. When their source of power disappears, so will they. And
so might you, if you've been catering to them.

How to Read the "Invisible" Company Power Chart

Every company or corporation has two power charts. The official one shows
the line-and-staff organizational structure. This chart is described in an
organization manual, usually called an SOP (standing operating procedure).
Formal power and authority lines are clearly shown. It is available for
anyone to read and study.

The unofficial power chart is invisible. You cannot find it on paper
so you can study it, but it is still there. You can understand this chart only

by constant and careful observation of people and their actions. Since many times it is the company's "real" power chart, it will affect promotions and raises, resignations, and dismissals.

The power lines in the invisible chart are formed by office politics. If you want to get ahead and stay there, you must thoroughly study and understand this invisible but very real power chart. Let me show you some of the things you should watch for. You may find others in your own organization, but the points I will give you are usually common in all companies.

1. WHO IS THE REAL INFORMATION SOURCE?   Rumors and gossip often flow through all levels of the organization. However, dependable information will normally come from someone who sets policy or makes decisions or from an individual close to him.

This does not necessarily mean that the person in authority on the official power chart will make the final decision on a crucial matter. It's up to you to find out who the real power is, who's behind the scenes pulling the strings on the puppet.

2. WHO IN THE ORGANIZATION SOCIALIZES WITH THE TOP BRASS? People who work together do not always play together. Many social relationships are established by membership in some organization outside the company. The connection can be political, religious, even athletic. It can result from club or lodge membership. It may be the result of the social standing of one's spouse. Whatever the relationship is, it gives that person an edge on power and an "in" with those who count. So be smart; know who these people are. Keep your guard up and watch your back and your tongue at all times when you are around them.

3. FIND OUT WHICH EMPLOYEE HAS REAL AUTHORITY IN THE INVIS-IBLE POWER LINE.   It can come as a complete surprise to you to find that someone outside the official power line has the authority to either okay or kill a project. Without his initials of approval, a proposal or recommendation can die.

When I first went to work as a junior executive with a big company, I submitted a recommendation to my superior for cutting costs in a particular department. "Take it to B.J.," my boss said. "Get his approval first."

"B.J.?" I said, surprised at his remark. "Why? He has no authority in this department."

"You're wrong," my boss said. "B.J. doesn't have any 'official' authority in any specific area, but he's been here since the place first opened up. He's sort of an unofficial troubleshooter for the chief who values his judgment highly. Without his initials of approval on your proposal, your recommendation won't stand a chance. It won't get anywhere at all."

4. WHO'S RELATED TO WHOM IN THE INVISIBLE POWER STRUCTURE? These people have an "in" simply because of a blood tie or a marriage relationship. If two people are equal in qualifications and ability, but one of them is the boss's nephew or his wife's cousin, guess who's going to be promoted when only one opening is available. So keep a weather eye on relatives of any kind. They may be powerless today, but have great power and authority tomorrow.

How to Analyze the Reasons Behind a Person's Push for Power

Keep in mind that people who use agency or borrowed power to attain their goals want the same basic things out of life that you and I want. They have the same needs and desires that all of us have.

What's the difference between them and you and me then? Well, you and I know how to get what we want by making sure our target person gets what he wants. But the person who's using borrowed or counterfeit power to achieve his purposes doesn't know how to use this kind of power. He doesn't understand the principles of power with people the way you and I do, so he has to use agency or borrowed power to get what he wants. He knows no other way.

So find out what that person really wants most of all. Discover what he's after. If you can help him fulfill his needs and *benefit yourself* at the same time, then do that. You'll gain a friend and an ally when you do. If you cannot, then at least you will know which side of the fence he's on, and you can govern your own actions accordingly. But even if he doesn't respond to your overtures, you don't have to despise him. Just categorize him.

Why You Should Know Your Business and Stick to It

Nine times out of ten, a person traveling on borrowed power is not an expert on much of anything. When the chips are down, you can force him to take cover by using your superior knowledge. The best way you can gain that superior knowledge is to know your own business better than anyone else does and then stick to it.

About two thousand years ago, Horace, the celebrated Roman poet, said, "I attend to the business of other people, having lost my own." Don't let that happen to you.

Your keystone to shoring up your own defenses and not letting other people overpower you is to know more about your job, your position, and your business than anyone else. Then your knowledge becomes real power. When you understand that, you are approaching wisdom. No one using borrowed or counterfeit power can assault such an impregnable position. He's too weak so it's impossible for him to overpower you and win.

Keep Them on the Defensive at All Times

The best defense is to attack—to go on the offensive. When you do this, you'll keep the other fellow so busy covering up and trying to protect himself, he can find neither the time nor the opportunity to attack you. One of the best ways to attack him is to use the word "Why?" Let me give you an example of how well you can make that work for yourself.

"This supervisor over in the belt building department was really trying to get me," says Ron Shelby, shift supervisor in the mill department of an Ohio rubber plant.

"He'd been demoted and transferred out of the mill department for his failure to get along with his subordinates. He was on fire to get even with someone, and since I had his old job, I was his best target.

"Now in the mill department we turn out calendar rolls of rubber to use in the various building departments of the plant. The thickness has to be measured by a micrometer, and the accepted tolerance is only 2/1,000 over or under. But more than just thickness is important. The density of the rubber has to be just right or a belt won't hold together on your car. It will fly apart in no time at all.

"Well, Pat was sending back every roll of rubber I produced for him. Each day when I came to work I'd find 20 or 30 rolls, half of my previous day's production, back in my area. Every roll had a green tag that meant it was unacceptable and couldn't be used in production.

"Naturally plant production fell off, and the next thing I knew Pat and I were in the production superintendent's office standing at attention in front of his desk. I was plenty scared, but luckily I'd been given some ammunition by one of the old-timers in my department who'd seen this game played too many times before.

"'Just ask Pat *why*,' he told me. 'And keep on asking him *why*? Make him tell you and the super *why* he can't use our rubber. It's good rubber. I know it is. After all, I helped make it. So ask him *why* he can't use it when everybody else can.'

"Well, the way it started, Pat said he couldn't use the rubber I was turning out—said he couldn't build good belts with it. Now I knew the tolerance was okay and the lab always checked the density of each batch before I ran it, and I told our production superintendent so. I also mentioned that the other departments were using the rubber and Pat was the only supervisor in the plant who'd been rejecting my production.

"I also said this: 'Since I don't know all the details of belt building the way Pat does, but only of making the rubber in my own department, I'd like to suggest that he tell us *why* he can't use the rubber, especially since the tolerance and the density are okay and all other departments are using it.

'I want to know exactly what is wrong with it so I can correct the mistake. I'd like to have him show us right on the production line *how* and *why* it can't be used.'

"The production superintendent agreed and now the situation was completely reversed. When we'd entered the office, I was on the defensive and Pat was on the offensive. When we left the office, it was the other way around.

"When it was finally over, Pat was demoted once more—right out the door and into the street."

If one of your associates is pressing you badly, back him off and put him on the defensive by challenging him with *why*. Make him prove his point. Make him prove that he knows what he's talking about.

One of the best ways to keep him on the defensive is to answer his questions with one of your own. Then follow up quickly with still another question.

In other words, use your challenge of *why* as a lead into a completely different aspect on the subject. That's what Ron Shelby did. When he went into the production superintendent's office, the question was *why didn't Ron produce quality rubber* that Pat could use in his department. When he went out of the office, the question was *why wasn't Pat building any belts?*

How to Challenge a Power with Complete Silence

Ever stub your toe on a rock and then hurt your foot even more when you kicked it? Or raise up and hit your head on a cupboard door and then make it worse by hurting your hand when you took a swing at that offending door? Well, it happens to writers, too!

A writer friend of mine became so frustrated one day when he couldn't say exactly what he wanted to say, exactly the way he wanted to say it, that he finally rose up in disgust and walked over and belted the wall! He broke two fingers, put a hole in the plaster board, and ended up with his hand in a cast for six weeks. And a writer who can't write is like a hunter without a gun or a fisherman without a pole and a hook.

The problem is, of course, the rock and the cupboard door are completely silent. They can't talk up and tell you how it happened. No matter how much you fume, kick, or cuss, they won't talk back. And the quieter they are, the madder you become.

You can use the rock's tactics on your challenger. Simply ignore him. More cases of divorce come from lack of attention than from adultery. No one, but no one, likes to be ignored.

Inattention is one of the greatest weapons ever used to cut a person down to size. It's used by employees, associates, customers, even by people who serve you in restaurants, bars, and motels. The dining car steward on yesterday's train has been replaced by the airline stewardess of today's airplane. These people are all experts at putting obnoxious individuals in their place by the simple method of ignoring them.

You can do the same. Take a lesson from them. You can destroy your most belligerent opponent's attack by ignoring him. Simply pay no attention to his requests, his opinions, his commands, his threats, his wishes. Watch the moderator at the next town council meeting. He studiously avoids the upstretched hand of the harassing troublemaker, the sharpshooter, and the rabble-rouser. If he's done his preparatory work properly, he'll have shills scattered throughout the group with enough questions to take up all the time.

When the porcupine rolls up into a ball, the fox or the coyote cannot harm him. All their attacks are in vain. Finally, the attacker gives up in disgust and walks away.

"I always play for time by turning a deaf ear to them," says Robert Scott-Smith, a high school principal I know. "I look old enough to wear a hearing aid even though I don't need it. Got perfect hearing in both ears.

"But teachers don't know this. When they come roaring into my office complaining about some extra assignment, a heavy workload, some uncooperative teacher, or a troublesome student, they have to wait until I turn on my hearing aid so I can listen.

"Course I've heard everything they've said. And pretending to need a hearing aid gives me a chance to ask them to repeat the question or the problem if I want still more time to think up my answer. And when they have to sit down, and repeat everything all over, maybe even a couple of times, it really slows them down. Sometimes they see the fallacy of their position for themselves even before I say anything. But in the meantime, I've had a chance to work out an answer to their question in my mind."

I was close to forty before I realized that my father always used the same technique on everyone, including his own children and, especially, the minister. He despised long-winded sermons, and it was his way of cutting the preacher's visit to our house extremely short. Reverend Clark got tired of yelling trying to make my father hear. But my dad always heard everything he wanted to hear, and that's for sure.

Why You Need to Build Some Strong Friendships and Alliances

Few people make it through life on their own. Even Thoreau gave the pond back to the frogs. The time comes, sooner or later, when you have to have a friend, even if it's only to cover your own grave.

You may have a lot of competition in your organization. If so, there'll be all the more need, then, for cooperation with others to meet that competition. If you're in business, for example, then attending trade association meetings or belonging to the Chamber of Commerce, the Rotary, Kiwanis, or Toastmasters is just good sound strategy and common sense. Get everybody on your side that you can.

You need to protect your own interests. If you're a member of some group and you don't attend their meetings regularly, you could well find you've been elected to some unwanted and time-consuming position like that of treasurer or secretary.

"That's how I ended up on the building and finance committee of my church," Roy S. told me. "Now I make sure to attend every Sunday to protect my vested interests!"

Gene Mason, a young salesman with the Cadillac Plastic and Chemical Company in Kansas City, Missouri, built strong friendships within the plant. He was ambitious and competitive, and he knew he needed to establish strong bonds with the plant's employees as well as with his customers on the outside. Customer demands were often greater than the available supply, and Gene wanted to make sure his orders were always filled first.

He soon became known as a "person you can really work with." And he moved into the sales manager's position and from there into the assistant general manager's spot in short order. Why?

"Because I built up strong alliances in the plant—that's why," Gene says. "I could get things done where other people could not because I knew the ropes in the plant. I knew the key people I could depend on and the ones I could get action from, while other management people in the company bogged down completely and didn't know whom to turn to in order to get the results that they wanted."

You should protect your own interests the same way. Build strong friendships with those people in your group who really count. Pinpoint those people who can help you become successful. You don't have to shine their shoes or polish the apple with them to get them on your side. Just make sure you fulfill their needs, remember? It's a surefire way of shoring up your defenses against the day when you'll really need them to help protect against any people who are out to overpower you.

How to Master and Control the Person with the Real Power

It might come as a surprise to you, but it is far easier to master and control the person with real power than the person who uses agency or borrowed power. People with real power are those who really count in the long run. They'll be around long after those with agency or borrowed power are gone.

All you need to do is practice the basic premise that I have stressed so many times that it's probably becoming monotonous to you. But it's so important, I'm going to repeat it once more. *Find out what the other person wants so you can help him get it* if you really want to become successful.

How You Can Find Out What He Wants.   Get a little notebook and keep your eyes and ears open so you can gather and record intelligence information about those individuals who are important to you and to your career. Use the basic needs and desires every person has as your guide for gathering useful information about your target.

Now don't get the wrong idea here. The data you record in your notebook are not to be used for improper purposes. You are gathering information only to find out what the other person wants so you can help him get it.

No doubt, the two key individuals who are vital to your success are your own boss, and, in turn, his boss. So find out everything you can about them: their likes and dislikes, their quirks and idiosyncrasies, their customs and habits, their strong points and their weak ones.

How You Can Help Him Get What He Wants.   Once you know what your boss likes, help him get it. If he is a bug about getting reports in early, then get them in early. If he wants his desk completely cleared off by quitting time, then help him by getting that done. If he frowns on people coming in late, then never be late. Whatever he wants, help him get it. After all, he's the one you want to keep happy and contented.

I do want to stress that while you are creating a strong alliance with your boss and with his boss by making sure they get what they want, don't make enemies out of those who can't do anything for you at the moment.

They may be able to help you in the future, for things always change. Promotion, retirement, death, dismissal, transfer, any of these can change the status quo in a moment, so always be prepared for any eventuality. No matter what happens in the circles of power, be ready to jump in any direction and you'll always come out on top.

And now I want to move on to the next chapter, one that is extremely interesting, for it will tell you how to use your unlimited people power to succeed in business, either in the big corporation or in your own company.

You'll meet one of the most enterprising and successful young men I have ever known, Bill Wilson, a Palm Bay businessman who is the owner of R & S Soft Water Services. Bill's philosophy is that total service is the real key to business success. As he says, "The customer must come first, last, and always."

Chapter 21 ✳ *The Twenty-First Day*

HOW TO USE YOUR UNLIMITED PEOPLE POWER TO SUCCEED IN BUSINESS

To be able to get ahead in today's business world, you must know how to solve people's problems. You see, it isn't problems with sales, production, or profit that will cause your headaches in business. It's people and people problems.

For example, you can solve your profit problems with better control over costs and expenditures. You can solve your sales problems and gain more customers with better sales techniques and procedures. And you can handle your production problems with more efficient methods, eliminating wasted motion and duplication of effort, improving the quality, cutting out excess waste, and various other ways.

Even when you solve all these problems, you are still going to find yourself with people problems, for *people are always needed to solve those profit, sales, and production problems*. You will always need people to help you become successful in the business world, for you can't possibly do it all by yourself.

That's why this chapter will be so valuable to you, for it will give you the techniques you can use to gain unlimited power with people in business. When you do that, you'll become an outstanding success in the business world just as Bill Wilson, the enterprising young man you'll meet later on in this chapter, did.

The Benefits You Will Gain

1. *You'll make much money.* Ever since the Phoenicians invented money several thousand years ago, the primary aim of every person has been to make as much of it as possible. This chapter will show you how to guide and direct the activities of people in the business world so you can go ahead and make more of it than you ever imagined possible.

2. *You'll have great power with others when you become a success in business.* You'll find that your influence will expand outward and you can become the leader, not only in business activities, but also in social, political, and community affairs as well.

3. *Personal power, prestige, respect and recognition will all become yours along with your financial success when you become prosperous in business.* People will look up to you.

4. *You can use the techniques you'll learn in this chapter to develop your own power tactics to master your boss and move up the business ladder of success.* If you are now at the bottom in a big company, you can use these techniques to move up to top management and executive levels. No matter who you are, what you do, or how low your position is right now, you can use your personal power with people to go up the ladder to the top so that every success you ever dreamed of can be yours.

Thirteen Tips for Climbing the Ladder to Success in a Big Company

Before I give you thirteen specific techniques you can use to climb the ladder to success in the big company, I want you to know that the top people in the executive suites above you are not especially anxious to see you succeed. In fact, if the truth is to be known, *no one is interested in your success but you, and you alone.*

The reason for that is this: Even the most efficient top-level executive will view each newcomer with suspicion and as a possible threat to him and to his position. If necessary, he will stop at nothing to protect his job and his way of life. If he feels that you are a menace to him in any way, he will go all out to get rid of you, no matter what your qualifications and abilities are.

So your first rule of survival in the executive suite is to be on guard at all times just as I told you in the previous chapter. Keep those thoughts in mind, and you'll be able to come out on top.

Now that you understand that and are willing to accept the risks involved in the executive suite, let me give you that first technique.

1. ATTRACT THE ATTENTION OF THE TOP BRASS. Although you do want to keep your boss happy with you and your work, your primary objective must be to move up and get ahead. For example, if you are a secretary, the best way for you to move up the ladder is to become known to your superior's boss as a knowledgeable and competent individual who really understands the workings of the organization inside out. Let me show you now by an example how to do exactly that.

Suzanne Peters is today the chief administrative staff officer for a large corporation. She reports directly to the president and chief executive officer of the company, to no one else. She has custody of important documents and corporation books, submits reports and statements to state and federal governments, is in charge of the transfer of corporate stock, and sees that the minutes of stockholders' meetings are properly kept and recorded. She has a large staff of her own to help her carry out these various duties. Yet Suzanne started out as a file clerk for a department foreman way down on the totem pole.

"I didn't want to be a file clerk all my life, so I made up my own plan of attack and my own timetable for successful achievement of my goal," Suzanne says. "The first thing I knew I had to do was to attract the attention of those who really counted. And I don't mean by wearing low-cut blouses and hip-hugging skirts either.

"Except for ordinary reports and routine memos, I quickly learned to keep important correspondence and major reports out of the interoffice mail. When I saw that a letter or a report was of a significant nature, I would suggest to my boss that I hand carry it to his superior. Of course, I would always imply that this would make my own boss look good.

"Once in his superior's office, I would bypass his secretary by saying, 'Mr. Black asked me to give this report to Mr. Green personally.' I wouldn't just lay it down on Mr. Green's desk and then leave. Instead, I would hand it to him and say, 'This is the report on production you've been waiting for from Mr. Black. I'll be glad to stay for a moment so if you have any questions I can answer them for you.'

"I always made it extremely clear that I understood the report and that I knew what it was all about. Before long, Mr. Green got in the habit of telling his own secretary to 'Call Suzanne and ask her; she'll know.' When his own secretary got married and left, he didn't look around to find a replacement. He immediately tagged me and I took my first step up the corporate ladder.

"But I didn't stay in Mr. Green's office for too long. That was only an intermediate goal. I used the same process, with a few variations, to come up to where I am today."

2. BECOME THE FOUNTAINHEAD OF INFORMATION AND KNOWL-EDGE. Just as Suzanne did, you will attract the attention of the people who really count when you fill yourself with accurate and useful information. The more knowledge you display, the more people will turn to you to find out what they need to know.

The more information you gain about the operation of the entire organization, that much more will your boss depend on you for the right answers to his questions and the correct solutions to his problems. It will soon reach the point where he will not go to a staff meeting without you. When he turns to you for an answer when the president of the company asks him a question, guess whose name is going to be remembered.

Let me tell you how I used this technique successfully when I was in the army back in World War II. I was a staff sergeant, and I had a major for a boss. As a regimental staff officer, he attended division staff meetings on a weekly basis. Since he was hard of hearing, he almost always came back with unintelligible notes. I suggested to him that I attend the meetings with him and take notes for him.

High-ranking division officers got used to seeing a sergeant come with the major to take notes and answer questions. One day the commanding general attended the meeting. I noticed that he watched me intently and asked several officers who I was and why I was there. After the meeting was over, his aide told me to report to the general's office.

"You shouldn't be an enlisted man," the General told me. "You should be an officer. You're already performing the duties of a major, but you're receiving the pay of a sergeant. I've called the division personnel officer for information about you from your records. You're highly quali-fied, so I'm recommending you immediately for a field promotion to first lieutenant."

Sixty days later, I was commissioned an officer in the U.S. Army without having to endure the physical and mental stresses of thirteen weeks of rigorous training in the Infantry Officer Candidate School at Fort Benning, Georgia.

3. NEVER COME EARLY, BUT ALWAYS STAY LATE.   If you show up early for work, the only people who'll ever see you are the janitor or the mailroom clerk. Neither one of them can help you get promoted.

Never, and I repeat, never, leave before your boss does. If you do, it will never fail but that he will want you that particular day. Always, and again, I repeat, always, leave after your boss does. He'll be impressed with your loyalty to the company and your devotion to duty.

If at all possible, try to time your departure to that of *his* boss. The more his boss sees of you, the more he will remember you. Carry some trade journals under your arm so he can see how interested you are in your profession. But don't carry anything that suggests you're doing your office work at home. This gives him the impression that you are not efficient enough to get your work done during regular working hours.

4. "BROWN BAG" IT SOME OF THE TIME.   You don't have to do this every day; a few times a week will do. This also implies great devotion to duty and never fails to create a good impression. But don't read a newspaper or a magazine or do your face or nails at your desk during the lunch hour. This spoils the effect you are trying to create. Instead, open a file or a report. If your boss wants to know why you're not going out to lunch, tell him that you want to absorb the details of this complicated report while everyone is gone and it's peaceful and quiet so you can really concentrate.

Don't worry that people will think you're cheap or antisocial when you brown bag it some of the time. You're in good company when you do. Leon Peters, chairman of the board of Cushman and Wakefield Realtors and consultant to RCA, does this, and so do a lot of other top executives. They can get much of their important work done when most of the office staff is out and there's little chance of telephone interruptions.

5. LOOK THE PART OF A TOP EXECUTIVE.   I am not going to go into the details of how you should dress. That will depend entirely on where you live and what the dress code and customs are for your company. I live in Florida and I know the dress code is much more relaxed here than it is in other places. But the important point is for you to show those above you that you will fit in perfectly well at their upper level.

6. IF YOU ARE BLOCKED VERTICALLY, MOVE HORIZONTALLY. It will sometimes happen that no matter what you do, you won't be able to move up where you are. In that case, try to move laterally from one job to another. You will not only learn much more about the company, but you will also sooner or later find the right slot where you can move up the executive ladder.

If anyone higher up wonders about your horizontal movements, you can always say that you want to get the broadest education possible about all departments in the company so you will be better qualified. This always impresses the top brass, and they will remember your name when the time comes.

7. NEVER MAKE AN ISSUE OF SMALL MATTERS. You should go along with minor or insignificant points when you can do so without causing damage to yourself or to your own position. When you do have to make an issue about something, be sure that it is a major point. Then your objection will stand out and you'll be remembered and well thought of for your professional attitude and conduct.

8. STATE YOUR OBJECTION CALMLY AND COURTEOUSLY. If you disagree with a major point, back up your disagreement with logic, reason, and facts. Objections based on emotion or how you "feel" about something won't carry much weight. If the final decision goes against your recommendation, don't carry a chip on your shoulder. Do your best to support the selected course of action of your superior. You will be respected when you do.

9. DEVELOP THE "GOLDEN TOUCH" IN HUMAN RELATIONSHIPS. The ability to get along with others is an absolute must if you want to get ahead in the big corporation. You cannot move up the ladder if you make an enemy out of everyone. In fact, knowing how to handle people is one of the hallmarks of executive leadership. If you cannot get along well with your associates, if you are constantly involved in verbal warfare with someone, you'll be let go, no matter what your qualifications and abilities are.

10. BE ENTHUSIASTIC ABOUT YOUR JOB. Don't expect to move up the executive ladder if you don't really have your heart in your work. Your boss can tell, for your attitude will be reflected on your face and in your actions.

If you can't go to work smiling because you love your job, I feel sorry for you. I recommend that you get enthusiastic about your work or that you change jobs before it's too late to do so.

11. DON'T BE AFRAID TO TAKE A REASONABLE RISK. Top-level executives expect their management people to have the courage to take reasonable risks. If you always play it safe, you'll never get anywhere. Good prior planning will prevent most major problems and greatly reduce the risks involved for you.

12. LOOK FOR MORE AND GREATER RESPONSIBILITY. The person who ducks responsibility will never go to the top. Top-level executives are always on the lookout for those who can accept more and more responsibility. The person who can do that is always labeled as a "comer."

Remember that every time you delegate a job to someone else, you are not passing the buck. Instead, you are freeing yourself to accept additional responsibility. Top management is always extremely happy to find a competent individual who is available to take care of new projects. If you want to climb the executive ladder and achieve success, then let that person be you.

13. DREAM UP YOUR OWN TECHNIQUE FOR ADVANCEMENT. Howard L. used one of the cleverest techniques I've ever heard of to climb the executive ladder to success. Shortly after he went to work for a large company, Howard realized that promotion was going to be a slow and tedious process. Then he had a flash of inspiration.

One of his college classmates had gone to work for an executive recruiting firm. He, too, was anxious to succeed. Howard gave his boss's name to his friend who was able to entice him away from the company. Howard then moved into his boss's slot. He used the procedure several times over the next few years to reach his present position in top-level management, leaving behind others with more seniority and experience.

You may not be able to use Howard's technique, but you can dream up one of your own so you can get ahead faster.

How to Succeed in Business for Yourself

Have you ever wondered why some individuals are so successful while others fail so miserably? Or why so many small business ventures fold only a year or so after starting? The answer is quite simple: *Those who failed didn't determine what people's needs were before they started.*

The most successful companies, corporations, and individuals find out what their potential customers want before they ever start. They don't waste time, energy, or money in guessing. They benefit by finding out specifically what a person's needs and desires are through psychological studies and marketing surveys before they ever open the door.

So, if you want to go into business for yourself and become successful, then you ought to do the same thing. Oh, I'm not saying you have to conduct expensive psychological studies and marketing surveys, but you should find out what people want before you start. You can do that by getting out and going from house to house talking to people to get the answers you need.

Only by talking to people can you get the answers you require to the questions you have. Even medical doctors, who are usually automatically successful or so it seems at any rate, must get information from the patient if they want to succeed. As my own family doctor said, "There is only one cardinal rule in medicine. You must always listen to the patient."

Let me give you an example now of how Bill Wilson, an extremely successful young businessman, followed these same basic principles to start his own company.

"Total service is the real key to business success—the customer must come first, last, and always," Bill says. Bill is the owner and president of R & S Soft Water Services, an irrigation contractor in Palm Bay, Florida. The company is comprised of five subsidiaries with forty-two employees involved in irrigation systems and water purification.

"Whatever a customer needs regarding water—whether it is a well, water purifier, irrigation system, or a pump—we provide it. We never send our customers elsewhere," Bill says.

But I'm getting ahead of my story. I first met Bill in 1973 shortly after I'd moved to Florida. Bill had come to Florida to live after leaving the military. He wanted to be in business for himself rather than work for someone else, but he was not completely sure of what kind to go into.

Before he made this decision, he decided to make a survey of the area so he could find out what people wanted or what essential service was lacking. He went from house to house, knocked on dozens of doors, and talked to a tremendous number of people to get his answer.

Bill found that the majority of people complained about the high cost of using city water to keep their yards beautiful and green. You see, in spite of all its lakes and having water on three sides, Florida never has enough rainfall. Grass must be watered constantly throughout the year or lawns will die out and become nothing but barren weed patches.

Based on his survey, Bill decided to go into the lawn sprinkling business. He digs a deep well so the homeowner has a source of free water for his lawn. Then he puts in a yard-watering system complete with pump, underground pipes, and lawn sprinklers.

Another major complaint that people had was the extremely hard city water that corroded plumbing fixtures, ruined washing machines and dishwashers, made clothes take on a dirty gray and grimy look, and left a filthy ring that could never be completely removed from the tub after a bath. So Bill also installs water conditioning units that convert the hard city water to soft water that no longer corrodes expensive plumbing fixtures or ruins washing machines and dishwashers as well as expensive clothing.

"At R & S we take a personal interest in our customers," Bill says. "I, or any one of my irrigation people, can tell you the name of the homeowner for whom we installed our first irrigation system and how many sprinkler heads it took.

"Some of our customers who are retired and living on a fixed income get special consideration on pricing. Hopefully, somewhere someone is treating my mother or father like we treat their's.

"R & S is open six days a week. We pride ourselves on same day service. We do very little advertising; the majority of our new irrigation business comes from personal referrals."

Another example of Bill's commitment to personal service to the customer was his firm's reaction to the December 1989 freeze which paralyzed Florida.

"The weekend before Christmas the temperature dropped to 28 degrees and the calls started coming in. Pipes were freezing, leaving homeowners and businesses without water," Bill says.

"I called my people in from their Christmas vacation and we stayed open during the entire crisis. We were even open on Christmas Eve and Christmas Day until 9 P.M.," Bill goes on to say. "We helped people get their water back. Many homeowners found they could depend on us in a pinch, so who do you think they'll call when they decide to put in an irrigation system?"

The Palm Bay community has learned that Bill Wilson is also generous with both his personal time and his money. "I believe in putting back into the community what I take out of it," Bill says, and he does exactly that for he sponsors Little League baseball, soccer, and bowling teams.

R & S Soft Water Service has also been the recipient of the Greater South Brevard Area Chamber of Commerce Small Business of the Year Award, plus dozens of state and national awards. Bill Wilson is an extremely successful young businessman and a credit to his community. I consider it a privilege to know him and to be his friend.

Bill has set the example for you to follow if you want to be successful. If you will follow his methods of finding out what people want so you can help them get it as he has done, and if you will practice his philosophy of total dedication and service to the customer, then you cannot help but succeed no matter what business you decide to go into. It will be absolutely impossible for you to fail.

Chapter 22

HOW TO HOLD AND INCREASE YOUR POWER WITH PEOPLE YEAR AFTER YEAR

You have now completed the *Twenty-one Days to Unlimited Power with People*. Your knowledge about how to gain unlimited power and mastery with people is now basically complete. You have all the information you need to achieve unlimited power, influence, and control with others. From now on, it is a matter of consolidating your gains and being prepared to expand your influence in an ever-wider and larger area. So this chapter is in a way a postscript to what has gone before.

However, I do want to point out that you cannot sit down and rest on your laurels now. There is still more to be done if you want to succeed. You must keep on working to get to the top or to stay at the top if you are already there.

The Key to Victory Is Your Follow-through

The young bowler seemed to do everything just right in his approach. He stepped off with the proper foot. He did not drift from side to side on his way to the foul line. Nor did he allow his eyes to stray from their target. He released the ball smoothly and watched it roll down the lane to break smartly into the 1-3 pocket just at the right moment, only to leave the 5 pin standing.

What happened? What went wrong? Why didn't he get a strike when everything looked just right?

"Your ball had no strength," his instructor said. "It had no power because you quit before the job was done. *You didn't follow through!*"

The same remark is made every day of the week by golf instructors, baseball and football coaches, executives and managers, foremen and supervisors in business and industry.

"You failed because you didn't follow through!"

To keep that from happening to you, follow these two techniques:

1. EXPLOIT YOUR INITIAL SUCCESS TO THE FULLEST.   In war, the final victory will go to the commander who has the ability and the foresight to follow up his initial advantage. Once the line has been breached and the enemy turns toward the rear, the opportunity has come to eliminate him completely. A confused enemy in disorganized retreat is an easy mark for a swift and determined pursuit.

In business, the same idea holds true. When you've sold him the suit, don't stop there. Follow through and sell him the shoes, socks, tie, and shirt to go with the suit.

The biggest profits in the automobile industry aren't made when only the car is sold. They're made when the smart salesman follows through and gets the customer to buy all those plush optional extras, from the stereo tape or compact disc player and FM radio with front and rear speakers to the push-button controlled power antenna, power seats, and so on.

This idea of following through applies not only to business, but also to the mastery of people. You can exploit your initial success and ensure a complete victory if you will *follow through with the utmost energy.*

2. ENSURE YOUR CONTINUED SUCCESS.   If you've developed your resources and made ready for the long haul ahead, you'll have sufficient reserve strength to follow through and ensure your continued success.

For instance, young musical groups come and go constantly. Out of every hundred, only one or two will still be around a year after they've started. Why? Well, as a popular TV night show host once said, "They don't have more than a couple of numbers they can do for an audience. They sound terrific for those two songs, but after that, they're dead. They can't get past the first encore."

You can avoid that death trap if you will develop your follow-through to ensure your continued success. To do that, you'll need to make an extra effort and be persistent above all else.

Remember How You Got to Where You Are Today

Don't become complacent and think you've got it made when you're on top of the heap. You must always keep in mind the basic needs and desires that all people have. Continue to be aware of your followers' needs, keep fulfilling those needs so they will always get what they want, and your position of leadership and unlimited power with people will be secure.

Politicians are voted out of office when they become so filled with self-importance that they forget the needs of their constituents. But the smart ones who continue to fulfill the needs of the voters in their state or district are elected time and again until politics becomes their sole career. For example, before Claude Pepper died, when you said *congressman* in Florida, his name automatically came to mind the same way people think Coke when you mention a soft drink.

Perseverance: The One Character Trait You Need for the Long Haul

The one major success factor that separates the men from the boys and the women from the girls is *perseverance*. It's easy to be full of fire about a project when everything's going right. But it's a tough proposition to persevere when it starts raining inside the house. That's when the boys and girls quit and the men and women keep right on going.

Without perseverance, you have no hope of success. Perseverance means to hold out, to last, to continue, to remain steadfast. It is the ability to put up with pain, pressure, fatigue, and distress. People who make it to the top have one character trait in common—perseverance.

One of our famous presidents described perseverance in effect this way: "Nothing in the world can take the place of perseverance. Talent will not; nothing is more common than unsuccessful men with talent. Genius will not; the world is full of educated derelicts. Perseverance and determination alone are omnipotent. The slogan 'Press on!' has solved and will always solve the problems of the human race."

That's the kind of perseverance you will need, not only to gain unlimited power with people, but to retain that power with them. Nothing else will ever do.

How to Use the Principles and Techniques in This Book as Part of Your Daily Life

You cannot possibly retain all the valuable information in this book with only one reading. After all, it's taken me a lifetime to collect the material that's gone into it. You should read and reread it until its principles and techniques have become second nature and are a living part of you.

Rather than read it from cover to cover again and again as some people do when they make a project out of reading the Bible once a year, do it this way. If you are having a particular problem that you need an answer to , find the appropriate chapter and read it before going to bed. Then sleep on it. Nine times out of ten, the answer will come to you crystal clear in the morning. If it does not, read it again and again until you do get your answer. Let me give you some examples so I can better show you exactly what I mean.

I recommend that you type up a list of the basic needs and desires that every single person has and slip it under the glass on your desk or place it somewhere so you can see it at all times. Always remember that to fulfill a person's basic needs and desires is the key to unlimited power with people.

Let's suppose you're having a problem with pin-pointing the key people who can help you become successful. Then go back and reread Chapter 6. Review the techniques that are in that chapter, and use them; you're bound to be successful in that area.

No matter whether it's a matter of understanding, predicting, and controlling people's behavior; making people feel important; projecting an aura of command that causes others to obey you immediately without question; giving orders that will always be carried out to the letter; building an army of loyal followers, or any other problem that is bothering you—you can find the answers that will help you when you refresh your memory by reading the appropriate chapter again.

Why am I so sure that *Twenty-one Days to Unlimited Power with People* will work for you? Because I've already seen it work for hundreds of others before. Hundreds, perhaps even thousands, of people have already attained unlimited power with people with this powerful yet virtually effortless program. They were just ordinary people in the beginning. But by the time they finished the power program—after spending only a few minutes a day for twenty-one days—in less than a month they became vastly more powerful than they ever dreamed possible. And if all those people could do it, then so can you.

INDEX